# EVIL SUMMER

The Elmer H. Johnson
and Carol Holmes Johnson Series in Criminology

*The Rita Nitz Story: A Life without Parole*
Larry L. Franklin

*The Atlanta Youth Murders and the Politics of Race*
Bernard Headley

*Negotiating Responsibility in the Criminal Justice System*
Edited by Jack Kamerman
Foreword by Gilbert Geis

*Hate Crime: The Global Politics of Polarization*
Edited by Robert J. Kelly and Jess Maghan

*Shattered Sense of Innocence: The 1955 Murders of Three Chicago Children*
Richard C. Lindberg and Gloria Jean Sykes
Foreword by Larry G. Axelrod

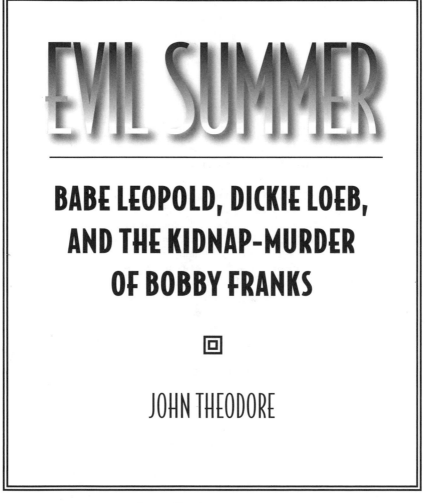

# EVIL SUMMER

## BABE LEOPOLD, DICKIE LOEB, AND THE KIDNAP-MURDER OF BOBBY FRANKS

JOHN THEODORE

Southern Illinois University Press
*Carbondale*

10  09  08  07    4  3  2  1

Publication of this book has been underwritten by The Elmer H.
Johnson and Carol Holmes Johnson Series in Criminology fund.

Library of Congress Cataloging-in-Publication Data
Theodore, John, 1946–
Evil summer : Babe Leopold, Dickie Loeb, and the kidnap-
murder of Bobby Franks / John Theodore.
p. cm.—(The Elmer H. Johnson and Carol Holmes Johnson
series in criminology)
Includes bibliographical references and index.
ISBN-13: 978-0-8093-2777-5 (cloth : alk. paper)
ISBN-10: 0-8093-2777-5 (cloth : alk. paper)
1. Leopold, Nathan Freudenthal, 1904–1971. 2. Loeb, Richard A.,
1905–1936. 3. Franks, Bobby, 1909–1924. 4. Murder—Illinois—
Chicago—History—Case studies. 5. Kidnapping—Illinois—
Chicago—History—Case studies. 6. Trials (Murder)—Illinois—
Chicago—History—Case studies. 7. Murderers—Illinois—
Chicago—Biography. I. Title.

HV6534.C4T54 2007
364.152′3092—dc22                    2007002454


Printed on recycled paper. ♻
The paper used in this publication meets the minimum
requirements of American National Standard for Information
Sciences—Permanence of Paper for Printed Library Materials,
ANSI Z39.48-1992. ∞

*Remembering Steve Neal*

# CONTENTS

# ILLUSTRATIONS

Young Dickie Loeb  1
Bobby Franks, victim of fate  19
Clarence Darrow, the Old Lion, and his young defendants  101
Illinois State Penitentiary at Joliet  165
New look for the former Jazz Age sophisticates  175

*Following page 100*
Elaborate ransom letter and envelope
Investigators examining the culvert where the body was found
Leopold's horn-rimmed glasses, found near the culvert
State's Attorney Robert Crowe and diver with typewriter
Babe Leopold
Dickie Loeb
Crowds outside Chicago's Criminal Courts Building
Darrow arguing his point
Crowe demanding the death penalty
Darrow sitting with his two defendants
Flora Franks describing the telephone call from "Mr. Johnson"
Jacob Franks escorted by his brother-in-law Edwin Gresham
Prison data for Leopold and Loeb
Clarence Darrow
Nathan F. Leopold Jr. upon his release in 1958 from Stateville
Former Franks home at 5052 Ellis
Franks mausoleum in Chicago's Rosehill Cemetery

# PREFACE

As childhood memories go, this one from the spring of 1951 has remained vivid: It's early morning, and I'm riding in a yellow school bus in Jackson Park. I watch the golfers walk in the wet grass, and then I stare at the buildings as the bus weaves through the University of Chicago campus before stopping at a big yellow-brick house at Hyde Park Boulevard and Ellis Avenue. I join the rest of the kids near fragrant, purple lilac bushes, and then, in an orderly line, we enter the Ffoulkes School. Once inside, I hang my jacket on a coat rack in the kindergarten room and settle in. I'm pretty excited. On this day, our class will walk to a hardware store on Cottage Grove Avenue to buy some sunflower seeds for the school's garden. I am six years old.

I had never heard of Bobby Franks. I'm not sure when I first learned about the crime, but it was a few years after I left the Ffoulkes School—probably in the third or fourth grade. One day my cousin asked me, "Didn't you used to go to school in that house where the boy was killed?"

I asked my mother what he meant.

"Bobby Franks lived there but he wasn't killed *in* the house," she told me. "Besides, that was a long time ago."

That's all she said.

Details about Bobby Franks's murder came to me slowly over the years in gruesome bits and pieces: how Bobby, age fourteen, walked home from school one afternoon, how two University of Chicago students lured him into their car, how they killed him inside the automobile—took a chisel to his head—right near his big yellow-brick home, how someone found him the next morning in swampland near Indiana, how the killers had poured acid over his nude body, how people still talked about it, even though it happened in 1924.

In 1924, the story of how Richard Loeb and Nathan Leopold Jr., brilliant collegiate sons of Jewish Gilded Age entrepreneurs, kidnapped and murdered one of their neighbors unfolded wildly in newspapers. Truth melded with fiction, and facts succumbed to rumors and gossip in Chicago's tabloids and broadsheets. The headlines and their stories escalated from late May to late September every morning and every evening with the discovery of the body to the killers' defense to the sentencing. The public feasted on every press run. The killers were emblems of 1920s' pampered youth—Leopold, a self-anointed "Nietzsche-colossus," and Loeb, a charming amateur detective. Because of the brilliance of their attorney, Clarence Darrow, Leopold and Loeb became vulnerable boys, killing not for the thrill but because of deep-rooted psychological reasons. "Their coming together," Darrow told the public, "was the means of their undoing." In Poe-like fashion, for an entire summer, the story paralyzed the wealthy neighborhoods of Kenwood and Hyde Park.

People began talking—and writing—about the crime the day a railway worker found Bobby's body. The killing of Bobby Franks still captures the imagination of writers, psychologists, and legal scholars because of the enormous scope of the crime with its Roaring Twenties theme: excess, overeducated youth, abnormal childhood behavior, anti-Semitism, sexuality, psychology, sensationalistic journalism, and capital punishment. "It is one of the worst crimes in the history of the city," Chicago's police chief Morgan Collins said. A *Chicago Daily Tribune* editorial claimed, "There have been few crimes in the history of the United States that have had more important implications than the killing of Robert Franks."

In his autobiography, Darrow wrote, "In the case of these two boys every motive that moves ordinary mortals to action was absent. There was no malice or hatred, or even dislike against the unfortunate boy. There was no motive for getting money connected with the foolish plot. The whole performance was childish and silly, and proved of itself a decided abnormal mentality." Darrow, a passionate enemy of capital punishment, based much of his defense on his clients' childhood during which, according to him, their "abnormal mentality" took shape.

*Evil Summer* emphasizes the fantasy-filled young lives of Loeb and Leopold and focuses on the summer of 1924 in Chicago. I want the reader to watch the narrative unfold as though looking through a vintage View-Master, each reel a distinctive part of the book, a moving presentation of the people in their Roaring Twenties' world.

In researching this book, trying to understand what it must have been like to live in Kenwood and Hyde Park at the time of the crime, I visited with Leon Despres, former Chicago alderman and lifelong resident of Hyde Park. As I sat in the front room of Despres's apartment overlooking the Jackson Park lagoon, I felt a peaceful civility coming from the man and understood why federal Judge Abner Mikva called him "the absolute conscience of the city." For twenty years, from 1955 to 1975,

Despres, a maverick in Mayor Richard J. Daley's city council, was the lone opposition voice.

Well into his nineties and in a wheelchair, Despres looked out the window to beyond the lagoon and Lake Michigan and talked quietly about the crime. From time-to-time, between thoughts, he reached over and held the hand of his wife, Marian, also in a wheelchair.

The facts came back to him in large waves. His retelling of the Franks's killing was consistent with his compassionate view of life—his mind filtered out the brutality.

He remembered Richard Loeb: "One time I saw him standing near the fence of a grammar school. The sun was setting, and it cast a warm glow across his face. I remember thinking how appropriate because he had such a glamorous personality."[1]

Despres recalled the hostile feelings in the neighborhood about the murder. "This stirred the community like nothing else, especially among Jews. But at least the victim was Jewish. Darrow did such a great job in educating the public. He was rough and crude-looking, but he had a most beautiful view of the world."

About the prosecuting attorney, Despres said, "Crowe wanted to string them up like trophies. He was so hateful and a master of dramatization. He had a lynch-mob way about him. I remember him looking like a pirate."

At the end of our talk, Despres looked across the room, a serene place where books dominated the décor, and said, "The judgment, though, the judgment was so wise."

After saying good-bye, I thought about how Despres had concluded his pensive recollection. In the millions of words used to recount the tragedy, it's a shame the word *wise* doesn't show up more often.

# ACKNOWLEDGMENTS

Library Special Collections reading rooms are great places to get lost in another time, in another place. Combing through the research boxes—not knowing exactly what you're looking for—and finding the right letter, a sensational newspaper headline, a special photograph . . . and the raucous era called the Jazz Age lives again. I spent many mornings and afternoons in these rooms across Chicago in researching this book. My sincere thanks to the research specialists at the Chicago History Museum, University of Chicago, Northwestern University, Newberry Library, Chicago Public Library, and the Spertus Institute of Jewish Studies.

My appreciation to Susan Neal and Tina Yarovsky for their early copyediting expertise and to Debra Yarovsky for guiding me across the wind-swept prairies of the Lake Calumet region. Thank you to Mary Lou Kowaleski for her excellent final-stage copyediting. A special thanks to Chicago artist Tim Anderson, whose striking portraitures grace the cover of this book, and to Dr. Paula Cormalleth for her sensitive insights into the behavior of Babe Leopold and Dickie Loeb.

Former Chicago alderman and civic leader Leon Despres was a young boy in the Twenties. I thank him for that special afternoon in his apartment overlooking the Jackson Park lagoon, when he talked so eloquently about growing up in Hyde Park during the summer of 1924.

I am grateful to Karl Kageff, Southern Illinois University Press editor-in-chief, and the entire staff at the press for their assistance and professionalism.

And, of course, thank you to my family—Maureen, Jackie, Meghan, and Michael—for their enduring love and support.

# Part One

## Fantasies

Young Dickie Loeb.
Chicago History Museum, DN0077990

■

The italicized portions in this book represent the fantasies, dreams, and thoughts of Richard Loeb and Nathan F. Leopold Jr. The representations are based on the Bowman-Hulbert Report, an extensive physical and psychological study of the boys that Drs. Karl Bowman and Harold S. Hulbert conducted for the defense. The report is cited often in this book.

## MISS STRUTHERS'S IDEAL BOY

Albert Loeb's third son knew at an early age what he wanted from life. In the dark of his bedroom, before sleep came, Dickie Loeb, age ten, held his teddy bear and shaped his secret life. *Picturization*, he called it, and it swallowed his ambition.[1]

*Each night, they came into his cell. The guards stripped him of his clothing and had their way with him. They shoved him against the bars and whipped him. The cold steel squeezed his chest, and he couldn't breathe. His back burned as the warm blood ran down his body. But the young prisoner felt no fear, only self-pity. He reveled in the attention. After all, he was a famous criminal, and this was the pleasure all masterminds must endure.[2]*

Like many wealthy families in Kenwood, the Loebs employed a governess. Miss Struthers nurtured and cared for young Dickie. He was her responsibility. Miss Struthers's definite ideas about strictness and obedience influenced his every move from age five to fifteen.[3]

The Loeb family enjoyed a regal life. By 1915, Albert Loeb, vice president of Sears, Roebuck, and Company, was building his fortune. His circle of friends included the most powerful people in Chicago. The grounds around his red-brick Elizabethan-style mansion on fashionable Ellis Avenue featured a greenhouse, fishpond, tennis court, and miniature nine-hole golf course. Inside the house, a polished staff of valets, chefs, chauffeurs, and nursemaids met the needs of Albert and Anna Loeb and their four sons: Allan, Ernest, Dickie, and Thomas.

The Canadian-born Miss Struthers and Dickie Loeb nourished each other. She educated, disciplined, and punished the boy. Her word was law, and he obeyed her to the minute.[4] In Miss Struthers, Dickie had an audience. He felt inferior to his two older brothers, but Miss Struthers treated him as an equal. Her passionate desire, he knew, was to make him into her ideal boy.

The Loeb library was one of the most complete private libraries in Chicago. It was a serious room, retired from the world, where volumes covered the walls, and tall, leaded-glass windows filtered the daylight. Here, after school, the bond between Miss Struthers and Dickie grew. She fed him only the best: Dickens, *Ben Hur*, and *The Rise and Fall of the Dutch Republic*. She tutored Dickie in his studies and encouraged him to move rapidly through school. She often looked into his soft green eyes and said, "Study history, and some day you will be an ambassador."[5] In this cloistered environment, Dickie Loeb became a willing prisoner to Miss Struthers's vigorous doctrine. She taught him well but never told him about her sister, who died insane. Outside, the children of Ellis Avenue played in the autumn sun.

Miss Struthers always accompanied Dickie to and from school. She forbad him from walking the shaded streets of Kenwood alone. Once, when he was seven, he refused to wait for her after classes. He ran home, knowing the punishment would be swift and stern. For this brief glimpse of freedom, he spent the rest of the afternoon in bed.

Lying, he quickly learned, was to be his way out. It was his pleasure and his art. Dickie lied by making false claims and by omitting facts. He even lied when it wasn't necessary. And nobody—not Miss Struthers, his family, his friends—suspected him. In high school, he lied about his prowess with girls. At times, he carried a gun and said he was a bootleg-ger. Dickie Loeb, you see, was a charmer. With a gentle face that always carried a smile, he politely lied his way through puberty and adolescence. Guilt and remorse never crossed his beautiful mind.

Dickie hid his nightly reading from Miss Struthers. Each night, be-fore picturization, he filled his mind with images of famous criminals and the detectives who chased them. Bank robbers, kidnappers, safe-crackers, they inspired Dickie and became his heroes. The authors and stories varied—Sir Arthur Conan Doyle's Sherlock Holmes in *The Sign of the Four*, Wyndham Martyn's *Anthony Trent, Master Criminal*, and Frank Packard's *Beloved Traitor* and *Adventures of Jimmie Dale*. They possessed him.

Dickie especially admired Jimmie Dale, a young gentleman crook, an expert criminal, very dashing and very noble.[6] Dale loves artistic pursuits, dines at New York's finest clubs, befriends the press, and eludes detectives. Everyone loves him. "He was the most puzzling, bewildering, delightful crook in the annals of crime," wrote Packard.[7]

*As the master criminal mind of the century, Dickie led others. Of course, they obeyed him. He was the ideal fellow: good-looking, smart, rich. And he knew all about being a criminal. He planned crimes all over the world and directed his confederates, who followed his lead to the letter. No detective could solve his crimes, and the country was in awe of Dickie Loeb, who hid from no one. He walked the streets with a nonchalant confidence, consulting with friends at his club and helping newspaper reporters on the crime beat. What a magnificent game—the ideal boy, the master criminal, the perfect crime.*[8]

## YOUNG MEN OF YOUR STAMP

Wealth and benevolence lined the leafing streets of Kenwood during World War I.

Albert Loeb, an easy-going, gentle man, was considered the best lawyer in Chicago when he joined Sears, Roebuck in 1901.[9] Seven years later, Julius Rosenwald, president and one of the partners of the giant mail-order house, named Loeb vice president. And when Rosenwald spent the war years in Washington counseling the War Department, Loeb became acting president.

Loeb and Rosenwald lived a block from each other on Ellis Avenue. Rosenwald's Prairie School three-story mansion, a neighborhood showpiece, included a spacious sun porch, lily pond, and stately ballroom. The homes of Kenwood reflected their owners' prosperous stature. Innovative architects—Charles Sumner Frost, Howard Van Doren Shaw, Frank Lloyd Wright, George Maher, George C. Nimmons, and the firm of Holabird and Roche—created the elegant look of Kenwood. They designed homes for the giants of Chicago: lumber merchants Martin A. Ryerson, who was a University of Chicago trustee and benefactor of the Art Institute, and William O. Goodman, who endowed the Goodman Theater; meat-packer Gustavus Swift; clothier Joseph Schaffner; and Sears executive Max Adler, Rosenwald's brother-in-law and benefactor of the Adler Planetarium. Kenwood reflected the style and philosophy of these men: fiscally conservative and socially liberal.[10]

Loeb and Rosenwald led a moving force in Kenwood's German-Jewish aristocratic and philanthropic legacy. Rosenwald enjoyed an especially imminent role. A generous supporter of the University of Chicago and founder of the Museum of Science and Industry, he contributed heavily to Jewish and other social causes, including model housing for Chicago's Negroes. Loeb and his brother Jacob, president of the Chicago Board of Education, were leaders in Chicago's Jewish community. Jacob Loeb raised nearly $2 million in relief for Jewish war sufferers and for his efforts received a personal commendation from President Warren G. Harding.[11] Albert Loeb, a thirty-second-degree Mason and member of the Standard Club and Chicago's two most prestigious Jewish golf clubs, Lake Shore and Ravisloe, instilled a philanthropic spirit in his family.

Dickie Loeb read daily newspaper reports of World War I. In 1916, when he was ten, he urged his father to send $700 to occupied France to assist local schoolteachers.[12] Dickie also sent his own allowance to help the French. But it was the air war that captured his imagination. Twentieth-century technology provided a new way to kill in World War I—from the sky. British and German bombing raids destroyed villages and killed innocent people across Europe. Random victimization. It escaped most nine-year-olds in Chicago but not Dickie Loeb.

Dickie and a few of his neighborhood friends created a small publication named *Richard's Magazine*. Dickie owned authorship. In an editorial he titled "Humanity," he penned his opinions on the horrors of war, including the random deaths of innocent women and children.

> Daily millions of dollars are being spent in the purchase of ammunitions and weapons. Think if that amount of money was spent daily in the beautifying of the world. Think if all the lives that have been lost in this war could have been spent in peaceful labor and happiness[. . . .] Think if Chicago was bombarded. Would not as many women and children die in the attack? Would not as many neutral foreigners die? The aeroplanes cannot pick out the men they are warring against. Such is war in the twentieth century.

Dickie Loeb sought a wider audience, one far beyond the prudish Miss Struthers. Rosenwald sent a copy of *Richard's Magazine* to his close friend Theodore Roosevelt. In May of 1916, Dickie received a hand-written note from Oyster Bay, Long Island, New York, praising him. In closing, Roosevelt wrote, "and I want to say that it does me good to see young men of your stamp growing up in this country."[13]

Random killing. An evil that would soon define Dickie Loeb.

## SHADOWING

At first, he worried she'd turn around and see him.

Dickie Loeb took his childhood of delusion and fantasy to the streets of Kenwood in a bizarre practice he called *shadowing*. It was a bridge, a rite of passage, and the next step the master criminal must take before committing the perfect crime. Reading detective stories, picturization, and shadowing consumed his young life.

For most eleven-year-olds, a fall Saturday afternoon meant playing in the golden leaves that painted the spacious lawns and avenues of Kenwood. For Dickie, it was not only a respite from schoolwork, library reading with Miss Struthers, and French lessons. Saturday was a day to play detective.

He first noticed the beggar woman in the alley alongside the Harvard School, about three blocks from his home.[14] *Here's someone I should shadow.* She wore an oversized raincoat, and a dirty bandana wrapped her head. Dickie hid behind an elm tree and watched the haggard woman sift through a garbage bin near the school playground. *Surely she's up to something.* He followed her down the alley and kept a safe distance as she made her way north on Greenwood. He grinned as she slipped between a fence and a chicken coop, lifted her clothing, and squatted to pee.

She turned onto Forty-Seventh Street and headed for Drexel Boulevard. *Sure, that's it, one of those mansions on Drexel.* Once on Drexel, a wide, fashionable boulevard with flowerbeds and trees adorning the median, Dickie walked closer to her. But when she suddenly turned around, he bolted across traffic for the safety of a thick willow.

The Indian Summer sun slowed her pace. They walked south for about a half hour. Dickie watched her duck in and out of alleys looking for food. *She's picking out a house to rob, a side door, an unlatched window. She'll come back later when it's dark.* He looked around. *Where are her confederates?* She stopped in front of an apartment building, took off her bandana, and stuffed it into a brown sack she held under her arm. *That's it, the bandana; it's a sign for her accomplices. There must be an apartment in that building she wants to hit. I'm on to her.*

At Fifty-Third Street, she crossed over to Ellis and headed toward the Gothic spires and towers of the University of Chicago campus in Hyde Park. Dickie had been trailing her for more than an hour when she stopped to rest on a bench by the massive medieval façade of Stagg Field, the campus football field. He darted across Ellis so she wouldn't notice him. *Where are her confederates? They must have scattered when she stopped.* He ran to the other end of Stagg Field but found no one. When he returned to the bench, she was gone.

A group of pigeons followed her through Cobb Gate into the gray quadrangle of the U of C. Dickie sprinted through the shadow of the ornate stone portal, but she was gone. He heard the gargoyles and griffins atop Cobb Gate laugh as he headed back to Kenwood.

## AS MOTHS AND BUTTERFLIES DO

For Dickie Loeb, wealth had its misfortunes.[15] As a child, he did his best to escape reality. He created a world of fantasy to avoid what others saw as a blessing: a privileged life filled with opportunity.

He loved his father, but he saw little of him because of Albert Loeb's responsibilities at Sears. The overzealous Miss Struthers overshadowed his mother in many aspects of his life, and Dickie felt inferior to his older brothers. So, he created a life of fantasy in which he played the leading role.

As he grew, his profound indulgence in fantasy grew. Miss Struthers's daily routine of reading and studying allowed little opportunity for Dickie to play outdoors with boys his own age. He was often alone, with too much time to think about his unsatisfactory life. Miss Struthers's strict rules took away his childhood pleasures, except for lying.

She pushed him in his studies. He entered University High on the U. of C. campus and received a high-school diploma in just two years. The baby-faced Dickie wore knee pants at his commencement. The parents of Ellis Avenue thought he was special, telling their own kids that Dickie Loeb was an example of a perfect child. Julius Rosenwald's daughter Marian said her father was jealous because his children were just ordinary kids.[16] Dickie enrolled at the University of Chicago at age fourteen. He transferred to the University of Michigan as a junior and graduated when he was eighteen. His voice still changing, Dickie Loeb became the youngest graduate in the school's history.

Miss Struthers continued to tutor Dickie during his first year in college and left him during that year, too. As she envisioned, Dickie's rapid scholastic accomplishments made him the ideal boy. But in Anna Loeb's eyes, Miss Struthers's role with Dickie had run its course. Anna believed the governess created disharmony in the family.[17] She assigned her youngest son, Tommy, to Miss Struthers's care, but the governess refused and left the Loeb home in 1920.

Polite and obedient to his family, Dickie continued to be the ideal boy at home following Miss Struthers's departure. But how would he grow in the real world, away from the hothouse environment of Miss Struthers?

Dickie had no trouble making friends. He began drinking alcohol at age fifteen, the same age he lost his virginity.[18] For the next three years, he carried a pocket flask of gin or bourbon. During this time, he also experienced facial tremors, especially when he became emotional. This affliction, however, failed to diminish his social skills, especially with the girls. Dickie's childlike face and wide smile attracted the opposite sex, but he actually lacked sexual potency.[19]

He traveled in the company of girls only because it was the thing to do. He really didn't enjoy sex. Dickie found it more stimulating to lie about his sexual exploits. He also lied about his grades, which were only average. He manufactured emotional satisfaction by demonstrating intellectual superiority over everyone. This feeling of superiority made him indifferent to the feelings of others. One close friend of Dickie Loeb said, "He blended [into] his environment as some moths and butterflies do. Dickie was at home with everybody but looked down on everyone."[20]

With Miss Struthers out of his life, Dickie became an addict looking for a fix. He frantically reached out for attention, for someone who would idolize him, someone who could fill his extreme needs. He found this in a U. of C. freshman named Nathan F. Leopold Jr.

## ONLY THE CROWS

He considered himself a cold-blooded intellect, so mourning was not an option.

Nathan F. Leopold Jr. looked down on his mother's grave with no emotion. He stood erect in the early morning mist, not giving in to the chilly air or the moment. His long, oval face carried no expression, no hint.

God took her away when she was needed; he would not worship such a God.

*Mother, poor mother, idolized by all who knew you. I know I'll never see you again. What was it you used to say to your Babe? "Happiness is a perfume you cannot sprinkle on others without getting a few drops on yourself."*

For Babe Leopold, age eighteen, there was no such thing as an immortal soul. And no beginning or end to the universe. Time, according to Babe Leopold, was merely the fourth dimension.

Babe left the grave and walked past the rows of ancient monuments in the cemetery's Jewish quarter. He headed for Jackson Park; it was migration season.

They returned every April—warblers, song sparrows, orioles, bluebirds, and starlings—enhancing the mysterious poetic effect on Wooded Island, Frederick Law Olmsted's sanctuary of natural beauty in Jackson Park.[21] By 1923, the thousands of trees and shrubs Olmsted planted for the 1893 World's Columbian Exposition had matured. The island belonged to the birds, their colors and songs living in harmony with the wild grasses and flowers, reddish jewelweed, and aquatic plants.

Babe Leopold's interest in birding followed his cataloging instinct.[22] As a youngster, he collected stamps, butterflies, and birds. He filled his second-floor bedroom with stuffed birds. When he was a teenager, he shot at a bird on the front lawn of his Kenwood home, narrowly missing the governess who lived next door.[23] By the time he was a junior at the University of Chicago, Babe had become an expert in ornithology. He conducted bird walks for high school students, married women, and grade-school children. They visited Wooded Island and nature preserves far south of the city. Babe usually preceded his birding classes with a visit to his mother's grave.

Nearing age two hundred, the giant oak in the center of Wooded Island was the oldest tree in the city. It rose sixty-five feet and its gangly arms stretched ninety feet, shading much of the island. Protected by two-inch-thick, black, corky bark, the oak's trunk measured more than three feet in diameter. Its low bow lured climbing youngsters, and thousands of birds, including robins, flickers, and great crested flycatchers, found a home in its hallows. In the fall, the sprawling oak covered the earth with its silken-fingered leaves the size of a hand.[24] The black walnuts, willows, catalpas, buckeyes, American lindens, and elms gave way to the mighty oak of Wooded Island. Only the crows disrupted the ancient oak. Aggressive and intelligent, the noisy crows dominated the oak's massive crown, eyeing their prey below.

Steady shrieks from atop the oak greeted Babe as he waited for his morning bird walkers. He lit a cigarette and peered through his field glasses at the predators in the high branches, ignoring the songs of a nearby scarlet tanager.

## SWEETIE

Babe was Florence Leopold's last child, born a sickly six pounds, four ounces.

Babe battled a series of childhood illnesses, including gastrointestinal disturbances that caused him headaches and vomiting. He was lethargic and had little energy until doctors removed his tonsils at age nine. Babe believed that before the tonsillectomy he had been a girl, but following it, he had become a boy.[25]

Precociousness marked his youth. His first words—"Nein, nein, mama"— came at four months.[26] At three, he recited his first prayer: "Ich bin klein, mein Herz ist rein" ("I am small, my heart is pure").[27] At age seven, he attempted to learn the word *yes* in every language. He would eventually speak twenty-one languages.

His mother, the daughter of German Jewish bankers, involved herself in many charitable causes. His father, Nathan, after a career in the Great Lakes navigation business, owned a box-manufacturing company, the Morris Paper Mills. He ran the business with his two oldest sons, Foreman "Mike" and Samuel. The Leopolds of Kenwood enjoyed a privileged standing in Chicago's German Jewish community. Their three-story home kept a company of workers, including a governess the boys called Sweetie.

An Alsatian immigrant who spoke no English, Sweetie entered Babe's life when he was in grade school. A homely, scheming woman, Sweetie wore gaudy red bows and thought she was beautiful. She did not get along with the other servants in the Leopold household. She possessed a violent temper and a twisted moral compass. Babe was thoroughly devoted to her.[28]

Sweetie took control of the boys when Nathan and Florence Leopold left the house. She bathed with Babe's older brother Sam and fondled him and then took him to bed to wrestle. She did the same with Babe. She offered nicknames for her breasts and nipples. She allowed the boys to examine her in a dressing closet and told them their mother wished she had a figure like Sweetie's. They believed her, especially Babe.

Sweetie always rewarded Babe's obedience. The governess and Babe wrestled on his bed, and she permitted him to rub his penis between her legs.[29]

Florence Leopold fired Sweetie when Babe was twelve. Although Babe's mother did not know the specifics of the relationships, she became indignant over the nursemaid's familiarity with her sons. Sweetie returned to Alsace and took up residence in Strasbourg, at 9 Rue de Bambino—Street of the Children.[30]

## KING/SLAVE

Babe idolized his oldest brother, Foreman. Handsome in his military school uniform, Foreman was the original catalyst for Babe's nightly fantasies, which began at age five. Simple in the beginning, the fantasies grew into complicated plots as Babe Leopold reached puberty and searched for his ideal companion.

Before he drifted to sleep, Babe hugged his pillow and took pleasure in the aroma of his own body. Only then was he ready.

*The slave-drivers beat the young boy until he could no longer stand. Bloody and dirty, they left him for dead. The King, tall and strong, came upon the Slave and saved his life. Under the King's command, he grew healthy and fit. The beautiful Slave resembled the Hart, Schaffner, & Marx man. In a heroic battle, the Slave saved the King's life. For this brave act, the King offered the Slave his freedom, but the Slave refused. He would always serve the King. To seal their bond, the King took the Slave to the gymnasium locker room of the Harvard School, where he branded a crown seal into the Slave's right leg.[31]*

*Lost at sea, Babe and his closest companion washed up on an unknown island. Two groups of people occupied this island: Nobles and Slaves. Babe spoke the natives' language. A piano survived the boat's wreckage, and Babe taught the natives about music. Because of his knowledge of music, Babe was a Noble. He selected his companion as his Slave. His Slave once belonged to another Noble, who mistreated him. Babe nursed him to health and gave his Slave three options: (1) to remove the brand on the Slave's right leg and set him free, although the Slave's original Noble could recapture him; (2) to remain his personal slave; (3) to sell him to another Noble, who would treat him far worse. On this island, the Nobles and Slaves use two words of endearment:* pussy *and* kitten.

## SUCH LITTLE FATE

As a boy, he believed a man was good until proven otherwise.[32] It was a philosophy he quickly outgrew.

Babe had a deep affection for his mother. She was, as he put it, "disgustingly and inordinately" proud of him. Easy to persuade, Babe always won her over. In the fall of 1921, Bright's disease, a kidney ailment she developed during her pregnancy with Babe, took her. Babe believed he caused her death, and it changed him forever.[33]

At age seventeen and after his mother passed away, his dreams had given way to distortion. Babe devoured the philosophy of Friedrich Wilhelm Nietzsche. It became his code and would eventually define him. He believed in Nietzsche's contemptuous and scornful attitude of life and adopted the philosopher's idea that evolution would create the superman. Man, Nietzsche wrote, has obligation only to his equals. The superman will be a law unto himself.

*God is a cruel and senseless God. Making friends will hurt you. There is no such thing as right and wrong. Justice has no objective existence. Happiness is the only thing that matters.[34] Anything that gives pleasure is right, even to steal or kill. The only way to overcome temptation is to give in to it.[35]*

According to Friedrich Nietzsche and Babe Leopold, only superior individuals—the noble ones—can rise above to create a heroic life.

## FLEA

His intellect consumed him.

Kenwood's wealthy sent their children to the Harvard School. Babe excelled in language, notably German and Greek. Languages, he knew, made him different. His prep school classmates agreed. Their sarcastic profile of Babe covered two paragraphs in the 1920 *Harvard Review*.

> Nathan Leopold, the crazy "bird" of the school.[36] The avicular member of the Fifth class is forever harping on birds, their advantages, and their twitterings known in all zoos, bird paradise, and bipedded creatures' communities. "Flea" has not found much difficulty in covering his yet unsprouted wings, and is always up to some . . . mischief. His favorite prank is proving Mr. Schobinger wrong or telling Mr. M. K. M. that he is laboring under a major neurosis.

"Flea, to leave the ridiculous—is proud owner of a large museum of birds, bugs, antiquities and . . . souvenirs," the *Harvard Review* yearbook said. "A favorite remark of this crazed genius every other Monday morning: 'Oh! Only 16 A's.'"

In October of 1920, Babe, just shy of his sixteenth birthday, entered the University of Chicago. He studied the prescribed major as a freshman: English, Latin, and psychology. He also devoured Russian, Latin, Spanish, Sanskrit, Modern Greek, ethics, and social origins before graduating in 1923 with a bachelor of philosophy, Phi Beta Kappa. He called his ability in school "ten percent work and ninety percent horse shit."[37]

## REVERIES

They were kids with an endless playground. As 1920 collegians, Dickie Loeb and Babe Leopold belonged to a growing elite group—sophisticated youth who worshiped prestige and conformity over achievement. Sophomoric in Fitzgeraldesque fashion, they recklessly raced through adolescence. Mentally, they possessed complete, unquestioned superiority; socially, they dominated all contemporary males.[38] And, like Amory Blaine, F. Scott Fitzgerald's young egotist in *This Side of Paradise*, they "saw people as automatons to their will. They would pass as many boys as possible to get to a vague top of the world."[39]

After Babe's first year at the University of Chicago, he and Dickie transferred to the University of Michigan. Both boys left the U. of C. because they felt it was like going to a neighborhood high school. As Amory Blaine told his generation, "You ought to go away to school, Froggy. It's great stuff." Dickie and Babe roomed together at Michigan until Dickie joined the school's Jewish fraternity, the Phi chapter of Zeta Beta Tau. Dickie's frat crowd did not care for his sullen friend. When rumors of a homosexual relationship spread, Dickie distanced himself from Babe, who left Michigan after one year and returned to the U. of C.

College life was all about conformity and peer pressure. The atmosphere was perfect for Dickie: Bragging, lying, and conducting heart-to-heart bull sessions with pretty coeds all came easily to Dickie. To fit in with the older students on the University of Chicago campus, Dickie started drinking regularly in his freshman year. It was a prerequisite, like English or history, and damn the Volstead Act. The freshman handbook noted, "in order to be collegiate, one must drink."[40] The more Dickie drank, the more he lied. He lost distinction between truth and falsehood.[41]

Babe's collegiate badge was a cocksure, jaunty arrogance. He patronized his friends and talked of himself in the third person. He dated only because it was expected of him and thought of women as intellectually inferior. Many times—to show his superiority—he stayed awake all night and then started his day by setting bird traps.

As other U. of C. students reveled in fraternity parties and bootleg gin, two confederates with very different personalities schemed to bring life to their childhood fantasies. Their unholy alliance grew under the cover of night.

While his family slept, Babe Leopold slipped out the back door and sneaked into the garage behind his house. He released the brake on his red Willys-Knight and steered as the automobile coasted down the driveway toward Greenwood Avenue. Once on the street, he started the engine, and the pain in the pit of his stomach returned. A few blocks from his home, he turned the car down Ellis Avenue and saw Dickie Loeb waiting. He was smoking a cigarette and leaning against the low brick wall that circled his parents' mansion. Calm and confident in the moonlight, Dickie watched the treetops bend in the summer breeze. *The Slave stopped the Willys and opened the door for the King.*

The late-night adventures began with drinking, usually in Jackson Park near the golf course.[42] Dickie carried a flask of gin, and Babe kept a bottle of whiskey in his car. Babe drove his Willys-Knight, lights dimmed, through the park, while Dickie threw bricks at the windshields of cars parked with late-night lovers. One night, Dickie picked the wrong victim. His brick smashed the target, interrupting a petting couple. The man bolted from the back seat and started shooting. Dickie roared with laughter as the Willys sped away.

Another night, they selected a drugstore. Dickie's brick smashed the plate-glass window, setting off the burglar alarm. A pair of beat cops heard the noise and fired. The boys got away, but a police bullet pierced Babe's Willys. Dickie loved the episode; Babe's stomach ached.

Dickie needed more involvement, more excitement, and a larger audience. Babe and he found a shack in a vacant lot, doused it with gasoline, and lit it on fire. After fleeing the scene, Dickie and Babe returned to witness the blaze. Dickie questioned people who had gathered to watch the fire. *So how do you suppose such a thing happened? Did anyone see any suspicious characters hanging around? Jimmie Dale would be proud.*

Dickie concocted an elaborate plan to rob the wine cellar of some friends who lived in Hubbard Woods, on Chicago's North Shore. Dickie knew when the owners of the home would be out of town. He bought a chisel and wrapped its blade with adhesive tape. He'd use it to break into the home. He brought a rope, should they need to tie up the maid. Dickie and Babe each carried a loaded revolver, should there be a night watchman. However, Dickie abandoned his carefully orchestrated heist when they failed to break into the securely locked home. Dickie was happy with the whole idea. The planning, not the bounty, pleased him.

In February of 1921, a light snow coated the elegant cars of the Twentieth Century Limited as it left LaSalle Street Station. Genteel African American waiters in crisp, white coats readied the heavy silver and starched napery on dining-car tables. A few cars up the track in a Pullman sleeper, Dickie Loeb taught Babe Leopold the finer points of card cheating.[43] The boys memorized hand signals so they could outbid the young patsies of Charlevoix, Michigan. Babe learned quickly. The weathered Indiana barns and farm homes kept pace with the speeding train through the sleeper's window while Dickie rewarded Babe for the first time.

Albert Loeb's Charlevoix estate in northern Michigan fit his stature as acting president of Sears, Roebuck. Cows and sheep grazed the sixteen hundred acres, and nearly a hundred workers and servants tended to the many medieval-looking fieldstone buildings built on a high bluff overlooking the wooded shores of Pine Lake. Loeb's main home featured a spreading lawn shaded by large poplars and pines. Architect Arthur Heun, who built Loeb's Kenwood home, designed the buildings to resemble the stone barns of Normandy.[44] Loeb used the land as a model farm where he raised livestock using farm equipment sold through the Sears catalog. Loeb built a new school for local children, one that included a motion-picture machine and recreation hall. He also provided a school bus for the small rural community. Loeb's property included a baseball diamond with stone bleachers. The ball field was open to the community.

The Loebs spent vacations and holidays in Charlevoix, and Dickie, one might say, acted as the Pied Piper of Charlevoix.

And where Dickie went . . . Babe followed.

Babe was a frequent visitor to Charlevoix, although the town kids thought he was aloof and patronizing. Babe, however, was more interested in the birds of northern Michigan than the people. In the summer of 1923, Babe and a few associates made ornithological news. Not far off highway M-10, in the middle of dense jack pine and yellow oak, they discovered the nest of the rare Kirtland's Warbler. His associate James McGillivray photographed Babe's hand-feeding the rare bird. The ornithological community praised Babe's discovery. *Auk*, a quarterly journal on ornithology, published his findings, "The Kirtland's Warbler in Its Summer Home." That October, he addressed the American Ornithological Society in Boston. It would be Babe's last major birding expedition.

Football paralyzed the University of Michigan campus on autumn Saturdays. On November 10, 1923, more than forty-five thousand giddy fans left Ferry Field after their team's victory over the Quantico Marines. Many attended campus parties, including one at the Phi chapter of the Zeta Beta Tau. In Kenwood, two former Michigan students had prepared a party of their own.

Dickie Loeb's plan, as usual, was complicated. Babe and he would drive 240 miles through the night and arrive at the Zeta Beta Tau house at the University of Michigan in early Sunday morning when everyone would be asleep. Dickie told his parents he would be attending a fraternity function at Northwestern University in Evanston and wouldn't be home until midday Sunday. He wrote a letter to himself outlining the Evanston event and mailed to his home in Kenwood.[45] The letter was his cover.

Zeta Beta Tau brothers and their guests were asleep in the attic when Dickie and Babe entered the three-story gabled home. Each carried a revolver and a flashlight. Dickie's weapon of choice was a chisel, its blade wrapped in tape.[46] He would use the blade end as a grip and strike a blow with the wooden handle. Babe carried a rope. They made their way easily through the fraternity's unlocked front door. Dickie and Babe went into the second-floor study rooms where the fraternity brothers left their clothing. They collected $74, several watches, fountain pens, and knives. Babe grabbed a portable typewriter. "We took everything we could get our hands on," Dickie said later.

A second fraternity house, one suggested by Babe, was also on their hit list. But after a few minutes inside the home, they heard a noise and made a hasty exit, stealing only a camera.

On the return trip, Dickie and Babe were tired, and they argued, but they knew they needed each other. On the dark roads between Ann Arbor and Kenwood, they struck a pact: The Master Criminal found his confederate, and the Slave won a personal premium each time he obeyed his King.[47]

## FOR ROBERT'S SAKE

Dickie and Babe were sons of millionaires, and money followed their every whim. Dickie nodded, and Albert Loeb's secretary wrote a check; Babe's stipend from his father was $125 a month.[48] Automobiles and the latest cottons and tweeds from Brooks' shaped their style, as did their Rudolph Valentino haircuts. Both boys wore their long, dark hair slicked down and combed back. The look failed to soften Babe's swarthy, angular face. Heavy eyebrows that met atop cold, gray-blue eyes gave him a sinister appearance. His smile was more like a smirk. Dickie, though, was radiant. The girls found him irresistible. One admirer said, "I always loved that childlike face of his—almost like a girl sometimes, when his eyes were soft and happy and he laughed."[49]

Sophisticated and raucous—even shocking—Dickie and Babe scampered through life as typical Fitzgeraldesque heroes: always laughing but never light-hearted.[50] Like Fitzgerald's Amory Blaine, they enjoyed each day as insolent University of Chicago graduate students in the fall of 1923, as they would "probably never enjoy it again. Everything was hallowed by the haze of (their) own youth."

Babe found Dickie to be totally alluring, physically and intellectually. Dickie's social grace—his savoir faire—captivated Babe.

"Dick could charm the birds out of the trees," Babe said.[51] "He could get along with anyone, make anyone like him. He always knew how to act, what to say. In any company."[52]

Dickie stood six feet—four inches taller than Babe—with a young face lighted by deep-brown eyes. The only blemish—a small scar above his chin from a childhood velocipede accident. Also, sporadic facial tremors—easily noticeable during stress—caused Dickie's charming smile to twinge in an awkward fashion.

Dickie's persona was a direct opposite to Babe's nervous and sullen nature. Babe believed Dickie was intellectually superior to him but lazy and without the same intellectual pursuits.[53] Babe's cataloguing instincts—and his biological proclivities—led him to develop a chart for the perfect man.[54] Dickie topped the list with a score of ninety; Babe's sixty-eight lagged behind. "At this time there was an almost complete identification of myself with Dick," he would say years later. "It was blind hero worship."[55]

It was, in reality, the fulfillment of Babe's King/Slave fantasy.

The orange glow from his cigarette illuminated a sliver of Babe's dark face as he drove through the Midwestern night toward home. A steady curtain of smoke hung inside the speeding Willys-Knight, but Dickie didn't mind. His confident words cut through the haze. After several years of childish notions, the Master Criminal was ready to take his pathological pleasures to a new realm.[56]

Their new compact would etch their destiny and forever link their names. These two overeducated and pampered eighteen-year-olds, these two aberrant personalities supplemented their abnormal needs in a unique way.[57] Babe's nicotine-stained fingers lit yet another cigarette as Dickie drank from a flask and articulated his plan.

Although they had known each other intimately since they were fifteen and had carried out many petty crimes together, neither wholly trusted the other.[58] They argued for hours on the ride home—mostly about each other's work in the robberies and about their personal relationships.[59] They had been on rocky terms for several weeks. Earlier that autumn in 1923, Babe sent Dickie a long, emotional letter that outlined a severe breach in their relationship: "When you came to my house this afternoon I expected either to break friendship with you or attempt to kill you unless you told me why you acted as you did yesterday."[60]

This new compact would now allow Dickie and Babe to live out their childhood fantasies and continue their relationship, albeit within certain parameters. "For Robert's Sake"—this was the catalyst.[61] When Dickie made a request of Babe using "For Robert's Sake," Babe had to do what Dickie suggested—usually a criminal act. (Under the pact, though, Dickie never commanded Babe to partake in any activity that would cause trouble with Babe's family.) This cryptic pact would remain alive until Babe traveled to Europe the following summer.

For Babe . . . *The King, tall and strong, came upon the Slave and saved his life. Under the King's command, he grew healthy and fit.* Each time Babe obeyed the "For Robert's Sake" edict, Dickie rewarded him. Babe had the privilege of inserting his penis between Dickie's thighs—once for every criminal deed.[62] *He would always serve the King.*

Babe quickly bought into the deal. He didn't care about Dickie's criminal plans, only that the covenant provided satisfaction for his desires, his own personal gratification.[63] It was enough for him.

They drove in silence after finalizing their perverse covenant. Dickie said nothing as Babe continued to smoke. Dickie Loeb, the Master Criminal, knew he was well on his way to committing the perfect crime. The exhausted boys stared far beyond the shaky glow of the Willys's headlamps as they passed the Illinois state line.

# Part Two

## Realities

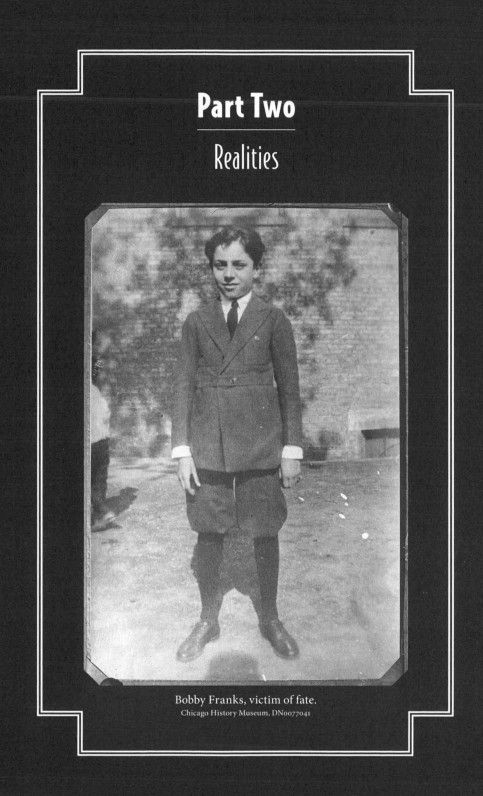

Bobby Franks, victim of fate.

## CITY OF THE BIG SHOULDERS

On the evening of November 19, 1923, Dickie and Babe led an urbane group of University of Chicago students to a few of their favorite cabarets near Hyde Park. It was Babe's nineteenth birthday. In typical Roaring Twenties' style—the men in baggy tweeds, the women in bright-colored bandannas around their heads and waists—they drank up what the Jazz Age had to offer. Raunchy and splashy, Dickie and Babe were part of a peer group who stressed prestige and popularity.

Alcohol played a huge role in the lives of the collegiate elite. Fraternity parties across the nation ignored Prohibition laws, and sophisticated college men never left home without their hip flasks. Drinking became such a problem at the University of Chicago that its dean sent a letter to all fraternity presidents. He threatened to "employ detectives" to weed out the booze. "Drinking has no proper place in the life at the University of Chicago," he wrote. "And it must go."[1] It didn't. And everything that went with it—the petting parties, the dancing, the jazz, especially the jazz—prospered in the gray shadows of the U. of C.

The Jazz Age lit up Chicago's South Side. Lured by the lively trumpets and trombones of the "colored folk," curious white Chicagoans became tourists in their own city. To protect their virtue, they left their quiet neighborhoods late at night for the black-and-tan cafes of Thirty-Fifth Street. There, lights sparkled, glasses tinkled, and the rhythms and laughter poured onto the crowded sidewalks.[2] There, black musicians, in crisp, tailored tuxedoes, flashed diamond-studded smiles and filled the smoky nightclubs with jazz. There, barely two miles from the mansions of Kenwood, white millionaires and philanthropists mingled with the sporting set, sneaking a glimpse at this new northern black culture. The white rich danced, flirted, and drank bootleg gin until dawn with these young black "immigrants."

How easy it was to become a victim on the streets of Chicago. Violence, like bathtub gin, was everywhere. The front page of the *Chicago Daily Tribune* kept its readers apprised by publishing a morbid, hand-drawn graphic of a death clock. The "Hands of Death" tracked the death toll in Cook County from automobiles, guns, and moonshine. In the last week of November, 1923, the Hands of Death alerted *Tribune* readers that 643 persons had died since January 1 from automobile accidents, 234 from guns, and 189 from moonshine.[3]

On the night of Babe's birthday celebration, a twenty-one-year-old taxi driver, Charles Ream, returned his Yellow Cab to its South Side garage after his shift. He had a quick bite to eat with some fellow drivers in the garage lunchroom and then, around midnight, boarded a cream and crimson streetcar for Hyde Park. Ream got off the rickety car at Fifty-Fifth Street and Dorchester Avenue and headed for his home a few blocks north.

On this cold Monday night, the bare catalpa trees on Dorchester provided little protection from the late-autumn wind. Ream didn't hear the automobile pull up behind him.

"Hands up!"[4]

The man who shouted the order held a gun. His accomplice—a young man with a long, hard face and murder in his eyes—shoved Ream into the car's back seat.[5] Inside the dark car, one of the men held a flashlight while his partner tied Ream's hands behind his back with a rope. He shoved a gag into Ream's mouth and wrapped a rope around his head to keep it in place. He blindfolded the cab driver, threw him to the floor, and covered him with a heavy blanket. The smell of ether hung in the car as it made a U-turn and headed south out of Hyde Park.

An orange sun slowly rose from Lake Michigan as Charles Ream regained consciousness. He awoke in great pain, his face buried in the long, wet grass of a prairie on the city's far southeast side. His clothing was half removed and soaked with blood. A county physician would call the castration a "bungling job."[6]

Freeman Louis Tracy was a social favorite on the University of Chicago campus. Many coeds called him "the handsomest man in the university."[7] A part-time student, Tracy earned $600 a month as an electrical worker for Commonwealth Edison.[8] He was pleasant and intelligent, and the girls found him to be an excellent dancer, despite his artificial leg.

After spending much of the evening at a union-sponsored dance on November 24, 1923, Tracy accepted a ride back to Hyde Park from a fellow worker. At half past midnight, his friend dropped him off at Sixtieth Street and Cottage Grove Avenue, in front of Frank Lloyd Wright's festive Midway Gardens. The Gardens, Wright's avant-garde commitment to public luxury, featured a five-tier, outdoor summer garden, a band shell, and a winter garden. Nearly one hundred Alfonso Iannelli graceful figures—the Midway Gardens' sprites—inhabited the block-long entertainment complex. Cottage Grove, at the western tip of the Midway

Plaisance, came alive at night. It was home to a string of nightclubs and theaters, including the Trianon, billed as America's most luxurious public ballroom. The Trianon's dance hall—inspired by the splendor of Versailles—sparkled with crystal chandeliers and marble columns. The music of Benny Goodman, Louis Armstrong, and Bix Beiderbecke poured onto Cottage Grove Avenue. Tracy enjoyed the Saturday night atmosphere for a few hours before heading for his apartment near the U. of C. campus.

Tracy had no clue the large touring car, its headlamps dimmed, was following him as he walked along Fifty-Eighth Street. As the car quietly pulled alongside him, a small, yellow flash flew toward his head.

Long after the nightclubs and dance halls of Cottage Grove closed, police discovered Tracy's crumpled body lying on Fifty-Eighth Street, a steel-jacketed bullet in his temple.[9] In the early morning hours of November 25, 1923, Freeman Louis Tracy, the handsomest man on campus, had become the latest fatality on the *Tribune*'s Hands of Death clock.

It seemed like every block in Carl Sandburg's "City of the Big Shoulders" was on the take.

Chicago's underbelly got fat on Prohibition. Organized gangs of beer-runners and bootleggers—more than thirteen hundred—ruled the city with a nightstick mentality.[10] Beer money greased the palms of cops, politicians, judges, and newspapermen. A young police officer made easy money if he looked the other way as the beer truck passed by; and his deputy commissioner made even more. Half the police force was crooked. The pipeline was easy for the gangsters. They bribed the ward bosses who had influence not only in City Hall but also in the courts. The notorious Torrio gang once tried to bribe the police chief—$1,000 a day if he allowed shipments of whiskey into the city.[11] Winds of corruption whipped across the Windy City, and like a hot summer's day in the stockyards, no one escaped its stench.

Perhaps Chicago voters had Sandburg's *Smoke and Steel* in mind when they went to the polls on Election Day, 1923.

> Play it across the table,
> What if we steal this city blind?
> If they want anything, let 'em nail it down.

For eight years, Republican William Hale Thompson, a boisterous political showman, ran a wide-open town. Chicagoans finally became fed up with their mayor's unabashed relationship with crime bosses, notably master criminal Johnny Torrio and his protégé Al Capone. Chicagoans were also disillusioned with Thompson on other fronts. They blamed him for reacting too slowly to calm a race riot in 1919 when fighting broke out at a South Side beach and spread to the neighborhoods. Thirty-eight people died before the militia stepped in. And there were the public schools. Educators called Chicago's schools a national disgrace.[12] Thompson has played politics with the schools long enough, Chicagoans said. Big Bill wisely decided not to run for a third straight term, leaving the door open for the reformers.

Toward the end of 1922, a group of socially prominent advocates of clean government met at the City Club, whose members monitored urban reform. Their aim: find someone who could restore dignity to the mayor's office. Clarence Darrow, Chicago's most famous defense attorney and popular liberal orator, told the distinguished gathering, "Chicago needs a mayor who has the courage to say 'no,' and to say it to his best friends."[13]

Democrats found such a man within the judicial system. William Emmett Dever of the Superior Court enjoyed a spotless reputation as a civic-minded judge. He told the city he was his own man and promised to "appoint men free from the taint of politics."[14] Dever's stylish, sixtyish looks—silver hair, trimmed mustache, honest, blue eyes—appealed to Chicagoans who hungered for a distinguished mayor to replace Big Bill. Dever won the election by more than one hundred thousand votes.

Chicago appeared ready for reform. On the night of Dever's inauguration, several thousand people celebrated on LaSalle Street outside City Hall. Inside, a huge throng of supporters packed the ornate marble lobby, and long lines stretched up two flights of stairs to the city-council chambers. Chicago's fifty aldermen stood and applauded as Big Bill placed the gavel in Dever's right hand.[15] The overflowing visitors' gallery erupted in deafening cheers and hurrahs.

Dever—"Decent Dever" as he was called—believed a blatant disrespect for the law existed in the nation following World War I, especially in Chicago. He said, "Restoring respect for the law rests squarely on my shoulders."[16]

Crooked cops were Dever's first challenge. Calling Chicago's police department a "constantly recurring source of trouble," Dever turned to a thirty-five-year police veteran, Morgan Collins, to shoulder the trouble.[17] During his second week as mayor, Dever named Collins chief of police. Collins's police career was impeccably clean. A North Side Republican, he received bipartisan praise. His appointment, politicos thought, proved Dever was serious about reform.

All his life, Collins had dreamed about becoming a doctor. He studied medicine but never earned his degree. Now, in his thirty-fifth year as a cop, he became responsible for healing a police force sick with corruption. A wide-chested man with sandy, wavy hair parted down the middle, Collins carried the look of a compassionate man. He wore a bow tie—usually crooked—with his formal double-breasted police coat.

On his first day as police chief, Collins held a frank meeting with his captains. He told them he knew that patrolmen, detectives, sergeants, and even some lieutenants had direct connections with bootleggers.

"Dealing in whisky and beer by members of the police department is at an end," he said.[18] "His honor, the mayor, has promised that all Chicagoans will be freed from commercial vice, gambling, bootlegging and other preventable crimes. He has promised a strict enforcement of all the laws, and we of the police department are going to make good on those promises."

He then placed responsibility directly on the captains. "No power will be greater than yours," he told them.

The next day, police raided gambling dens and brothels across the city. District captains led many of the raids themselves. Collins reshuffled the department. He moved seventeen captains to new districts and transferred more than one hundred patrolmen.[19]

The South Side was the first area to feel the Dever-Collins muscle. The mayor ordered a crackdown on the black-and-tan clubs. Dever called the interracial cabarets "vile in the last degree." Cops arrested hundreds of people.

Collins then took on Chicago's most notorious gangsters—the Torrio-Capone syndicate. The Four Deuces—at 2222 South Wabash Avenue—was more than a crime headquarters. The modest, four-story, red-brick building was a metaphor for Chicago's lifestyle under Big Bill Thompson. Located in the middle of the old South Side Levee—an area of brothels, bordellos, gambling and opium dens, and penny arcades—the Four Deuces had it all: saloon, bookkeeping office, gambling floor, and whorehouse. Dever and Collins even went after small-time "alky cookers," who made moonshine in restaurants and private homes.

As 1923 came to an end, the face of Chicago still belonged to gangsters—their killings, their bribes, their control. Murder was commonplace. Nearly one thousand people were slain in Chicago in the decade's first four years.[20] But the crime that would shock the city like no other brewed silently in the minds of Dickie Loeb and Babe Leopold.

## ACCIDENTS OF SERIOUS NATURE

A childhood of studying crime—in books, in magazines, in newspapers—came to fruition for Dickie Loeb in the winter months of 1924. "For

Robert's Sake"—his pact with Babe—firmly in place, Dickie began for-
mulating his plan with his permissive confederate. The thrill for Dickie
was in the planning and the more complicated the better. The cleverness
of the crime—that's what aroused him.[21] It was time for Dickie Loeb to
replace the dashing Jimmie Dale as the master criminal, kingpin of them
all. Dickie's crime, he knew, would stir the nation—like the abduction
of young Charley Ross.

> On a warm July day in 1874, a buggy carrying two men comes to
> rest on East Washington Lane, a tree-lined cobblestone roadway in
> Germantown, Pennsylvania. Handsome homes—on high ground,
> set back some distance from the road—sit comfortably behind acres
> of well-kept lawns covered with tress and shrubs. Charley Ross, a
> four-year-old with a round and full face surrounded by drooping
> flaxen curls, plays with his older brother Walter as the carriage
> stops in front of their home. One of the men—the one with the red
> whiskers and a deformed, turned-up nose—offers the boys candy.
> As he takes the peppermints from the man's hand, Walter notices
> two gold rings on one of the man's fingers. Charley follows Walter
> into the buggy. A few blocks up East Washington Lane, the men
> give Walter some money and tell him to run into the general store
> to buy some fireworks. They'll wait for him. When Walter returns,
> the carriage is missing—his brother Charley gone forever.[22]

Charley's abductors sent twenty-three ransom letters to his father.
They threatened to kill Charley if his father hired detectives: "if you
put the cops hunting for him you is only defeating yu own end . . . if
any aproch is maid to his hidin place that is the signil for his instant
annihilation."[23] The second letter demanded $20,000 ransom: "This is
the lever that moved the rock that hides him from yu $20,000. not one
doller les—impossible—impossible—you cannot get him without it."[24]
Christian Ross communicated with the men through the personal columns of the local newspaper for nearly a year.

The Pinkerton Detective Agency looked for the boy, distributing cir-
culars with a photo of Charley, including a reward offer of $20,000.[25]
The entire nation followed the case of Charley Ross in the newspapers.
A song, "Bring Back Our Darling," swept the country in sheet-music
form. Ross agreed to pay the ransom, but the complicated payment ar-
rangements failed, and communications ceased.[26] Christian Ross never
saw his son again.

Two years after his loss, Ross wrote a book detailing the mysterious
disappearance of his son, America's first kidnapping for ransom. *Charley*

*Ross, the Kidnapped Child—A Father's Story* was nightly reading—before picturization—for a young Dickie Loeb.

Inside the homes of Kenwood and Hyde Park lay unspoken fears of kidnapping.

Young, cocky, and well-to-do, Frederick C. Robie knew what he wanted in a home.[27] And only Frank Lloyd Wright could deliver it. When Robie, a bicycle manufacturer and creator of the experimental Robie Cycle Car, selected the site in 1908 for his new house, he envisioned a home of wonder and enchantment.[28] Robie found a long, narrow lot on the northeast corner of Fifty-Eighth Street and Woodlawn Avenue, a block north of the Midway Plaisance.

Wright's design proved true to his reputation: "sheltering overhangs, low terraces and outreaching walls sequestering private gardens."[29] Robie's three-story brick home stretched low to the ground, like a sleek ship, its clean lines reflecting Wright's adoration of the Midwestern prairie. Wright designed Robie's house to be at peace with nature, a stark contrast to the architecture of the University of Chicago, which Wright called "hybrid Collegiate Gothic."[30]

In the garden area—between the garage and the house—a brick retaining wall protected Robie's young children. He had insisted upon it: "These kids could not be gotten out of the yard, nor could they help themselves to foreign travel. They were fully protected; and that should eliminate accidents of serious nature."

Frederick C. Robie would call the house "the most ideal place in the world."[31] It sat barely a mile from Dickie Loeb's home.

In Chicago, the color green usually arrives late. Chicagoans welcome spring's first warm burst of air with open arms: lawns are tended to, spirits rise, and young voices fill the neighborhoods. The spring of 1924 meant much more to Dickie and Babe. After an anxious winter of discussions and planning, they were at last ready to commit their perfect crime: They would steal a child.

The idea—ambitious and complicated—was chiefly Dickie's. Like the picturization of his youth, the malignant plan grew nightly in his mind, clearly, as though he saw it all unfold through a stereoscope viewer: each phase leading up to the crime a different photo card, each scene a vivid, three-dimensional picture. The plan read like a story from one of his childhood detective stories: "Dickie Loeb—Master Criminal—Plans His Perfect Crime."

*Young Son of Wealthy Businessman Missing—*

*He's young, small. Easy to handle. And he knows us so we can lure him into our car. Babe wants to snatch a girl. No chance, girls are watched too closely. Too difficult. His father's wealthy, has plenty of money. No trouble paying the ransom. Hey, why not my kid brother Tommy? We know his dad has money. Plenty of boys in Kenwood fit the bill, at least half a dozen; shouldn't be a problem grabbing one. We don't care who.*

*Rendezvous with Death—*

*Need to kill him. He'll never escape, never be able to identify us. Killing—it's an inevitable part of the perfect crime. No trace. Strangling's the best way to do it. Babe and I each pull one end of the strangling rope. Share the culpability. As soon as he gets in the car, we cover his face with a gag soaked in ether. Then knock him out with a chisel—a cold chisel because it's strong. We've already wrapped the blade with tape for a good grip. Lay him facedown on the floor of the car, and cover him with an auto robe. Drive all the way to the state line, and get rid of the body in the dark.*

*Burial at Night—*

*No one will look for a kid way out here. Nothing around but swamps and birds. Leave it to Babe to find a place like this. Strangle him out here. Strip the clothing off him, everything. Pour the acid over his face. If they do find the kid, they won't be able to identify him. Pour it over his penis, too. Shove the body inside a drain culvert, nice and tight. He'll rot in the water. Never be found. Take the clothes back with us; burn 'em.*

*The Long Ride—*

*The car. Can't use ours, especially Babe's; it's red. Rent one. From one of those places on Michigan. But we need to get a phony ID. Can't use our names. Babe goes twice to the Rent-A-Car Company—once to establish himself as a reliable customer, the second time to get the actual car for the crime.*

*First, we need to set up a false identity for Babe. He opens an account for $100 at the Hyde Park State Bank under the name of Morton D. Ballard from Peoria. He's a salesman working the Chicago area. At the same time, I register at the Morrison Hotel downtown under the same name—Morton D. Ballard. I bring a suitcase with me, most guests do. It's filled with books from the U. of C. library.*

*Babe and I address several letters to "Morton D. Ballard c/o Morrison Hotel." This way Babe—Morton D. Ballard—can show the Rent-A-Car people he has a residence in Chicago. I go to the Morrison and pick up the letters and give them to Babe so he has them when he goes for the car.*

*I also give Babe $400 in cash—my own money—in case he needs a deposit. Babe also shows his Hyde Park Bank deposit book. You see, we need to prop up Babe— Morton D. Ballard—as a man of means. He tells the Rent-A-Car Company that he's from Peoria, and he's currently selling in Chicago. The only person in towns he knows* *is Mr. Louis Mason, and here's his telephone number. The Rent-A-Car man calls. A pay phone rings in a booth at a cigar store at Sixteenth and Wabash, a few blocks away. I answer the phone as Mr. Mason. "Sure," I say. "Mr. Ballard is absolutely dependable." Of course, they rent him the car. Babe tells the clerk to forward his Rent-A-Car identification card to the Morrison Hotel, so the next time he rents from them, he won't need a personal reference.*

*A few weeks later, when Babe visits the Rent-A-Car Company—for the perfect crime—he's established as a reliable customer. Perfect.*

*Set Ransom at $10,000—*

*Getting the ransom money is always tricky. We decide to have the father throw the money off a moving Illinois Central train, at a designated landmark—the Champion Manufacturing Company. It's a red-brick, clearly marked building, at Seventy-Fourth Street. He can't miss it. Now we've got to notify the boy's father.*

*The day before the crime we get everything ready at Babe's house: the strangling rope, chisel (sharp end taped), acid, ether, rags to be used as gags, hip boots for the swamp, auto robe. We also write the ransom note and sketch out our telephone messages. I dictate the note while Babe types.*

*The plan involves a number of relays. First-off we call the boy's father on the night of the kidnapping. We tell him his son has been kidnapped and to expect a letter the next morning. The letter, which we send special delivery on the night of the crime, tells the father his son is being held for ransom. If he obeys our instructions we will release his son in six hours; if not, we kill the boy. Gather $10,000 in the following denominations: Eight thousand dollars in fifty-dollar bills; two thousand dollars in twenty-dollar bills. And please, no tricks. Get old, unmarked bills.*

*Place the money in a cigar box, securely tied at both ends, and wrap it in white paper. Seal the ends in sealing wax. We want him to think the box is to be delivered personally to a messenger of the real executives of the plan. The note explains that he will receive a phone call in the afternoon. Keep the line open. The letter is signed, "Yours truly, George Johnson."*

*Babe does the telephone calling because he has a normal, low voice; my voice has a very distinct quality to it and can be easily remembered. The caller—George Johnson (Babe)—tells him there is a Yellow Cab outside his house. Take the cab to the corner of Vincennes and Pershing where there's a "Keep the City Clean" box. Inside is a note which tells him to go to a specific drugstore, which has a public phone. Johnson calls him at this phone, instructs him to head for the I. C. station at Sixty-Third Street and board the next train to Michigan City. Now, the drug store is close to the I. C. station; he has just enough time to buy a ticket and catch the train—no time to contact police. I, of course, being the Master Criminal, had the I. C. schedule and specific car information all mapped out weeks before.*

*We tell him to go to the rear car and look in the telegraph receptacle. Earlier that day, while the train was still in the downtown station, I bought a ticket, entered the train, and placed a note in the telegraph box. The note instructs him to go to the rear platform of the car, face the seat east, and look for the first large red-brick factory adjacent to the tracks, the one with a large black water tower with white lettering "Champion." Count to two or three after that, and throw the cigar box as far as he could. (I, of course, test every possible contingency, including making a simulated package of money so I can try throwing it off a moving train.)*

*Babe and I wait in our rented car—its license plate covered with a black cloth. The money lands near our car. We grab the box and leave the scene.*

*Only We Know the Facts—*

*A total success. The kid's not found, and Babe and I are $10,000 richer. We enjoy the next few weeks as the cops and everyone look for the boy and the killer. It's all people talk about. The newspapers go crazy. Only Babe and I know the real facts. I walk the streets of Kenwood and help the detectives and the newspapermen. They don't have a clue and never will. I try to help them. "Have you guys checked this out? Have you talked to so-and-so?" It's all about being the Master Criminal.*[32]

## SPRING MIGRATION

Having no scruples, Babe had no real objections to the crime.[33] While he believed kidnapping and killing a child were far too dangerous, and that the acts really wouldn't bring him much pleasure, Babe decided to go ahead with the plan "For Robert's Sake." But foremost on his mind was spring migration season.

Wearing hip boots and a tailored business suit—and pointing a revolver into the soft glow of a setting sun—Babe Leopold splashed across the Lake Calumet wetlands. Knee-deep in the marshes and shrub swamps, he shot erratically at three Wilson's Phalaropes.[34] The rare, delicate shorebirds, their long, needle-like bills leading the way, darted over Hyde Lake into the amber sky, eluding the bullets and the likelihood of becoming a stuffed trophy in Babe's bedroom.

Eggers Woods, at the southern edge of Lake Michigan, became Babe's sanctuary during the spring migration of 1924. The Lake Calumet region, a sprawling carpet of shallow lakes, wetlands and beach ridges, was a haven to Chicago-area birders.

Perhaps at a different time—with a clearer mind—Babe would have downed one of the phalaropes. He spent Saturday and Sunday, May 17 and 18, traversing the prairies on the Illinois-Indiana border. An important constant in his life, birding had captured his imagination since childhood. As a youngster, Babe was extremely close to his mother's sister—Aunt Birdie. Babe thought of her as an ethereal woman, and he continued to pay homage to her in his ornithology sketchbooks: Several drawings of birds have their heads replaced by a sketch of Aunt Birdie's head.[35] The weekend in the Lake Calumet wetlands would be Babe's last birding expedition for some time.

## MAY 21, 1924: A CHILLY WEDNESDAY

Songbirds filled the lush trees of Kenwood each May. The old oaks, cottonwoods, and Norway maples that lined Ellis Avenue stirred each morning to the songs of robins, scarlet tanagers, and Baltimore orioles. So, too, did their neighbors in the stately mansions. Maids drew open curtains, and daylight poured into parlors and kitchens. Chauffeurs readied automobiles, and nursemaids prepared children for school.

Jacob Franks's home at 5052 Ellis Avenue sat proudly on a terraced lawn at the northwest corner of Hyde Park Boulevard and Ellis. Tall, arched windows in the Italian Renaissance tradition and rows of decorative balustrades gave the yellow-brick house a regal appearance. Each spring, lilac bushes along the south lawn bloomed in purple, and Flora Franks's flower beds provided a splash of color to the front yard. It was a calm home.

Like many of his Kenwood neighbors, Jacob Franks had millions. Money first came his way in the late 1890s. Franks's Collateral Loan Bank in Chicago's notorious First Ward enjoyed a stellar reputation. There, gamblers down on their luck got a fair shake. If "Uncle Jake" knew you—and he knew most every faro or poker player near his Clark-and-Madison pawn shop—you'd get one-half or three-quarters of the value of your watch or ring or diamond stud.[36] Mike "Hinky Dink" Kenna, First Ward Irish political stalwart and proprietor of the Workingman's Exchange saloon, had high praise for Franks: "He ran the business strictly on the square and had the respect of every man who ever made a loan."

Franks parlayed his hock-shop earnings into real estate, but he made his first real fortune by investing in the Ogden Gas Company. Franks reportedly realized $1,000,000 when he sold his shares to People's Gas and Coke Company.[37] He then became principal owner of the Rockford Watch Company and continued to invest heavily in real estate, his true love. In 1908, a year before the birth of his youngest child, Robert, Franks bought the spacious lot at Hyde Park and Ellis from Albert Loeb, his distant relative who lived across the street.[38] Born Jewish, like many of his Kenwood neighbors, Franks and his family adopted the Christian Science faith.

At age sixty-seven, Franks still dabbled in real estate. As he put it, "I tried golf once, but I like real estate better." A gentle man, Franks spoke slowly and in a low voice. His serious, pale face and gray hair made him look more like a mortician than a semi-retired millionaire. Tall and thin, he walked in a stooped manner. Sad, dark eyes peered out from behind nose glasses, and the long, narrow ribbon that hung from the spectacles added to his formal appearance. He usually wore a black derby and always carried an octagonal timepiece from the Rockford Watch Company. The watch featured the letters of his name—instead of numbers—on its face. On the morning of May 21, 1924, a chilly Wednesday, Franks said goodbye to his family and headed downtown. He wore a black, wool overcoat. It seemed to fit his demeanor.

Dressed fashionably, their hair slicked back, the two boys appeared at ease standing inside one of the cloisters on the University of Chicago campus. To watch them chatting amicably one would think they were typical grad students. Perhaps they discussed their dates from the previous night or their upcoming final exams. Hardly. Dickie Loeb and Babe Leopold were ready to kill—as Babe put it, "just to get a thrill."[39]

They left the campus in Babe's car and headed for the Rent-A-Car Company at Fourteenth Street and Michigan Boulevard, a short ride from Hyde Park. They were confident and cocky in Babe's red Willys-Knight, a sport model with red disc wheels, nickel-plated bumpers and lamps, reflectors, and a tan top. The automobile fit their image as Roaring Twenties college men but far too flashy for the somber task at hand.

Dickie's complicated plan for establishing identification for Babe had broken down when letters addressed to Morton D. Ballard never arrived at the Morrison Hotel. They tried a second hotel—the Trenier at Oakwood Avenue and Grand Boulevard, closer to their homes—and called the car agency to mail Babe's ID there, but it never arrived; nor did their letters penned to Morton D. Ballard. When Babe entered the Rent-A-Car Company, he had no official identification. But he had cash—$400—and the lease number from the first time he rented a car at the same agency.[40] Babe left a $35 deposit, agreed to pay seventeen cents per mile, and promised to return the vehicle the next day. He drove away in a dark-blue Willys-Knight, a five-passenger touring car. "This fine car keeps youth in your veins," claimed a recent Willys-Knight advertisement in *National Geographic*.[41]

Dickie waited in Babe's Willys a few blocks away. And when Babe passed by in the rental car, Dickie followed his confederate to Kramer's, a restaurant at Thirty-Fifth and Cottage Grove. Time for lunch. It promised to be a long day.

Bobby was Flora Franks's youngest child and her favorite. Flora and Jacob called their fourteen-year-old son "Baby," much to his dismay. "Don't you realize my age?"[42] Bobby would ask his father. Still, each night—sometimes three or four times—Flora tiptoed into Bobby's bedroom to kiss him while he slept. He always responded with a hug. Bobby and his brother Jack, a year older, were planning on attending Dartmouth College, and their sister, Josephine, seventeen, planned to go to Wellesley College.

After eating lunch with his mother, Bobby walked back to school on Ellis, a joyful hop to his step as he passed the Loeb mansion where he frequently played tennis. He was looking forward to umpiring a baseball game after school. Small for his age—five-feet, eighty pounds—Bobby excelled at the Harvard School, where Kenwood's elite sent their boys. Harvard's headmaster called him "one of our most brilliant students."[43] Bobby, the star of Harvard's debating team, recently argued against capital punishment. His brother, Jack, took the other side. "Murderers should be hanged," he told Bobby.[44]

A handsome lad with dark wavy hair combed in pompadour fashion, Bobby wore a wool, belted knickers suit, four-in-hand necktie, tan golf stockings, tan cap and oxfords, recently purchased at Marshall Field.[45] A black-and-gold Harvard class pin decorated his jacket lapel. As Bobby neared the red-brick Harvard School, a soft breeze sighed in the tall cottonwoods, and tiny, white seedlings floated to the ground.

A few blocks away, on Greenwood Avenue, two autos pulled up to the garage behind the Leopold home. Sven Englund, the Leopold chauffeur who cared for the family's four cars, greeted Dickie and Babe. The boys transferred their equipment—rope, chisel, gags, robe, acid, boots—from Babe's Willys to the rental. After filling the touring car with gasoline, Babe asked Sven to pull his car into the garage and oil the squeaky brakes.

The young men drove to Jackson Park.[46] Dickie and Babe needed to kill time and wait for classes to end at the Harvard School. They parked near the golf course and discussed their plan. The afternoon hours unfolded slowly, like the nightly fantasies of Dickie Loeb's twisted childhood—picturization, shadowing, and finally random victimization:

The dark-blue Willys heads back to Kenwood to an alley just south of Forty-Seventh and Ingleside, a block west of the Harvard School. Dickie leaves the car and begins to orchestrate his adventure. He walks to the school playground and first chats with a tutor who is supervising the children. He is easing into his plan.

Then he spots Johnny Levinson, a nine-year-old classmate of his brother Tommy. Most boys in the neighborhood know Dickie well. Most find his personality glamorous.[47] Levinson, though, doesn't care for Dickie. Levinson is the perfect victim: small and easy to handle. And he has a lawyer for a father—no trouble getting the ransom paid. Levinson doesn't give Dickie much time; he's got a ballgame to play. Dickie makes his way to the front of the school on Ellis. There, he finds Tommy, but Babe gets his attention by whistling from across the street. He tells Dickie he's found a group of boys—possible prospects—playing at an empty lot at Forty-Ninth and Drexel, about three blocks away. There, they find Levinson. They sneak to a spot behind the lot from which they can observe the boys without being seen. But the kids are too far away. Dickie and Babe need Babe's birding glasses.

While Babe drives back to his house to get the glasses, Dickie walks to a nearby drugstore. He needs to look up Levinson's address. So relaxed, so cocksure, Dickie buys a couple of packs of Dentyne. He chews rhythmically as he pages through the telephone directory. Address in hand, Dickie leaves and meets Babe at the Drexel lot, but when they peer through the field glasses, they can't find young Levinson. Dickie runs to an alley but no luck. When he notices the tutors leaving the lot, he knows it's time to look for new prospects.

At Forty-Eighth and Greenwood, across from the Leopold home, some boys are playing baseball. Perfect. Dickie spots two likely candidates. Dickie and Babe watch for a few minutes but then decide to drive by Levinson's house on Lake Park Street. Johnny's still the number-one prospect, but he's nowhere to be found. They return to Greenwood to spy from a window in Babe's house.

After a while—by now it's five o'clock—they return to the Willys to take one more ride by the lot on Drexel where Levinson had been playing. No luck. They drive south on Drexel to Hyde Park Boulevard and then turn north on Ellis.

Just south of Forty-Eighth Street, Dickie spots Bobby Franks walking home. He's headed south on the west side of Ellis. Bobby is less than three blocks from his home. The Willys passes Bobby, makes a U-turn at Forty-Eighth, and heads south on Ellis, the same way Bobby's walking. The large car pulls alongside Bobby just before Forty-Ninth Street.

"Hey, Bob," Dickie yells as he opens the passenger door. "Do you want a ride home?"

"No, I'll walk," the boy says as he walks over to the car.

But Dickie persists. The Master Criminal knows this is the one.

"Come on in. I want to talk to you about a tennis racquet."

Flora Franks's Baby climbs into the front seat.

"Do you mind if we go around the block?" Dickie asks.

The Willys turns east on Fiftieth Street, one block from Bobby's home.

Two quick blows from the blunt end of the cold chisel dig into the back of Bobby's head.[48] He falls back against the seat, and two more blows crush his forehead. A pair of hands grabs the youngster at the shoulders and yanks him into the back seat. He is small, easy to handle. The same hands shove a gag deep into Bobby's throat and cover his body with an automobile robe. The Willys, the fine car that "keeps youth in your veins," is only three blocks from Bobby's home.

The Willys winds slowly through Jackson Park to South Shore Drive, wraps around the South Shore Country Club, and hugs the edge of Lake Michigan all the way to the Lake Calumet wetlands at the Indiana state line. Babe knows the ten-mile route well, as do most Chicago birders. Bobby's head bleeds through the auto robe and into the floorboards.

At Calumet Boulevard in Indiana, the Willys takes a series of country roads before stopping in a deserted area. Still plenty of daylight, but there's no one around. Dickie and Babe remove Bobby's shoes and hide them in thick bushes. They take off his trousers and stockings but leave them in the car. They toss his belt and buckle in the brush, along with Bobby's class pin.

Dickie and Babe need to kill time before they can get rid of the body in the dark. The Willys drives back and forth along Calumet Boulevard and Indianapolis Avenue. It stops at a roadside sandwich shop—Dew Drop Inn. The boys dine on red hots (Chicago nickname for hot dogs) and root beer inside the car as Bobby's head bleeds into the tonneau.

As the twilight sky turns black, the Willys heads back across the state line into Illinois and takes a road that leads out toward Hegewisch (a working-class community at the southeastern tip of Chicago) from 108th Street and Avenue F.

Dickie and Babe drag Bobby from the car. They place his lifeless body in the auto robe and haul him through the dark prairie—they believe no one will look for a kid way out here. Dickie carries the head, Babe the feet. After three hundred yards, they stop at a large, funnel-shaped culvert beneath a railroad embankment. No need to strangle him; the chisel had done the job hours ago. They finish disrobing the boy. The body is stiff, and the eyes are blank when Babe pours the hydrochloric acid over Bobby's face, stomach, and penis.

Babe takes off his suit jacket, puts on his hip boots, and steps into the shallow stream that runs through the culvert. He grabs Bobby's feet and pulls him into the water. He shoves the boy into his watery grave, head-first toward the smaller end. He pushes as far as he can but the pungent fumes of the acid cause him to abandon the task. Bobby's feet hang out of the culvert.

Dickie runs up the embankment to make sure no one is around. He washes his hands in the stream as Babe takes off his boots and puts on his jacket. They gather up the pieces of Bobby's clothing and carry them back to the car in the blood-soaked auto robe.

The Willys drives out of the wetlands and stops at a neighborhood drugstore. Babe calls home—he'll be a little late. Dickie checks the telephone book for Jacob Franks's address and phone number. In the dark car, on the road back to Kenwood, Babe writes the Franks's address on the ransom envelope.

A lonesome figure, the old man in his black derby and overcoat walked slowly along the empty sidewalk. In his heart, Jacob Franks feared the worst. It was well past the dinner hour—unlike Bobby to be this late. He looked around corners, down alleys, and peered through thick shrubs that ringed the spacious lots of Ellis Avenue. Franks stopped in front of the low brick wall that wrapped around the Loeb property—maybe Bobby was playing tennis.

Inside her home, Flora Franks made frantic phone calls to Bobby's school chums. Do you know where he might be? Did you see him leave school? When's the last time you saw Bobby? Their answers gave her no comfort. They all said they assumed Bobby walked home after the baseball game.

Franks tried to console his wife, who had convinced herself that something terrible had happened to her "Baby." She paced around the living room and stared through the tall, arched windows hoping to see Bobby come up the walk. Franks knew he needed help. He telephoned his good friend Samuel Ettleson, a well-connected lawyer. Ettleson, who lived next door to the Leopolds, once served as corporation counsel to Mayor Bill Thompson and was also a state senator. Sam would know what to do. Franks was sure of that.

Ettleson suggested that maybe Bobby got himself locked inside the Harvard School. It was nearly ten o'clock when Franks and Ettleson drove to the school. They found a basement window open and climbed inside. The two men walked through the deserted school calling Bobby's name.[49] They covered each floor, every classroom but found no one. When they left, they realized the obvious—if the basement window was open, surely Bobby could have got out.

The Willys cut through the night.

Babe saw it in Dickie's eyes, heard it in his voice. He was in high spirits.

"You saw how smooth this all went off," Dickie boasted.[50] "Just like I told you over and over it would. Are you convinced now it was as easy as falling off a log?"

Dickie rattled on, his voice filling the car. But Babe's doubts spun through his head: *Somehow I never believed that it would happen—that we'd actually go through with it. But it's done. And now, at least, there aren't any decisions to make. I'll be able to put all my thought on not making any slips—or staying one step ahead of the police. But that's nonsense. Nobody's ever going to suspect me.*

Babe tried to relax. He lit another cigarette and listened to Dickie talk about getting the ransom.

"That'll be a snap, Nate. Nothing to it. We don't have to get within a hundred yards of anybody. Just sit safe and snug in that alley and wait for them to toss us the dough. The rubes have about as much chance of catching us as a snowball in hell."

It was nearly half-past ten before Dickie and Babe were ready to telephone Mr. Franks. Once in Kenwood, they parked the Willys on Fiftieth Street at the side entrance of the Loeb home. They burned Bobby's clothing in the Loeb furnace and then hid the auto robe alongside the greenhouse. They tried their best to scrub the blood off the floor of the car but decided to wait until morning. They needed more light. The final step before the phone call—mail the ransom envelope marked "SPECIAL" at the Hyde Park Post Office.

Dickie and Babe squeezed into the phone booth at the drugstore. Babe would do the talking. A few blocks away, a maid in the Franks's home answered the ringing telephone. A voice asked for Mr. Franks, and the maid handed the phone to Mrs. Franks.

"Mr. Franks is not here," she said.

"This is Mr. Johnson.[51] Of course, you know by this time that your son has been kidnapped."

Flora Franks trembled. She could barely speak. "Who is this?"

The voice, cultured, not gruff, continued. "We have him, and you need not worry. He is safe. But don't try to trace this call or to find me. We must have money. We will let you know tomorrow what we want. We are kidnappers, and we mean business. If you refuse us what we want or try to report us to the police, we will kill the boy. Good-bye."

The line went dead, and Mrs. Franks fainted.

A few moments later, Franks and Ettleson returned home following their search of the Harvard School. Franks found his wife on the floor. They revived her, and after she told them what the kidnapper said, Franks took her upstairs to bed. Ettleson called the phone company and demanded a trace be put on the Franks' line.

Franks and Ettleson then waited for another telephone call. At 2:00 A.M., they decided to drive downtown to the detective bureau. Ettleson had a good relationship with Chief of Detectives Michael Hughes and Lieutenant William Shoemacher. Their advice, Ettleson told Franks, would be sound. Neither Hughes nor Shoemacher was at the bureau, but Franks and Ettleson did speak with the lieutenant on duty. Ettleson told the officer in no uncertain terms that the conversation they were about to have was strictly private. Off the record. After explaining the circumstances at length, they all agreed that putting Bobby's disappearance on the police blotter at this time could endanger the boy's life. Franks would wait until later that morning before filing an official report.

In the early hours of May 22, patrolman Charles Enos drove his flivver along Greenwood Avenue. It had been a routine night until Bernard Hunt, a night watchman in the neighborhood, stopped him at Forty-Ninth Street. Hunt told him that earlier that night, he had seen someone toss something out of a moving car. And when he picked it up from the gutter, he noticed it was covered with dried blood.[52] Hunt thought the police should have it. Enos accepted the object, and at the end of his shift, he filled out a brief report at Fourth District Police Headquarters. He also marked his initial *E* on the cold chisel with tape wrapped around its blade.[53]

## DEATH WILL BE THE PENALTY

"We are kidnappers and we mean business."

The words kicked inside Jacob Franks's stomach. He spent the night alone in his library, waiting for the phone to ring. Fear and silence filled his home. Deprived of sleep, he tried to visualize the recent events, to bring each snapshot into focus. But like a dream spinning out of sequence, he couldn't make sense of it: walking the street, looking down alleys for his son; searching the darkened school, calling Bobby's name, finding Flora passed out on the floor.

At 9:30, a sharp rap at the front door jarred his thoughts. The small boy handed Franks a special delivery letter. A handwritten envelope—Jacob Franks, 5052 Ellis, City—contained a two-page, typewritten note that struck terror in his heart.

Dear Sir:

As you no doubt know by this time, your son has been kid-napped. Allow us to assure you that he is at present well and safe. You need fear no physical harm for him, provided you live up care-fully to the following instructions and to such others as you will receive by future communications. Should you, however, disobey any of our instructions, ever slightly, his death will be the penalty.

1. For obvious reasons make absolutely no attempt to communicate with either police authorities or any private agency. Should you have already communicated with the police, allow them to continue their investigations, but do not mention this letter.

2. Secure before noon today ten thousand dollars ($10,000.00). This money must be composed entirely of OLD BILLS of the following denominations:

$2,000 in twenty dollar bills

$8,000 in fifty dollar bills

The money must be old. Any attempt to include new or marked bills will render the entire venture futile.

3. The money should be placed in a large cigar box, or if this is impossible, in a <u>heavy</u> cardboard box, SECURELY closed and wrapped in white paper. The wrapping paper should be sealed at all openings with sealing wax.

4. Have the money with you, prepared as directed above, and remain at home after one o'clock. See that the telephone is not in use. You will receive a further communication instructing you as to your final course.

As a final word of warning, this is an extremely commercial proposition and we are prepared to put our threat into execution should we have reasonable grounds to believe that you have com-mitted an infraction of the above instructions. However, should you carefully follow out our instructions to the letter, we can assure you that your son will be safely returned to you within six hours of our receipt of the money.

Yours truly,<br>George Johnson[54]

GKR

The strain was too much for Flora Franks. She fainted, and her hus-band summoned a physician. Franks then called Ettleson and read the entire ransom letter. Ettleson instructed Franks to secure the ransom money and to exactly follow the instructions. Ettleson then took charge.

He called his friend Chief Hughes and explained the situation. He then asked the telephone company to call off the tracing of telephone calls to the Franks' residence. "I was afraid to do one little thing that would incur the wrath of the kidnappers and thereby endanger the life of the boy," Ettleson said.[55]

Alone with his early-morning thoughts, Tony Minke walked through the isolated marshes along the Illinois-Indiana state line. Migrating birds dotted the low, cloudy sky, their songs carried away in a brisk wind that whipped across the high grass. He followed a path that hugged a shallow channel on the western edge of Wolf Lake, one mile from Lake Michigan. A lonesome place, the nearest home sat a mile away. Minke, a Polish immigrant, lived on the Indiana side of Wolf Lake. He was headed for Hegewisch. His watch needed repair.[56]

At one point, a single railroad track crossed the channel, and beneath the railway embankment, a large culvert swallowed the runoff water. Minke stopped his walk as he approached the culvert—something white floated in the murky water. He carefully inched down the embankment to investigate. Panic overcame him when he saw the small, nude body stuck inside the drain pipe. Minke raced up the embankment and saw two gasoline-powered handcars coming toward him from the north. He waved excitedly for them to stop.

Paul Korff, a signal repairman for the Pennsylvania Railroad, halted his crew as they approached Minke. Minke's English was poor but he frantically tried to tell Korff "feet sticking out" as he led Korff down the embankment. When Korff saw the body, he yelled for his three coworkers. In an awkward tangle of hand motions, Polish, and broken English, Minke told the men he had nothing to do with the body. He was just walking by.

Korff took the initiative. He stepped in the cold water and tugged on the boy's bare feet. The body scrapped along the pipe—face down—as Korff pulled it free. Korff carried Bobby to dry land. Each man frozen in his own thoughts, Korff's crew stood motionless. No one spoke. The men looked down on the small boy. The water had flattened his wavy hair. His bushy eyebrows appeared painted on. Copper-colored stains covered his face and lips.[57] His swollen head was bruised—two wounds in the forehead, two more in the back of the head. Deep scratches ran from his shoulders to his buttocks. Similar scrapes marred his forehead.

After a brief discussion—Did he drown? He couldn't have been swimming in the channel. How did he get in the culvert?—one of the men wrapped Bobby in a tarpaulin and carried him to a handcar. Korff, disturbed by the boy's naked body, looked around for clothing. He only found a pair of eyeglasses. He wiped the mud from the lenses and placed the glasses in his pocket before joining the others on the railroad track. He told his crew he'd call the police once they got to the Hegewisch railway station, about a mile south.

The men started up their machines, and a family of startled yellow-headed blackbirds darted from its nest in the marshy earth. The two cars clattered slowly down the track before picking up speed.

## PLENTY LEFT TO DO

The Master Criminal bubbled with exuberance.

"I knew if we just put our heads together and gave ourselves time enough we could come up with a fool-proof scheme," Dickie said. "Let's see them unravel this one."[58]

Dickie planned a busy day. After Babe's law classes, they lunched with a mutual friend, Dick Rubel, at the fashionable Cooper-Carlton. Dickie and Babe had actually thought of killing Rubel but discarded the idea because Rubel's father was stingy. Too difficult to get the ransom money, they theorized. Babe freed his afternoon by asking a fellow birder to take his Wooded Island class. The afternoon would be important. Dickie's plan involved a series of intricate actions—the wheels-within-the-wheels.[59] It all had to run smoothly. Precise. Plenty left to do after lunch.

Jacob Franks awaited communication about the ransom. Dickie was ready.

"Who says there's no way of getting delivery of the ransom without letting anybody getting a look at you?" Dickie assured Babe. "Or giving them a chance to plant a gang of dicks to watch you pick it up."

But first there was some clean-up work. They drove to Babe's house to finish cleaning the blood-stained rental car before they drove it back to the agency. Bobby's blood covered part of the floor, the seats, and a fender. Sven Englund couldn't believe his eyes when he saw the two pampered sons of millionaires washing the car. Both boys had their hands in a pail of water, scrubbing cakes of Bon Ami all over the Willys. This was a first. Sven was sure of it. The chauffeur offered to help. No thanks, Dickie told him, and then the Master Criminal proceeded to make up a glib story about spilling red wine on the car.[60] *Only Babe and I know the real facts.*

While Dickie and Babe washed the car, their neighbor Jacob Franks readied the ransom money. After consulting with Ettleson, Franks went downtown to his bank and withdrew the cash: $2,000 in twenties and

$8,000 more in fifties. The young bank teller behind the cage followed the old man's instructions: "Make them all old, worn bills." When he returned home, Franks put $10,000 in a cigar box and wrapped it in white paper. He secured the package with sealing wax.

Franks then joined his wife by the telephone.

## A RUSHING RIVER

Like a spider's web, the Master Criminal's "fool-proof scheme" widened during the afternoon of May 22. It stretched from Kenwood to Hegewisch and back again. It had already grabbed and killed a young boy, and now it reached out for more.

While Jacob and Flora Franks waited for their phone to ring, a cub reporter approached the city desk at the *Chicago Daily News*. "Here's a tip worth chasing down," the editor told James Mulroy.

Mulroy walked across the Loop to Sam Ettleson's office. "He's supposed to know something about a kidnapping" was all the editor knew. The young reporter was really just a legman, someone who ran down leads for veteran reporters. Mulroy stood respectfully at the desk of the seasoned attorney. Ettleson became enraged when he realized the press knew about the kidnapping of his friend's son.[61] The cub got the details but agreed not to go to press at this time. A story now might endanger Bobby's life, Ettleson told him. When Mulroy left, Ettleson phoned the *Evening-American*, another afternoon paper, and told an editor that the youngest child of Jacob Franks had been kidnapped. And as he did with Mulroy, Ettleson made the editor promise not to publish prematurely.

"The events swept before us like a rushing river," Sam Ettleson would say about the remaining afternoon hours.[62]

### The One O'clock Hour

Following his conversation with Ettleson, Mulroy calls the *Daily News* city desk. The editor tells him to get over to the Jacob Franks house. Mulroy is told that a source at the East Side police station says they're investigating the apparent drowning of an unidentified young boy. The paper assigns Alvin Goldstein, another cub. Maybe there's a connection, the editor says. He tells Mulroy to stay by a phone at the Franks' home.

After meeting Paul Korff and his crew at the Hegewisch railway station, police officer Anton Shapino brings the dead boy to the Olejniczak Funeral Home. Shapino gives the mortician the pair of eyeglasses Korff found near the culvert. They presume the glasses belong to the boy. Police believe they're dealing with a drowning, but on closer inspection of the head wounds, they suspect foul play. At first, police think the boy might be Phillip Denny, who disappeared from his home a month ago.[63] Denny's mother rushes to the mortuary but says the boy is not her son.

Detectives from the East Side Station continue their investigation where the body was found. Paul Korff, his crew, and Tony Minke accompany police to the culvert. Sergeant Edward Anderson finds a tan, wool golf stocking in the mud.[64] He also discovers several bricks, and police theorize that someone thought about weighing down the body and throwing it into Wolf Lake.

Police question whomever they can find in the isolated swampland. They first find Michael Barrett, a worker for the Ford Motor Company assembly plant in Hegewisch. Barrett tells police that late last night—a few minutes after midnight—he saw three men walking up the Pennsylvania Railroad tracks at 118th Street,[65] "all young fellows, probably between 18 and 30, and they all wore caps . . . and acted suspiciously." It's the first of many false leads.

Because Adam May lives in a tiny hut just four hundred yards from the culvert, he's rounded up by police. They take the elderly icehouse watchman into custody. Captain Thomas Wolfe is sure May knows something.

Cub reporter Mulroy knocks on the front door of the Franks house. Jacob Franks doesn't want the reporter inside his home, but he changes his mind when the persistent Mulroy tells him it would look suspicious if the kidnappers saw a reporter hanging around the front lawn. In Hegewisch, Goldstein is the first newspaperman to arrive at the Olejniczak Funeral Home.

### The Two O'clock Hour

Dickie and Babe dry off the Willys. In two cars—Dickie in the rental, Babe in his red Willys—they drive a short distance to the intersection of Pershing Road and Vincennes Avenue, where they stop at a "Keep the City Clean" box.[66] They've prepared a note for Jacob Franks, part of Dickie's complicated relay plan to obtain the ransom money. The note tells Franks to go immediately to the Van de Bogert and Ross drugstore at Sixty-Third and Blackstone in Woodlawn. Franks should wait in the far easterly phone booth. He'll receive a telephone call from the kidnappers. But Dickie's elaborate scheme runs into trouble when the note won't stick to the "Keep the City Clean" box. Fearing it will blow away, they decide to omit this step from their calculations. When they call Franks, instead of telling him to go to the "Keep the City Clean" box for further instructions, they will tell him to go directly to the Van de Bogert and Ross drugstore.

The phone rings at the Franks home. Cub reporter Goldstein asks to speak with Mulroy. Goldstein describes the boy in the morgue to Mulroy, who relays the information to Bobby's father. Jacob Franks tells Mulroy that this can't be his son because his son doesn't wear glasses. But Ettleson's not so sure. He suggests that Mulroy drive Bobby's uncle, Edwin Gresham, who is at the house with other family friends and relatives, to Hegewisch . . . just to make sure.

Dickie and Babe drive to Sixteenth and Wabash, park the red Willys, and head to the Illinois Central railway station in the rental car. Once there, Babe heads for a phone booth. He calls the Yellow Cab Company and then the Franks house. Dickie, wearing eyeglasses for disguise, buys a ticket to Michigan City. While the train is being readied for departure, Dickie enters car 507. He places a note in the box provided for telegraph blanks. It instructs Jacob Franks to go immediately to the back platform of the train, to watch the east side of the track, and to wait until the train passes the first large red-brick factory with a water tower on top of it, with "Champion" written on the tower. Then, count quickly to five, and throw the package as far as he can.

The phone rings again at 5052 Ellis. "Mr. Johnson" tells both Ettleson and Jacob Franks that a Yellow Cab will arrive shortly in front of the house. Franks is to go to the Van de Bogert and Ross drugstore at Sixty-Third and Blackstone, enter the far easterly phone booth, and await a call with further instructions. Babe first gives the message to Ettleson, who then hands the phone to Franks. Again, Babe repeats the message. When Franks hangs up, he can't remember the address. Nor can his attorney.

### The Three O'clock Hour

A Yellow Cab sits in front of the house at 5052 Ellis.

Inside, the phone rings. Franks hopes it's the kidnappers. He'll get the address right this time. It's Bobby's uncle. It's Robert, he says.

William Taylor, a family friend of the Franks, leaves the house and gives the taxi driver fifty-five cents, and asks him to leave.[67]

Dickie and Babe drive to the Walgreen drugstore at Sixty-Seventh and Stony Island to call the Van de Bogert and Ross drugstore, where they believe Franks is awaiting word from Mr. Johnson. But Dickie is shocked when he notices a stack of afternoon papers at a newsstand. "BOY SLAIN BY KIDNAPPERS" screams the banner headline of the *Chicago Daily Journal*.

"When are these damn papers printed?" Dickie demands.[68]

"Hell, I don't know," says Babe. "Maybe a couple of hours ago."

"That was a swell place you picked to leave him. They'd never find him, huh. Not for twenty minutes anyway."

Dickie and Babe deliberate as to what to do now. Babe insists they call the drugstore anyway.

The telephone in the far easterly booth at the Van de Bogert and Ross drugstore rings. A porter answers. Someone asks for a Mr. Franks. The porter looks around the empty store and tells the caller no one by that name is in the store.

Dickie and Babe decide to drive to yet another drugstore. They'll make one more phone call.

Again, the telephone rings in the far easterly booth at Van de Bogert and Ross drugstore. This time Percy Van de Bogert tells the caller there's no one there by the name of Mr. Franks.

### The Four O'clock Hour

About a mile and a half south, the train headed for Michigan City rumbles past the Champion water tower. No package flies out of the last car.

Babe returns the rental car to the agency, and the young men drive back to Kenwood in the red Willys.

Jacob Franks identifies his son at the Hegewisch morgue.

### The Five O'clock Hour

Dickie and Babe stop at a drugstore across the street from the Harvard School. Over sodas, they read the latest editions of the newspapers. The papers have Bobby's name and the details of the ransom note. On the way out of the drugstore, they run into a teacher from the school, Mott Kirk Mitchell. Although his plan has failed miserably, Dickie can't help but talk up the crime. Holding up a newspaper, he tells the instructor, "Isn't that terrible what happened to poor Bobby Franks?[69] He used to play tennis all the time on our court."

Babe heads home, and as Dickie walks down Ellis to his house, he notices a crowd in front of Bobby Franks's home. He spots Goldstein, who has just arrived from Hegewisch. Goldstein is a U. of C. chum. They chat for a while about the crime, and Dickie asks about the condition of the body at the morgue.[70]

An exhausted Sam Ettleson stands in a cold drizzle and talks with reporters. Inside, Jacob Franks tries to comfort his grieving wife and their two children. Alongside her home, Flora Franks's lilac bushes bloom in a long row of purple.

# NO ORDINARY DAY

As usual, the limousines rolled up to the Harvard School Friday morning, May 23. Their chauffeurs and valets in hand, the young masters of Kenwood and Hyde Park prepared for another day of studies. Many carried golf clubs and tennis racquets. But this would be no ordinary day.

Like aftershocks, an epidemic of rumor and suspicion jolted the neighborhood. And the stylish Harvard School sat in its epicenter. Principal Charles Pence, usually an affable man, felt the strain of the surging police investigation. Three of his instructors spent most of the night in custody. Police grilled the teachers until 3:00 A.M., sent them home, and then ordered them back for further interrogation. Pence canceled classes and made his way to the detective bureau. "We are doing everything we can to help the officers," he said.[71]

Inside the school, parents gathered in Pence's office to discuss the kidnap and murder of young Franks. Pence told teachers to remain in the building the entire day and to cooperate thoroughly with police. On the playground, Sergeant Edward Powers questioned a large group of students. They shed little light on Bobby's disappearance. Only one of their classmates, Irving Hartman, age ten, had something to say:

"I started home from school Wednesday. . . . I saw Robert walking down Ellis Avenue, about half a block in front of me. Between Forty-Seventh and Forty-Eighth I noticed he was just opposite a big gray Winton touring car with the curtains down. My teacher had told us to look at tulips, and I saw a big bed of them and stopped to look at them. I looked just about a minute and when I turned around Robert had disappeared and the big Winton was coming lickety split up Ellis going north. It whizzed past me. I thought it was pretty funny."[72]

Irving's mother discredited her son's story. "The boy is probably suffering from an excited imagination. He told me this morning he dreamed all night about the case. I believe if too many people question my son, he soon will have the whole mystery solved."

The police had orders to follow all leads. They searched the city for gray Winton touring cars, and the unfortunate Mr. Johnsons who drove them had to account for their actions on Wednesday, May 21.

School gossip drove the early stages of the police investigation. One mother told authorities that her son had told her stories of immorality at the Harvard School. "Things are going on I wouldn't even tell you, mother," the boy said.[73] Some teachers speculated about their associates. They talked about an instructor who once said, as Bobby Franks walked by, "His father has nothing but money. He would be good pickings for someone."[74] There was so much hearsay that police felt justified in holding anyone for questioning. And they did just that.

Chicago Police Chief Morgan Collins put Chief Detective Hughes in charge. "Such a crime strikes at the very vitals of our school system," Collins said.[75] "Such men as have planned and committed this terrible crime must not be permitted to prey upon our youth with impunity."

Collins' initial statement about "our school system" appeared to be centered on the Harvard School. Hughes followed his chief's lead, "I firmly believe that someone in the neighborhood, probably someone who knew the boy at school, invited Robert to his home near the school. There, with the instincts of a moron, the slayer mistreated the lad."[76]

A shadow had always followed Mott Kirk Mitchell.

Mitchell had a muliebral way about him. Many children thought he was different from the other teachers. Babe Leopold was quick to tell people that Mitchell—known as Mr. M. K. M.—had solicited boys at Harvard School to have sexual relations with him.[77] Mitchell, the school's English teacher, was just what Hughes was looking for—an easy target. Police were so impressed with the wording of the ransom note they decided the writer must be a well-educated person. Perhaps an English teacher. Because of Mitchell's suspected sexual proclivities—and his English skills—police made him a prime suspect in the killing of Bobby Franks. Hughes's men even dug up the sewer in front of Mitchell's home hoping to find some of Bobby's clothing.

Hughes's detectives also held Walter Wilson, Harvard's good-looking mathematics instructor from Boston. When police learned that Flora Franks called Wilson's rooming house the night Bobby disappeared, they called Wilson in for questioning. The teacher lived about a block from the school. Wilson wasn't home but his landlady took Mrs. Franks's call.

"She was nearly frantic with worry," Mrs. George Chase said. "When Mr. Wilson returned, I gave him Mrs. Franks' message, and he went to her home immediately. He has lived in my home two years, often taking his dinners here. He has unusually fine habits, only smokes a little, and although he is 29 years old he is in reality only a big boy—or so I always regarded him."[78]

Wilson was indignant about the way the press and the police treated him. A *Chicago Tribune* reporter who went to Wilson's Kenwood rooming house wrote that Wilson had taken Bobby Franks and his brother, Jack, to an amusement park about a year ago and kept the boys out until 1:00 A.M. "But that's nothing," Wilson replied. "It's a long way from our neighborhood to Riverview Park, and it takes two hours to make the trip one way."

The paper also reported this brief dialogue between Wilson, whose home is in Lawrence, Massachusetts, and the reporter:

"Have you a sweetheart?"

"No, I don't know any young ladies in Chicago."[79]

He was attired in a bathrobe and appeared nervous. He said he had no theory about the murder—had had no time to think about it.

Wilson, who knew the police were looking for a pervert, later defended himself in the *Chicago Evening-American*: "I am a healthy, normal man. If the insinuations printed in a morning newspaper get back to Massachusetts, I will be a ruined man. It is an atrocious attack on my character."[80]

While Wilson defended himself, police ransacked his room in Mrs. Chase's house. They took a pair of eyeglasses. Police also took some notepaper from Mitchell's apartment. They would try to match the paper against the ransom notepaper.

Police also interrogated athletic director Richard Williams. He became a prime suspect because Jacob Franks and Sam Ettleson attempted to telephone him before they searched the Harvard School. Police searched Williams's apartment and found several small bottles filled with liquid. They presumed the bottles contained some sort of poison. Investigators initially believed the killer poisoned young Franks. The bottles, Williams explained, held lotions he used to rub sore muscles.

The poisoning theory also led detectives to Fred Alwood, the school's chemistry teacher. Alwood lived a block from the Van de Bogert and Ross drugstore. Alwood, like the other three suspected Harvard instructors, had a solid alibi as to his whereabouts on Wednesday, May 21.

Principal Pence spent most of the day vouching for his teachers' integrity. "No instructors are brought here unless their character has been investigated thoroughly," he said. "This school caters to only the very best pupils and the faculty must correspond."[81]

Police released Williams but Mitchell and Wilson remained in custody.

Midday Friday. Somber bundles of silver-gray clouds darkened the U. of C. campus. The way a doctor monitors a patient's recovery, the Master Criminal prepared to take the pulse of his crime.

Before leaving his house for Hyde Park and the U. of C., Dickie Loeb examined the morning newspapers:

"DID YOU SEE KIDNAPPING OF ROBERT FRANKS?" asked a page-one, boxed headline in the *Tribune*.[82] Dickie read about the intense interrogation of the Harvard instructors. He chuckled when he learned that a reporter caught Walter Wilson in his bathrobe. To his delight, the press was already calling the kidnap-killing "famous"—right up there with the Charley Ross case.

Dickie's mother made him smile when she told him, "Whoever did it should be tarred and feathered."[83] But Albert Loeb's sullen reaction to the murder of his friend's son worried Dickie. *Did Dad suspect something?*[84]

Anxious to discuss his crime with his peers, Dickie took lunch at the Zeta Beta Tau house. If he worked fast, like a good public-relations man, he could get some first-page play in the afternoon papers. As luck would have it, Dickie spotted Howard Mayer, the campus stringer for the *Evening-American*. Dickie had known Mayer for about a year; he called him over to his table.[85] Within minutes, Dickie's persuasive charm took hold.

"Yeah, that makes sense," Mayer said when Dickie suggested that the kidnappers would never meet Franks at the drugstore.

"You know, these kidnappers would not meet a man on a busy street like that," Dickie said. "That is common sense. Franks would have been directed to take the money somewhere else."[86]

Mayer agreed, but since the *Evening-American* hadn't officially assigned him to the story, he wasn't going to pursue Dickie's theory.

"Howie, why don't you make the rounds of these drugstores on East Sixty-Third Street and see if you can't find one at which some word was left for Mr. Franks?"

Mayer didn't respond. Just then, Goldstein and Mulroy walked into the lunchroom.

"If you won't take my proposition, I'll put it to them," Dickie told Mayer as he called over the two *Daily News* reporters. The two cubs jumped at Dickie's idea.

*I walk the streets of Kenwood and help detectives and newspapermen. They don't have a clue and never will. I try to help them. "Have you guys checked this out? Have you talked to so-and-so?"*

But neither Goldstein nor Mulroy had a car, and it was raining. Dickie persuaded Mayer to use his automobile. Dickie and the three reporters got into Mayer's big Marmon and headed for Sixty-Third Street. Dickie told Mayer to pull over at Blackstone Avenue. He suggested that the *Daily News* guys check out a cigar store while Mayer and he go to the Van de Bogert and Ross drugstore.

*As the master criminal of the century, Dickie led others. Of course, they obeyed him.*

Once inside the store, Dickie and Mayer approached the black porter. Mayer identified himself and asked, "Any calls come in yesterday asking for a Mr. Franks?"

"Yes." James Kemp put down his broom. "Two calls come in, but the store was empty."[87] There was no Mr. Franks around, he told them, when the phone in the far easterly booth rang. He told the caller as much.

Dickie burst with excitement.

"You see, I told you we could find it. Now you have a scoop," he told Mayer.

After talking with the porter, Mayer called the *Evening-American* city desk. He then phoned police. Dickie told Mayer that he should keep the information for himself and not tell Goldstein and Mulroy, but Mayer said that wouldn't be right because they all started out together.

Like the stage manager of a play, Dickie relaxed at the marble soda fountain and watched the characters play out their roles.

Dressed in an overcoat, a vested suit, and fedora, Chief of Detectives Hughes entered the drugstore with a handful of detectives. Hughes, leading the investigation for Police Chief Collins, loved the thrill of the chase and enjoyed a reputation as a "thief-catcher." The detectives questioned Kemp and the store's manager, Percival Van de Bogert. Goldstein and Mulroy did the same when they arrived. Dickie checked his watch: Still plenty of time to make the afternoon papers.

A steady rain splattered the sweeping fenders of Mayer's Marmon. Its large tires, with their black spokes, splashed over puddles as the three newspapermen unknowingly escorted the killer to the Furth Mortuary in Kenwood. The afternoon was going Dickie's way. He looked forward to Bobby's inquest.

Knowing Dickie lived across the street from the victim, Mulroy wanted some human-interest background. "So what kind of kid was Bobby Franks?"

Dickie heard the question but didn't answer at first. He looked out the car window. He'd pause—for drama—before answering. *He walked the streets with a nonchalant confidence, consulting with friends at his club, helping newspaper reporters on the crime beat.* Finally, Dickie turned toward his companion in the back seat.

"If you were going to kidnap and murder someone, it would be just the sort of cocky little son-of-a-bitch as Bobby Franks."[88]

Quietly, and looking ghostly, a lifeless Jacob Franks spoke at his son's inquest. His words floated across the crowded room, like small clusters of fog. Several of Bobby's schoolmates sat alongside witnesses, police, and newspapermen. In a monotone voice, Franks patched together the events following the disappearance of his son:

"When he did not come home we began to investigate. About 10 o'clock we got into the school building. Not finding him, I reported the information to the Woodlawn police.

"While I was gone, my wife got a telephone call. His name was Johnson. My boy had been kidnapped, but . . . he was all right. We would receive more information. The next morning . . . a special delivery letter . . . kidnapper wanted $10,000."

Franks took a seat next to Sam Ettleson and cupped one hand behind an ear to listen intently as strangers described in detail what happened to his dead son. The ransom letter was read in its entirety for the official record. In the back of the room, Dickie Loeb stood with a group of newspapermen. The witnesses had their say, and the reporters scribbled notes. Dickie evaluated it all, how their roles fit into his childhood fantasy.

Edward Anderson, a policeman from the East Side Station, said how shocked he was when he saw Bobby's nude body at the Hegewisch morgue. Anderson then traveled to the culvert beneath the Pennsylvania tracks. "I found a golf stocking about forty feet from the spot where the body was found," he testified. Anderson also discovered some house bricks along the path near the culvert. He picked them up and brought them back to the station because they appeared to be unlike any used in the neighborhood.

Joseph Springer, the coroner's physician who conducted the autopsy in Hegewisch, explained the wounds on the back of Bobby's head and forehead. They were delivered by downward blows, he said, from a blunt instrument.[89] He also described scratches that ran from Bobby's right shoulder to his buttocks and some scratches on his forehead. Bobby's face, he said, was a copper color, caused by an irritant—such as hydrochloric acid. The autopsy showed discoloration down the windpipe into the right lung. It was caused by absorption of fumes and suffocation, he said. He added that Bobby died of an injury to his head, associated with suffocation.

Coroner Oscar Wolff concluded that Bobby struggled violently with his captors but that he was not sexually abused.

Following the inquest, Jacob Franks stood amid a small group of reporters in a mortuary ante-room. Frail and exhausted, Franks answered more questions. He didn't notice—nor care—that his neighbor, Dickie Loeb, was part of the group.

By the time Dickie arrived home, newsboys all across Chicago yelled out the *Evening-American*'s headline: "KIDNAPPER'S PHONE CALL NEW CLUE IN BOY'S DEATH MYSTERY!"[90]

Dickie called her "Patches." At first, during the winter, he only gave her the lousy days of the week—Tuesdays and Thursdays—but the dark-eyed beauty from the North Side soon progressed to weekend dates. A shocker, Patches wore her brown hair in an Egyptian bob. She teased and tantalized Dickie with her flamboyant style and quick tongue. A good match for the collegiate killer.

Hours after the inquest, Dickie took Patches dancing at the Edgewater Beach, an enchanting medieval-looking pink hotel on the shores of Lake Michigan. Dickie and Patches spent much of the night on the romantic, moonlit Beachwalk, where a pier led couples across a sandy beach into the dark lake. It was a beautifully planned, sensual date. For Dickie, the planning—the seduction—that was the thrill. As far as the sex—the act itself—the Master Criminal could easily get along without it.

## TABLOID MENTALITY

Writer Ben Hecht put it best: "Chicago is a sort of journalistic Yellowstone Park, offering haven to a lost herd of fantastic bravos."

Chicagoans witnessed the kidnap-murder of Bobby Franks unfold in their morning and afternoon newspapers. In a bizarre mix of facts, rumors, and innuendos, the city's "lost herd of fantastic bravos" spun the crime into a sensational melding of truth and fiction. Many years after he stuffed the dead body of Bobby Franks in the culvert, Babe Leopold wrote, "What a rotten writer of detective stories Life is."

Newspapermen enjoyed a certain swagger in the city of the big shoulders. Newspapers changed dramatically in the years following World War I, reflecting the attitudes of their readers. People sought out good times, and their newspapers didn't let them down. Readers, tired of dry, factual reporting, wanted human-interest news, where they could be drawn into the stories—a little yellow journalism to go with their bathtub gin and black-and-tan clubs.

In Chicago, where no single newspaper dominated, competition was legendary. Reporters had free and easy access, especially in police stations and ward headquarters. And many were dirty, profiting through cozy relationships with gangsters and city officials. Writers attracted readers with glitzy, front-page stories of crime and scandal. Journalistic ethics were sketchy, so when a newspaper did take the high road, this in itself became page-one news. Chicago's *Evening-American* proudly told the city that its editors held back publication of the Franks kidnapping until the family was certain the dead boy at the Hegewisch morgue was identified as Bobby. Its late edition on Friday, May 23, carried the following cover story:

### The News—and the Heart of a Great Newspaper

The Chicago Evening-American was in possession at 11 am yesterday of the fact that Robert Franks had been kidnapped. . . . It is sometimes necessary, at the plain dictates of humanity, that a newspaper withhold important news despite the fact that, in doing so, it runs the great risk of being beaten by its competitors. Such a problem faced the Evening-American yesterday.

This paper got in touch immediately with the family. It asked to withhold the news in its possession because the family felt there was some doubt as to the identity of the body found, and that any publicity might endanger Franks' life if still alive. Despite the fact that this newspaper realized it had what is known as a "big scoop," the story was withheld from 11 am–4 pm, although it is the policy of the Evening-American to be "First with the Latest."[91]

The press, thanks to Sam Ettleson's benevolence and Dickie Loeb's fascination with reporters, became part of the story from day one. Newspapers would eventually make Dickie and Babe public property throughout the summer.[92] Their crime was a perfect fit for the tabloid mentality that was Roaring Twenties' journalism.

Along with detailed stories, initial newspaper photos captivated readers: the angelic Bobby with his long, wavy hair and bushy eyebrows, a ghostly looking father in his black derby hat and formal nose spectacles, the worried looks of the suspects from the Harvard School, the desolate crime scene in the middle of the Lake Calumet wetlands, "Home of Sorrow"—the stately house at 5052 Ellis where Flora Franks lay "prostrated with grief."[93]

The *Evening-American* took readers to another realm. One of their writers recreated what Bobby Franks actually thought as he walked along Ellis.

I had turned for a final, lingering breath of the flowers-scented air when, like a flash, a rough hand was clasped over my hot lips, white with terror, to halt any outcry, and my arms were pinioned behind my back. I matched my strength, born of desperation, with that of my fiendish captors, with the tides of hell running like molten lava through their accursed veins.

"The Murderer," a page-one editorial cartoon in the *Chicago Daily Tribune*, took Chicagoans inside the killer's hideout: a drawn shade covers a window, and a chair holds the door shut; an alarm clock ticks loudly while the walls are covered with eyes; the panic-stricken murderer reads about his "brutal murder" in the newspapers while the caption assures readers, "As he knows the circle is closing in."[94]

Detective chief Michael Hughes was part of this circle. Just a few hours after the afternoon newspapers of May 23 hit newsstands, police began getting tips from concerned citizens. Hundreds of tips poured into the detective bureau and the home of Jacob Franks.[95] "We aren't going to overlook a thing," Hughes said. "I'm not sticking to any theory, or slighting any possibility. We'll run down anything that looks like a clue."[96]

Police Chief Morgan Collins urged everyone to "look around" and to report any unusual activity to police. "This undoubtedly is one of the most brutal murders with which we have had to deal," Collins told the press. "Never before have we come in contact with such a cold-blooded and willful taking of life."[97]

Collins offered a $1,000 reward for information leading to the capture of the murderer: "All information will be treated as strictly confidential, thoroughly analyzed and run down to the end. Some one of Chicago's three million people other than the person or persons who committed the crime must know or have some suspicion of the one who did it."[98]

While Collins pleaded for people to "look around," the *Chicago Herald and Examiner* created a preposterous contest asking readers for theories—for cash.

How and why was Robert Franks, a fourteen-year-old heir to $4 million, killed? Police investigators may clear that up. But have you a theory now? Can you write a logical theory, telling step by step how the crime was committed and what motivated the participants?

The *Herald and Examiner* will give a prize of $50 to the reader who writes the best theory. The winner also will be eligible for a share in the $10,000 reward if his theory should aid in the solution of the slaying. The judgment will take place when the slayers are apprehended, if they are, and if they are not, upon the logic and probability of credence obtained in the written theory. The theories should be written in condensed, concise form, cleanly written or typed, on one side of the paper, and should be addressed to the City Editor, Herald and Examiner.

Somewhere in Chicago, behind a desk, or in a streetcar, or in a foundry, may be a keen and analytical mind adapted but not trained to detection and the reconstruction of past events, as a hunter reconstructs the story of the chase from the muddy records of the spoor. It may be yours. Send in your theory.[99]

Readers mailed in more than three thousand theories within a few days. The *Herald and Examiner* contest, along with passionate statements by Collins and a reward pot that swelled to $16,000, led to a frenzy of false leads.

## YET ANOTHER DIRECTION

Daybreak Saturday, May 24. For most Chicagoans it was a calm start to the weekend. Lake Michigan's blue-green water carried gentle waves into the stone retaining wall at Ontario Street, the halfway point between the Edgewater Beach and Kenwood. The city behind him, Sylvester Wenjenski stood alone at the water's edge, an insignificant silhouette against the rising sun. No one witnessed his suicide leap.

Later that morning, the phone rang in Sam Ettleson's downtown office. She had been living with this confidence man, the young voice told the attorney. She suspected the man might have engineered the plot to steal Bobby Franks. He had talked to her several times about kidnapping, and she believed he had actually been mixed up in one. That's why she left him. This man, she said, always kept poisons around the house, and he hung around a pool hall at Sixty-Third and Cottage Grove. Oh, yes, he had a typewriter, too.

Ettleson repeated the conversation to the Cook County State's Attorney Robert Crowe. Ettleson then told the press, but he withheld the name of the woman and of her confidence-man friend. "We will not make them known until we have investigated this information," he said.

In the afternoon hours, after someone discovered Wenjenski's body floating in the lake, a letter arrived at police headquarters. The typewritten note, which made headlines in the late editions, was addressed to the police chief:

Morgan A. Collins—Dear Chief:
I am the murderer and kidnapper of the Franks boy. When you get

this letter I will probably be a dead man. I intend to commit suicide. I am very sorry I did this inhuman piece of work.

A SORRY MAN[100]

Collins quickly told the public he now had another tangible clue to follow: "There is no doubt in my mind that the man who wrote this letter was the one that wrote the letter to Mr. Franks."

Detectives rushed to a funeral home just north of the Loop to examine Wenjenski's body, but they were never able to make a connection to the Franks case.

While Collins talked to the newspapers, a postman on the South Side delivered an unsigned, handwritten letter to the home of Jacob Franks. The crude note threatened Franks's daughter and sent police in yet another direction:

> Questioned are innocent, so watch her—Josephine. She is next. You dirty skunk—bah! So you are so smart. To give your future to save your boy, why you stingy. . . . You could have saved her but . . . very bad. If I had you here I would have strangled you to death. You couldn't keep your dirty mouth closed. Well, we will go a little further, so watch yourself. To hell with the police. There's that now. A big watch. You are crying. You made your money honest? Hah, hah. "Honest Jake." But the world don't know you. But you shall suffer minute by minute, you low down skunk. So low that you could walk under a snake. So you are very low. And now every time you disobey us we will strike. Go ahead.

It was Robert Crowe's nature to play the role. A gifted orator, "Battling Bob" used the courtroom as a stage. Striking a pose, the ambitious forty-five-year-old state's attorney would raise a fist high, hold an arm behind his back, and deliver his plea. A fancy, white handkerchief adorned the pocket of his suit jacket; wavy, sandy hair matched his tortoise-shell eyeglasses. Crowe's brashness—and his Irish baby face—appealed to voters. Once a popular member of the William Hale Thompson machine, he first made a name for himself crusading against the anti-Thompson press—the *Daily News* and *Daily Tribune*. (He eventually split with Thompson after a falling out with Police Chief Charlie Fitzmorris, who attempted to stop Crowe from closing down some vice dens.)

Crowe, a former chief justice of the Cook County Criminal Court, owned a poor record for convictions as state's attorney. In 1923, his large staff dropped or mitigated nearly 24,000 charges; only 1,959 were sent to prison.[101] Now, six months from an election, the Bobby Franks case—only forty-eight hours old—seemed to be the perfect drama for the flashy Crowe. He told the newspapermen, "If the slayers of Robert Franks are caught, they will be brought to trial within the shortest time permitted by the law."

Crowe and Collins merged their forces following the death threat to Josephine Franks. Eight detectives guarded Jacob Franks's home on Ellis. They checked every automobile that stopped in front of the house, and they kept the curious moving down the block. Long, slow lines of cars passed by the home at all hours. They also came on foot—gawkers trying to peer inside the Franks home. Police allowed only relatives or the most intimate friends to enter.

Crowe and Collins set up special headquarters at the new Drake Hotel on Michigan Boulevard, about a block from Lake Michigan. Crowe appointed one of his top assistants—Kenwood resident Bert Cronson, a nephew to Sam Ettleson—to coordinate efforts with detective chief Hughes. "The process of elimination will not fail us," Crowe said.[102]

The city's top law enforcement officials promised to sift through the mountain of leads and tips—from the plausible to the ridiculous—to find the killers.

- Police searched the city for gray Wintons. A Kenwood chauffeur echoed young Irving Hartman's words, "the big gray Winton was coming lickety split up Ellis." The chauffeur told police he saw such a car—a 1919 or 1920 model—parked in front of the Harvard School on Wednesday afternoon. Its curtains were drawn, he said, and a red-faced man sat at the wheel.

- Anna Licht, a secretary at Harvard, said she saw a drunk lurking outside the school Wednesday. "I was looking out the window," she told Hughes. "Robert was just leaving. Sitting on the curb was a man who looked drunk. As Robert went through the gate, this man got up and waved, as to a car." Hughes called her story "important."[103]

- Mrs. Alfred Anderson, who lived on the far South Side, had police looking for a woman. After all, she told them, think about what she knew.

   I was walking west on 113th Street, just west of Michigan Boulevard. A car approached . . . a sedan. It slowed down, and in the front seat I saw a man of about 35, driving, wearing a dark fedora hat. Beside him sat a woman about 30 or 32. . . . In the rear I noticed a bundle on the seat, which appeared upright about a foot and a half above the window sill. It was covered with a brown wrapping, like a blanket, and it seemed to me to be a material somewhat like burlap, only of finer texture. As I looked, it swayed from side to side, and a point at the top of the bundle that might have been a head—although no outline showed—moved back and forward. It seemed to me to be the motions of a person trying to get free of the covering.[104]

- It was either a Nash or a Moon, and it had a broken front bumper, the railroad switchman told police. His story had so much detail that authorities considered it their best lead. John Shackleford, who lived in Gary, Indiana, said he saw a black or blue sedan at 118th and the Pennsylvania Railroad tracks. It was nearly midnight on Wednesday when "three men and a woman, one of them got out with a bundle in his arms. It looked like a tent wrapped up, and I said to myself, 'This is a hell of a time to go camping.' I lost sight of him for a few minutes, and when I saw him again he didn't have the bundle." Shackleford actually played a role in his own story. The Nash or Moon tried to pull away in the darkness but got stuck in the mud. Shackleford, who was parked in his car a short distance away, offered to help. He put chains on the car's tires and towed it free, but the car's front bumper was damaged during the towing. Crowe called Shackleford's story "one of the most important clues we have obtained so far." Police began searching for a sedan with a broken front bumper.

- Sergeant Harry Goldstein, a county highway patrolman, was sure he knew two men in the Hegewisch area who could be involved in the Franks killing. Goldstein said the men had written letters similar to the ones received by the Franks family. And the suspects lived in the area where the dead boy was found. He would bring them to the Drake for questioning.

- Tips from amateur sleuths poured into a special unit at the Chicago Detective Bureau, and Lieutenant Ernest Meuller was in charge of receiving and cataloging them.[105] A young man approached Meuller with a detective diploma from a correspondence school. One of Meuller's men gave him a test and asked the aspiring detective if he could find a two-bit piece Meuller had hidden in the room. The young man never found the quarter. That same day, a woman from the Northwest Side gave detectives the name of a man she knew who recently bought a portable typewriter. This man, she said, also read dime novels and detective stories. A telephone operator called Meuller to say that morning she had passed a woman at State and Madison streets who was wearing a pair of eyeglasses exactly like the ones found at the swamp.

- Because the kidnappers killed Bobby Franks before his father had a chance to deliver the ransom money, many people believed the crime was the work of a "moron." One Hyde Park alienist—Dr. James Whitney Hall—theorized that a degenerate killed Bobby after he was "spirited away in an automobile."[106] Hall and others reminded police of the 1919 killing of Janet Wilkenson. A janitor, Thomas Fitzgerald, molested and strangled the five-year-old girl and then buried her in a coal pile. Robert Crowe, then chief justice of the criminal court, sentenced Fitzgerald to hang.

- Michael Hughes even assigned some detectives to look into the past of Jacob Franks. Hughes theorized that because Franks was once a pawnbroker to gamblers, maybe revenge figured into the killing of his son.

- Two salesmen said they saw something suspicious near the Pennsylvania tracks early Thursday morning. A Dodge touring car, with the headlamps extinguished, was parked alongside the tracks at 105th Street. Two women stood nearby, they said, and one of them was cleaning a shovel. They also saw some men in a nearby swamp. Police dispatched digging teams to the area.

- On Wednesday afternoon, Gertrude Barker, a seventeen-year-old who attended St. Xavier's girls school, disappeared on her way home. She lived at Forty-Eighth and Blackstone. The girl's relatives believed she may have seen the Franks abduction and had become a victim herself. Newspapers printed a detailed map: "Where the Kidnapping Trails Met?" Miss Barker eventually appeared safe and sound a few days later. She said she became tired of school and wanted an "adventure." Police found her keeping house for the owner of a Kenwood stable on Forty-Ninth Street, where several wealthy men kept their horses.

- A couple walked into the Hyde Park Police Station and showed the desk sergeant a note they claimed was found at the crime scene. They said they discovered the note (along with a piece of a pillow slip) in the long grass a short distance from the culvert. "You dirty skunk—G. J. I will get you yet," the note read.[107] Police sent the items to the Drake Hotel.

- An oculist told Hughes that he had recently prescribed a pair of eyeglasses to a Mr. Johnson—the same kind found in the swamp. "He was nervous and high strung," the oculist said. "He seemed intelligent yet of such nature as would stop at nothing—cruelty, crime, anything. Instinctively at looking at that face one would know the possessor capable of murder."[108]

- In Detroit, a psychic—Eugenie Dennis—saw a vision, one that was quickly relayed to Chicago police. According to Dennis, a red-haired woman and two men abducted young Franks, and one of the abductors is already in custody. "The other one, the one with the light complexion—he has sort of gray streaks in his hair—is hiding," she said. "He is in a big place, not a hotel, somewhere in the southwest part of the city. The Franks boy's clothing are there."[109]

- After nearly a week in custody, a judge ordered the release of Mott K. Mitchell and Walter Wilson, the instructors at the Harvard School. Police pressured the teachers to confess but were never able to gather enough evidence to formally arrest them. Crowe, several of his assistants, and Lieutenant William Shoemacher made a final attempt to gain confessions. They grilled the two men extensively in the final hours before the habeas-corpus hearing. Mitchell and Wilson walked out of the Criminal Courts Building free men, but detectives continued to follow them. Police still considered them "prized suspects."

A gray Winton, a dark-blue Nash or Moon with a broken front bumper, a red-haired woman in a psychic's vision, a piece of a pillow slip, Mr. Johnson's eyeglasses, were just a few of the false leads that consumed authorities. But the two clues Collins and Crowe had since day one—the eyeglasses and the ransom note—were the only ones worth following.

## IF WURST COMES TO SAUSAGE

How ironic. The eyeglasses were supposed to relieve Babe's head pains. Now they gave him the headache of his life.

Babe followed the investigation in the daily newspapers. He didn't read every edition of every paper like Dickie did, but he examined them closely, cataloging in his mind any bit of information that could be linked to him. When he saw the photo of the horn-rimmed glasses under the headline "Whose Spectacles Are These?" he began to worry. The papers had all the details: the owner was nearsighted; the glasses were peculiarly shaped, the size to fit a woman or small boy, but the nose bridge was wide, suggesting they belonged to a man with a narrow, angular head and wide, prominent nose.[110]

At first, police assumed the eyeglasses belonged to young Franks, but later, they told the press they believed the glasses were dropped near the culvert by the killer. Babe hadn't worn the glasses in months, but he knew they must be his. Just to make sure, he searched every inch of his room—they weren't there.[111] *They must have slipped out of the breast pocket of one of my birding suits. What now, go to the police on my own? Why? They were common prescriptions; they'd never be able to trace them back to me. I had a good excuse why they'd be in that swamp—it's one of my favorite birding spots.*

But he knew he'd better talk to Dickie.

The Master Criminal was annoyed. How could his confederate be so sloppy?

"Are you sure, Nate?" Dickie asked when they talked in Babe's bedroom Saturday afternoon.

"I looked all over for them, and I can't find the damn things."

"Look, can they trace them, do you think?" Dickie asked, his eyes sweeping across the room, looking past the stuffed birds that overwhelmed Babe's second-floor sanctuary.

"They're a common prescription, Dickie. Had a degree of stigmatism, the doc said. There must be a jillion pairs of them in the city. So I don't think there's much chance of their being traced."

Babe assured Dickie he had a perfect excuse if the police did question him—since he goes birding in that area all the time. "What do you say if I go and claim them? Kind of spike their guns in advance."

"No, I think that'd be a fool caper. Don't get mixed up in the case at all. They might try some rough stuff on you. And besides, it might take you a hell of a while to talk your way out of it. Of course, the crucial thing is what chance there is the things can be traced to you."

"Well," Babe said, "as I said, I know the prescription is a very common one. The doc told me so. And how are they going to know what oculist they came from? They'd have to go through the records of every oculist in town and then check on a couple of thousand people."

"Hell, let it go," Dickie said. "You don't know your glasses are gone. Make 'em come to you. Then, if wurst comes to sausage, you can be so surprised that the glasses are yours. Then's the time to tell your story about losing them birding."

The two killers weren't the only ones concerned about a pair of eyeglasses.

At the Drake Hotel, State's Attorney Crowe assigned one of his assistants, Joseph Savage, to trace the horn-rimmed spectacles. Babe thought there were "a jillion" similar pairs of glasses in Chicago. He was dead wrong. Savage's investigation eventually traced the lenses to Almer Coe and Company. The firm identified the glasses as theirs by a faint, diamond etching on the lenses. As Babe said, the prescription—written by Dr. Emil Deutsch—was common. The Xylonite frames were also ordinary. But the hinge, which connected the earpiece to the nosepiece, was a specialty item. Bobrow Optical of Brooklyn, New York, manufacturer of the hinge, had sold only three frames in Chicago—all to Almer Coe.[112] An attorney who was traveling in Europe had bought one pair; a woman purchased the other. And Savage would learn that in November, according to Coe's records, one of its stores sold a pair of Bobrow horn-rims to a young University of Chicago law student.

In Hegewisch, police continued their investigation in the Lake Calumet wetlands. Officer Edward Anderson of the East Side Station interviewed the game warden at Eggers Woods. After examining the visitors' book, Anderson noticed a recent entry of "N. F. Leopold of Greenwood Avenue" in Kenwood, Bobby Franks's neighborhood. Sure, the game warden told Anderson, young Leopold is an ornithologist and is a regular visitor.

The city's brightest criminologists focused on the ransom letter.

Assistant State's Attorney Cronson and Sergeant Charles Egan devoted themselves exclusively to the typewritten note. Early analysis suggested it was written on a Corona. Cronson and Egan enlisted the expertise of H. P. Sutton, a veteran at the Royal Typewriter Company. The killers used an Underwood portable to type the ransom letter, Sutton said. He explained that certain characteristics in the note were consistent with the actions of the Underwood portable, especially the way the 3 trailed off into a tail at the bottom, and the lower half of the 8 was much larger than the upper. And the writer was a novice at typewriting. "The person who wrote this letter never learned the touch system," Sutton said. "A person using the touch system strikes the keys pretty evenly, with an even pressure on the keys. The man who wrote this was either a novice at typing or else used two fingers. Some of the letters were punched so hard they were almost driven through the paper, while others were struck lightly or uncertainly."

Handwriting experts scrutinized the ransom envelope addressed to Jacob Franks. The lettering came from a professional hand, they said, "in a manner taught mathematics, physics and mechanical art students, and emphasized in art school cartoon courses."[113] The experts concluded that the handwriting was not of one who was trying to letter well but from an individual who attempted to letter poorly.

Detectives studied the letter's precise language and specific format. James Gortland, secretary to Michael Hughes, discovered that the note resembled a fictional ransom letter that appeared in "The Kidnapping Syndicate" story in the May 3 issue of *Detective Story Magazine.*

"Look for the suspect with that magazine in his possession, and you'll pretty nearly have the man who killed Robert Franks," Hughes's detectives claimed.[114]

In "The Kidnapping Syndicate," the victim is a wife instead of a child. But the details in the magazine's ransom letter—including the numbered paragraphs, a warning against going to the police, and a relay procedure for future communications—closely mirrored the letter sent to Jacob Franks.

> Your wife is in our custody, and as long as your conduct toward us warrants, she shall be treated with every courtesy and respect, and, in so far as the circumstances permit, will be made comfortable. Any change in this attitude will be the result of your own defiance to our terms, which are:
>
> 1. That you make no appeal to the police or to any private detective agency. In that event the amount stated below is automatically doubled, and, let us assure you, it will avail you nothing and only bring great anguish to yourself and wife.
>
> 2. Upon receipt of $50,000 in bills of $10 and $20 denominations delivered at the place, the time, and under the conditions which you will receive later, Mrs. Griswold will be returned to you within a few hours thereafter.
>
> 3. Acceptance of these terms are to be conveyed to us as follows: You'll leave your house tomorrow morning wearing a white carnation in the lapel of your coat and wear it all day.
>
> 4. Following this we shall send you further instructions as to how, when and where the money shall be paid.
>
> The Kidnapping Syndicate

The *Chicago Daily Journal* offered readers a novelist's perspective of the crime and commented, "It is presented for what it may be worth."

> Assuming two persons (involved) in the crime, their roles would be about as follows:
>
> John Doe, an educated, clever man, probably a clever failure, conceived the idea of the kidnapping. He takes into partnership

Richard Roe, who is probably a more ignorant person or coarser type. Together they kidnap the boy and take him to a hiding place where he is left under the care of Richard Roe. John Doe goes back to his quarters to phone the parents and write the ransom letter, or to mail it if already written.

At the hiding place, Robert gives trouble. He is an active lad, with a keen mind, and at the age when one has most confidence in his physical prowess. He makes an attempt to escape or to attract attention, and is killed.

The fact that death was caused by suffocation indicates that the hiding place was somewhere within earshot of people, and that his captors were trying to keep the boy still. It also indicates the killing was not intentional, though that does not lessen the guilt of the criminals in any way . . .

It is possible that John Doe did not learn of the death of the victim at least until after mailing the ransom letter. Perhaps he did not learn it until after the second telephone message . . .

Richard Roe, finding himself with a dead boy on his hands, tries to hide his crime. He strips the body, to hinder identification, and plans to sink it in the lake, changes his mind, as a panicky criminal so often does, and flings the corpse in a swamp. John Doe may or may not have taken part in this attempt to dispose the body. The odds are that he did not; two crooks are less likely to change their plans than one . . .

The fact that the boy was suffocated by something pressed over his mouth makes one feel that his guard was neither very powerful, nor much of a fighter.

Opticians say that the glasses found near the scene of the crime belonged to a woman. Women seldom take part in crimes of violence against children, but the attempt to smother a boy's cries does have a feminine look. If that be the case, Richard Roe is a woman.

John Doe should be traceable by his typewriter. Either John Doe or Richard Roe, most likely the latter, should be traceable by his spectacles. Those spectacles, with the provision for a broad nose and a narrow face, suggest a colored person, since that combination of features is a common African characteristic, but very rare among white people.

The theory that any man sat down and wrote that ransom letter, perfectly phrased and correct in spelling and spacing, within a few hours after taking part in a brutal murder is too preposterous to be worth discussing.[115]

The writer concluded that the motive for killing Bobby Franks was strictly for money.

While Dickie and Babe discussed what to do about the eyeglasses, more than thirty-five thousand boys marched down Michigan Avenue on Saturday afternoon in a snappy parade to end "Boys' Week"—a combined celebration of the R.O.T.C. and the Boy Scouts. The *Daily Journal* used the occasion to issue a piercing editorial, one aimed at the efforts of State's Attorney Crowe and Police Chief Collins:

### A Grim Comment on Boys' Week

At the climax of Boys' Week, one of the city's finest boys is found murdered, and at the close of that week the authorities are still running around in circles trying to pick up a clew to the murderer. . . .

Much—though not a word too much—has been said on the need for better protection for the city's girls. Here is an object lesson on the need of better protection for the city's boys. . . .

The safety of the lad depends on the community, and the community has not done its duty. . . . But if Chicago had put the fear of the law into the criminal world, Robert Franks would be alive today.

He is dead because nearly every killer in Cook County beats the rope, because the records are full of unsolved mysteries, because crooked bondsmen, unscrupulous lawyers and sentimental juries have stacked the cards in a game against justice, because even when a criminal goes to prison "influences" are working for his pardon or parole. . . .

Let there be no misunderstanding, no hysteria. This is not a case for blind vengeance. There must be no torturing to secure confessions which a jury will disregard, even if the judge does not throw them out, as judges have a habit of doing. This is a time for patient, painstaking, unremitting, unrelenting work until the mystery is solved. . . . The boys of Chicago are entitled to protection which only the community can give them. Get to work.

Sunday, May 25, 2:30 in the morning. The gilded Statue of the Republic wore a moonlit sheen in the middle of Jackson Park. The three-story-high replica of the Columbia Exposition's Lady Liberty watched over Frederick Law Olmsted's sleepy lagoons. She stood alone, this golden sentry, except for the two killers beneath her.

Babe cut the headlamps and allowed the sporty Willys to coast to a stop. Dickie sat in the front seat and finished prying off the tips of the

Underwood's keys with a pair of pliers. A strong wind shook the tree tops in Wooded Island as Dickie tossed the small bundle of keys into the lagoon.[116]

The typewriter and its case met a similar fate at the southeastern corner of Jackson Park. Headlamps dimmed, the boys drove to an ornate granite-and-sandstone bridge decorated with carvings of hippopotamus heads, ship prows, and water deities. Dickie walked to the top of the bridge and threw the Underwood into the channel below. The splash momentarily disrupted the white ribbons of moonlight on the black water.

Babe's Willys crossed over the bridge and followed South Shore Drive to Seventy-Third Street. The Leopolds' blood-soaked automobile robe would be the last piece of evidence to destroy. Dickie and Babe carried the robe and a can of gasoline to a makeshift timber pier at Lake Michigan. They doused the robe with gasoline and set it afire in the darkness.

Both boys carried the smell of smoke into the Willys as they drove back to Kenwood. They still needed to finalize their alibi. Babe was especially anxious because the police already had his eyeglasses in custody. Proficient liars, they had no trouble concocting an alibi: On May 21, after morning classes, they lunched at Marshall Field's Grill. Then it was birding in Lincoln Park, north of downtown. They also did some drinking before heading back to Kenwood for something to eat at the Cocoanut Grove. After dinner, they picked up a couple of girls in Washington Park, just west of the University of Chicago campus. They drove around with the girls but were not able to come to a mutual agreement, so they dropped them off in Jackson Park.

They disagreed on how long to use the alibi. If questioned by the police, Babe wanted to keep the alibi in place until he left for Europe in early June.

"Gee, Nate," Dickie said, "they can't expect you to remember just where you were every day. Where were you a month ago? You don't remember. Sure, if they pinch one of us today or tomorrow, it'll look fishy if we say we don't know where we were Wednesday. But after four or five days, how can anyone expect you to remember?"[117]

"I think you're wrong," Babe said. "I'll bet they won't let up that easy. Besides, it's so much cleaner and easier simply to use the alibi if we have to. Sure, if one of us does get picked up, he'll do his level best to talk his way out of it without using the alibi. He'll insist as long as he reasonably can that he can't remember where he was Wednesday."

Babe considered himself more conservative than Dickie, more cautious. And more timid. If questioned by police, he knew he would not be able to get away with failure to remember.

"If it becomes apparent to him that it isn't going to work," Babe continued, "then I say he ought to give up the alibi. I say we use the alibi right up to the time I leave for Europe."

"Hell, no!" Dickie screamed. "That's way too long. That's ridiculous. I say five days or so—say through next Thursday."

That was it—next Thursday. The Master Criminal had put an abrupt end to the argument. They'd use the alibi for one week. After that, they'd say they couldn't remember their exact actions on May 21.

Dickie ended the long night confident. They cleaned up after their crime, figured out a plausible alibi, and agreed how to use it. The planning seemed perfect. Babe wasn't so sure.

## AN UNTIMELY RITE

They assembled slowly at first—a handful of people at the corner of Hyde Park and Ellis and a few groups near the lilac bushes at the side entrance of the sad, yellow house.

Within a few hours, a couple of hundred people had converged on a chilly and windy Sunday morning, May 25. A dozen policemen kept the crowds away from the walkway leading to the front door. Only relatives, close friends, and select schoolmates entered. The curious also gawked from cars. A smoky, ragged stream of chugging automobiles clogged the intersection outside Jacob Franks's home. A solemn awe hung over the elegant neighborhood.

Inside, scattered throughout the first floor, youngsters talked in hushed, nervous voices. For most, it was their first funeral, an untimely rite. Eight of the boys would serve as Bobby's pallbearers. In the library, in front of the fireplace, their friend lay inside a small, white coffin covered with a blanket of red rosebuds. The mixed fragrance from the lilies of the valley, orchids, roses, and peonies on the mantle created an inappropriate aura for a fourteen-year-old boy. Flora Franks sat nearby in a quiet daze. She looked away from her son and waited for the procession, for the future without her Baby.

Jacob Franks stood by his wife, his head bowed in silent grief. Josephine and Jack Franks sat next to their mother, while the pallbearers—the oldest being fourteen—circled the coffin.

After a brief prayer service, a soloist from the Fifth Church of Christ, Scientist sang, "O, Gentle Presence" and "Shepherd, Show Me How to Go."[118] Eight boys in heavy overcoats then carried their friend out the front door and down the two sets of concrete steps that led to a hearse parked on Ellis. Dickie Loeb watched from the street. He showed no remorse, but he would admit that he felt uncomfortable when he saw the small, "bright-faced boys" carrying the coffin.[119]

Six police motorcycles led the twenty-five-car procession out of Kenwood for the ten-mile ride to Rosehill Cemetery, north of the Loop.

At Rosehill, the funeral cars passed slowly under an arched, castle-like limestone portal. The procession wound its way beyond the orderly rows of white grave markers of fallen Union soldiers, past a tall Civil War monument—"Our Heroes"—into the secluded Jewish section.

The hearse stopped in front of an understated granite mausoleum. A small oak stood alongside, and two stone planters sat on either side of the leaded-glass doors. Leading up to the crypt from the gravel road, a velvet carpet, with flowers strewn on each side, awaited the Franks family. Bobby's classmates placed his coffin inside the small mausoleum while Flora Franks, her face trembling, stood by the door with her daughter, Josephine. Someone from the Fifth Church of Christ read prayers and sang, "I Will Lift Up Mine Eyes to the Hills."

Flora looked down on the small, while coffin—still adorned with the blanket of crimson buds—and turned away. Josephine helped her mother into the limousine. Neither watched as two cemetery workers set the long marble slab in place.

> *Life is because God is, infinite, indestructible and eternal.*
> *Robert E. Franks*
> *Sept. 19, 1909–May 22, 1924*

Among the many floral deliveries sent to the Franks' home on the morning of Bobby's funeral, one would find its way to the state's attorney's office and into the newspapers. A $10 wreath of tiger lilies held a small, handwritten card: Sympathy from Mr. Johnson. Police confiscated the flowers and questioned all florists in the area. The bouquet was purchased at a store on Forty-Third Street late Saturday night. The shop owner said the man who bought the wreath was about thirty years old and wore horn-rimmed glasses and a light gray telescope hat. Police interrogated anyone who fit this description, but Mr. Johnson never materialized.

Babe had much on his mind that morning of Sunday, May 25. He never heard the knock on the door.

Lying in bed, he wrestled with the sudden confusion in his life. He wasn't completely comfortable with Dickie's alibi, and he didn't know what to do about this thing with the eyeglasses—the clue everyone seemed to be talking about. He also faced final exams in all five of his law classes that week, along with the entrance test to Harvard Law School. But, in early June, he'd be sailing for Europe and a trouble-free summer.

Edward Anderson and Hugh Byrne were a long way from their blue-collar neighborhood. It was rare that two cops from the East Side Station had business in Kenwood. They rang the bell a few times before Babe's father answered.

"I'd like to see N. F. Leopold," Anderson said.

"I'm N. F. Leopold."

Anderson quickly explained that he and Byrne were looking for the N. F. Leopold who studied birds. Leopold summoned a maid to wake up his son.

Leopold invited the two Chicago policemen into his home. They waited for Babe in the parlor and, of course, discussed the Franks case. "Some maniac probably caused Bobby's death," Leopold said as his son came down the long staircase.[120] He wore purple pajamas.

Anderson told Babe that Captain Thomas Wolfe at the East Side Station wanted to talk with him. It wouldn't take too long. Babe told the cops he had a date in the early afternoon and asked if he could drive to the police station in his car. They struck a compromise—Babe drove Anderson in his Willys and Byrne followed in the patrol car.

Captain Wolfe was pleasant but direct. "The game warden at Eggers Woods says you're out there quite a bit," Wolfe said.

"That's right," Babe said, not knowing exactly where his answer would lead.[121] Anderson had offered no clues in the car as to what Wolfe was looking for. "During the spring especially I go out to the Hyde Lake–Wolf Lake district two or three times a week. I was out there as recently as last Sunday."

"Well," Wolfe said, "that's just why I asked you to come. I'd figured you know a lot of people that go out there. Would you give us a list of the people you know who go there?"

Babe thought about George Lewis, who had been with him last week. He mentioned Lewis, and he also gave Wolfe the names of some other birders. Then the other shoe dropped.

"You don't wear glasses, do you?"

Dickie's words flashed through Babe's mind: *Don't get mixed up in the case at all. They might try some rough stuff on you.*

"No, sir, I don't." *At least I don't now,* he told himself.

"Well, will you tell me which ones of these people do wear them?" Wolfe asked, referring to the names Babe had given him.

Babe threw out a few names. He made a mental note to call Lewis to tell him his name had come up during his brief chat with the police. Babe actually felt good about his encounter with Wolfe. He had now gone on record saying he was at Eggers Woods last Sunday, the 18th. He figured the interview was kind of an insurance policy. After all, he reasoned, if they ever trace the glasses to him, he'd have a clean explanation as to why they were found at the crime scene. He'd also have a character witness—Captain Wolfe.

Before heading back to Kenwood, Babe wrote and signed an official statement:

> I have been going to the general locality of 108th Street and Avenue F for six years. I have been in the locality about five or six times this year. The last two times were Saturday, May 17th, and Sunday, May 18th. On May 17th, George P. Lewis and I drove out through the forest preserve and down south along the east shore of Wolf Lake to about 126th Street. We then returned, arrived about 2:30 P.M. and left again about 5:00 P.M. On Sunday, May 18, at the conclusion of the day's birding, Mr. Sidney Stein, Jr., George Lewis, and I drove along the road to the forest preserve and out to May's shack between Wolf and Hyde Lakes. We arrived about 6:30 or 6:45, walked east to the ice house, back to the railroad track and left by the same road about 7:20 or 7:30. The purpose of all these trips was the observation of birds.[122]

Babe left the police station in a hurry. He had a date. Babe dated only because it was the thing to do, but the girl still had to measure up. She had to be intelligent and come from a high social stratum.

Susan Lurie fit the bill. She was attractive and sophisticated and came from a prominent Jewish family on Chicago's North Side. And Susan Lurie, a dainty, pretty philosophy major at the U. of C., enjoyed Babe's company. They shared a mutual interest in French, met for afternoon tea, and spent many evenings dancing. Susan admired Babe's intelligence. "His brain works fast," she told students who disliked Babe because he was aloof and conceited.[123]

The young coed had no idea just how fast Babe's brain worked. On Friday night, forty-eight hours after he and his friend poured acid over Bobby Franks's nude body and stuffed the child in a culvert, Babe took Susan Lurie dancing. They laughed the night away, she said.

And after his Sunday visit with Captain Wolfe, Babe called on Susan again. They shared a romantic lunch at a wayside inn, rented a canoe, and then paddled away the rest of the day on the Des Plaines River. Babe played a ukulele as Susan sang softly. They read French poetry, and Babe called the afternoon the happiest of his life.

## CINDERELLA TEAROOM

Each day, the small, stooped man in the black derby hat walked slowly through the great limestone arch into the Criminal Courts Building. Each day, he passed under its two female figures—one carrying a book representing law and the other holding a sword signifying justice. Each day, he hoped someone inside would provide closure.

Jacob Franks's face, once pale but strong, had turned gray and sunken, a fading shadow of grief cloistered under his derby. Franks rested on a bench in the corridor outside Robert Crowe's office. He talked quietly with a newspaper reporter about who killed his son.

"They are persons Robert knew," he said, his words fading away in the long, noisy hallway. "They are persons I know. I have been racking my brains trying to think who they could be. Robert knew the murderer. That is why they chocked him to death. And since Robert knew them, I must know them. Whoever it was who kidnapped my boy did so for the ransom. It was the money they were after. They knew his habits. They knew my love for him and that I would willingly pay any sum to have him back. But Robert recognized them, and they grew afraid, and they strangled him."

The young newsman from the *Chicago Tribune* scribbled in his notebook and waited respectfully while the old man lit a cigarette. Franks placed his hands on his crossed legs and stared at nothing.

"They tell me I bear up under the strain very well, but they do not know. I know it will not help that Baby any to keep brooding. I try to put things out of my mind, but they come back. My wife keeps showing me pictures of him. And I lie awake until dawn thinking about it all, thinking about that Baby."

A secretary from Crowe's staff interrupted and asked Franks to come into the state's attorney's office. Franks rose to his feet and told the reporter, "It is someone I know. But I cannot think who."

That same day, Dickie Loeb couldn't wait to get to the Zeta Beta Tau house. It was the weekly meeting for Phi chapter members, and Dickie knew it would be a good one.

"Where were you last Wednesday?" someone asked him.[124]

He threw back a lame excuse and settled in. The luncheon fit well into Dickie's Master Plan—everyone sitting around chatting about *his* crime, bewildered, looking to Dickie for his thoughts. Dickie was in his element.

The Franks case was the major subject under discussion. The frat men asked Alvin Goldstein of the *Daily News* about the latest developments in the case. Dickie jumped in and told Goldstein he thought it would be a good idea if they checked some more drugstores—this time along Fiftieth Street—maybe some suspicious phone calls were made. Goldstein, who usually listened to Dickie, liked the idea. *What a magnificent game—the ideal boy, the Master Criminal, the perfect crime.*

Babe waited for her in the quadrangle, in the warm spring sunshine. Most of May had been cold and rainy, but Chicago's weather had finally turned, and it seemed to lift Babe's spirits. It had been three days since his visit with Captain Wolfe at the East Side Station, and nothing had come of it. Now, he just had to get through his law exams, and he'd be off to Europe.

Susan Lurie was also in a pleasant mood when she met Babe. They walked along the Midway on their way to the Cinderella Tearoom on Cottage Grove. On the way, Babe bought two newspapers. Susan and he discussed his upcoming trip. Babe said his father had promised to give him $3,000 for the three-month vacation in Europe. Susan told Babe that was an absurd amount for such a short trip. Babe responded with his usual aloof chuckle.

Inside the Cinderella Tearoom, Babe excitedly covered their table with the newspapers. A "sure-enough" smile cut across his swarthy face as he began to read.

"Let's see what has happened in the Franks case," he said, almost laughing.[125]

Under dark, insidious-looking brows, Babe's eyes scampered up and down the broadsheet columns. His brain was working fast, as Susan would say, and it tickled his fancy. When he read about the crank letter sent to Jacob Franks, calling him a "dirty skunk" and threatening his daughter, Babe howled: "That's a good one. What a great joker."

Susan was a bit uncomfortable, but, in an attempt to join in Babe's fun, she told her date that it would be a good joke if he went to the police and confessed to the crime. Babe thought that would be the perfect joke. "Sure, I'll confess and you'll get the $16,000 reward money."

They both laughed. Another perfect afternoon for Babe and Susan.

After the gaiety at the Cinderella Tearoom, Babe took one of his final exams at the University of Chicago law building. Most of the students were still taking the test when Babe placed his completed exam on Professor Ernest W. Puttkammer's desk. He then asked for a few words with his instructor.

"Professor Puttkammer, in the Franks case, suppose the intent was simply to kidnap, nothing else apparently?" Babe asked.[126]

"Kidnapping is a felony in Illinois," Puttkammer said.

"Yes."

"Supposing a man causes somebody's death while he is intending to commit a felony, is that murder or manslaughter?" the professor asked his student.

"Well now, suppose that intent was simply to take improper liberties with the boy?" Babe asked. "I understand that this is a misdemeanor here in Illinois."

"Well, wholly without regard to that, on your assumed case," the professor said, "you still are talking about someone who had an intent to kidnap at the time, so that it is nonetheless a case in which the intent is to commit a felony, even though other crimes might enter into it that are simply misdemeanors."

Puttkammer then told Babe he really didn't know a great deal about the Franks case, but that the boy, too, attended the Harvard School.

Babe then asked Puttkammer what he knew about Mott Kirk Mitchell from Harvard. While the other students buried their heads in their exams, Babe tried to implicate his former high school teacher. This was a continuation on a theme. When Babe was a senior at Harvard, its yearbook recalled how he accused Mitchell of "laboring under a major neurosis."

"Mr. Mitchell, as far as I know, is a very upright, high-grade sort of man," Puttkammer said.

"Well," Babe said, "I don't know. I'm not so sure about that."

In a hushed conversation in front of the other law students, Babe told his professor that Mitchell had solicited boys, presumably boys in the school, to have sexual relations with him.

"Are you sure of that?" the astonished professor asked.

"Yes. He made that sort of proposition to my brother. That is straight enough, isn't it? I wouldn't put it past that man, Mitchell. I would like to see them get that fellow."

His case presented clearly, Babe walked a few steps away from his teacher's desk and then came back. "But, I didn't say he did it."

## MAKE 'EM COME TO YOU

Like a pair of songbirds advancing from tree to tree, the two detectives blended into the neighborhood. No one seemed to notice as they parked their car up the block on Greenwood, in front of an apartment building, and walked leisurely in the warm air to the Leopold house. For the second time in four days, the police wanted to have a word with Babe.

Babe was in his bedroom preparing for his Thursday afternoon birding class when one of the two men identified himself to the maid as "Mr.
Johnson." She asked them to wait in the library.

The Leopold's longtime servant Elizabeth Sattler knocked on Babe's
door and told him two gentlemen wished to speak with him.

"Who are they?" Babe asked.

"Only one gave his name, Mr. Babe. A Mr. Johnson."

*Johnson.* The name jarred Babe. *The same as the ransom note. Had
someone found out? Is this blackmail?*[127]

"What can I do for you gentlemen?" Babe asked, as he entered the
library.

Detective Sergeants Frank Johnson and William Crot, both in suits,
showed Babe their police identification cards. "The chief wants to see
you downtown," Johnson said.

"What about?"

"I don't know," Johnson said. "He just said to come out here and ask
you to come downtown."

"This is mighty awkward. I was just on the point of leaving to meet
my bird class at the University Elementary School. They'll be waiting
for me."

"Sorry," Johnson said. "But this won't take too long."

*Make 'em come to you,* Dickie had told Babe. That's just what was
happening as Johnson and Crot drove Babe into the Loop, where the
state's attorney had a suite of rooms at the fashionable LaSalle Hotel.
Robert Crowe and Michael Hughes were poised. Some persistent police
work and Almer Coe and Company's efficient recordkeeping had traced
the Bobrow horn-rims found near the body of Bobby Franks to Nathan
Leopold Jr. of 4754 Greenwood.

Johnson and Crot escorted Babe to Crowe's sixteenth-floor headquarters. "Battling Bob," eyeglasses in-hand, greeted Babe respectfully but
wasted no time.

"Are these your eyeglasses?"

"They sure look like mine," Babe said. He sat in a large, winged chair
and examined the pair. "If I didn't know that mine were at home, I'd
almost think they were."

"Oh, yours are at home?"

"Yes," Babe said, without hesitation.

"Well," the state's attorney said, "I'll have the boys drive you out there
to get them."

*Wurst,* as the Master Criminal would say, *was about to come to sausage.*

Foreman "Mike" Leopold wasn't the type of man to become easily upset. So when his youngest brother came in the house with two police detectives, he knew Babe would have a plausible explanation.

Babe quickly recapped the situation for Mike, who then helped Babe and the cops look for the glasses.

"Didn't you say the other night, Babe, this place where they found the body is right where you often go looking for birds?" Mike asked, loud enough so Johnson and Crot could hear. "You must have dropped them out there and never noticed they were gone."[128]

"Maybe so, Mike," Babe said.

At that moment, Babe thought about asking Mike to get a lawyer. Johnson and Crot were busy looking for the glasses, so he had plenty of time to talk privately with Mike. But Babe did not want to admit to his family that he was a murderer. As he would say years later, "I couldn't do it. It was unthinkable. I'd gamble the whole hog or none."[129]

Their search a failure, Mike tried to take control. "Look," he said to the detectives, "Mr. Ettleson, Samuel Ettleson, is our next-door neighbor and a friend of the family. He's known this kid since he was a baby. Let me call him on the phone. He'll be able to straighten this out in a jiffy."

Johnson and Crot had no problem with that, but when Mike phoned, he found out that Ettleson was at the Franks home. Mike then suggested they all go over to the house on Ellis and talk to Ettleson in person. Babe was confident Sam Ettleson would believe that he lost his glasses while birding.

Ettleson and Jacob Franks both answered the door. Mike politely explained that they needed to talk with Ettleson for a minute. Franks asked everyone to step into the parlor. It was the first time Babe had met the father of the boy he killed. Franks watched as Babe clearly and calmly described his dilemma. Babe looked at the old man when he said he had been in the same vicinity that Sunday before, and that's when he lost his glasses.

Franks seemed a bit overwhelmed, but Ettleson appeared to buy into the story.

"There's some mistake here," Ettleson told the detectives. "I've known this boy all his life. I know the whole family. It's a fantastic coincidence. You tell Mr. Crowe that it's all a mistake. I'll take the responsibility."

All seemed perfect for Babe. He thought maybe he'd make his afternoon birding class after all.

Until Johnson asked to speak with Ettleson privately. The conversation was brief, and Babe now felt very uneasy in the presence of Bobby's father. Following the short talk, Ettleson turned to Mike and Babe.

"The whole thing is absurd, of course," he said. "But the officers feel that they are duty bound to take Babe back downtown to Mr. Crowe. If it's not too inconvenient, perhaps that would be the better thing to do."

Babe and Mike thanked Ettleson and said good-bye to Franks. Mike decided to follow Babe and the detectives to the LaSalle Hotel. On the way downtown, Babe still believed he had an airtight explanation as to why someone found his glasses at the murder scene. As they drove along the lake, Babe ran it all through his mind: *Just check with Captain Wolfe, he's got it all on record. What did they have, after all? Not a thing. They had the glasses, sure. So they were mine. So what.*[130]

Crowe and two of his assistants, Joseph Savage and John Sbarbaro, greeted Babe when he returned to the LaSalle Hotel. They politely asked Mike to wait in an anteroom while they resumed the questioning.

Babe admitted ownership of the eyeglasses, saying they must have dropped out of his suit jacket pocket when he was birding near Eggers Woods on the weekend of May 17. Relaxed but not arrogant, Babe said that's the only reason someone found his glasses in the swampland.

"Well, I always had them in my coat pocket, and it is possible that Sunday, with big rubber boots on and running over this culvert, I might have tripped and dropped the glasses in that manner," he explained.[131]

"Do you know where the body of Robert Franks was found?" Crowe asked.[132]

"Yes, sir."

"Where?"

"It was found, as I understand it, under the railroad embankment of the Pennsylvania Railroad tracks at the location of 118th Street, if it were extended," Babe said.

"Are you familiar with that spot?"

Babe then gave Crowe a detailed account of his weekend in the wetlands, sticking closely to the statement he had given Captain Wolfe: How he and George Lewis crossed the railroad track and ran to the lake and how he tried to shoot the Wilson's Phalaropes. "I fired three shots at them, missing like a tenderfoot," he told the prosecutors.

Crowe asked Babe if—during that time—he paid any attention to the drain culvert where the killers hid Bobby's body.

"No, sir," Babe quickly responded.

"But you're familiar with the drain at that particular spot where the body was found?"

"Yes, sir. I didn't know there was a pipe there. I knew that this little channel flowed from one side of the track to the other. I knew of course just where it went under, but I never bothered to investigate to see how it got under there."

Savage asked Babe to demonstrate how his glasses fell. Babe put the eyeglasses in his suit jacket pocket, walked across the hotel room, and tripped. He fell to the floor, but the glasses didn't fall. He did it again. And again, but the Bobrow horn rims remained in the pocket. Sbarbaro then suggested that Babe place his jacket on the floor and then pick it up. Babe followed the instructions, and the glasses fell to the plush LaSalle carpet. The attorneys knew this little demonstration proved nothing, but at least they got Babe to admit for sure that he and his glasses had visited the scene of the crime.

It was like Dickie had told him: They might try some rough stuff on you.

Like a pair of tag-team wrestlers, Savage and Sbarbaro came at Babe at different times, with different moves. And to make sure Babe stayed off-balance, Crowe came in and out of the room throughout the proceedings.

"So what did you do on May 21st?" Savage asked.

"Gee, I don't know," Babe said.

For the next few hours, they jabbed at Babe about his good record at law school and reminded him how smart he was. Surely he could remember what he did a week ago. When one paused, the other would jump in and start a new round of questions.

At one point, as Babe lit a cigarette, he asked if he could go to the washroom. On his way, he passed his brother Mike, who waited in the anteroom.[133]

"How are things going?" Mike asked.

"Fine," Babe said.

Again, Babe had a chance to ask his big brother to get a lawyer to file a writ of habeas corpus. They had already held him for several hours and had not charged him with anything. *Way beyond a reasonable time, and besides, what did they have to charge me with?*[134]

When Babe returned, he decided to use the alibi he and Dickie concocted, even though it was eight days after the crime—one day past the agreed deadline. He started slowly, cautiously, not wanting Savage and Sbarbaro to think he had something rehearsed. He played hookey on that day, he told them. He and a friend—Richard Loeb—drove downtown in Babe's red Willys-Knight and took lunch at the Grill at Marshall Field's. After lunch, they drove to Lincoln Park to do some birding. They also did some drinking.

"I should say we might have been a little bit happy, but neither of us was drunk," Babe said.

He went on to say that Loeb was worried that he had liquor on his breath and didn't want to go home, so they ate at the Cocoanut Grove, not far from their homes. After dinner, they drove up and down Sixty-Third Street and picked up a couple of girls.

"What were their names?" Savage wanted to know.

"Edna and Mae, but I don't know their last names."

Savage and Sbarbaro gave Babe a nod to continue.

Babe said they parked the car near Wooded Island and had a few drinks with the girls. "But we couldn't come to an agreement with the girls, so we asked them to leave, and we went home."

Crowe's men finally had something new to attack. They wanted details: How old were the girls? When did you get home? Did you make any phone calls that night? And what about this Richard Loeb?

Not long after Babe mentioned the name Richard Loeb, police returned to Kenwood. They whisked the Master Criminal from his mansion and brought him to a different room at the LaSalle Hotel. Then, several of the detectives searched his room. They found a letter Babe had sent Dickie. Crowe used its contents to interrogate Dickie.

After Dickie told the state's attorney he couldn't remember his activities on May 21, Crowe wanted to know about his relationship with Babe.

"Are you frat brothers?"[135]

"No."

"What about the letter he sent to you in which he said it would not do for cocksuckers to fall out?" Crowe asked. "What significance do you attach to that?"

Dickie was shocked by this question. A tremor distorted his face, but he regained his composure. "The fact that he wanted to say that a rumor had gotten around that he was a cocksucker," he said.

"What difference would that make?"

"We did everything in our power to avoid any possible scandal in regard to that thing for two years, since it happened. That was three years ago, when this rumor started, and for two years, we were very careful never to be seen alone together in public, seen together any place or to be alone together any place, where we could be seen. We were careful so when we wanted to go to a theater on a particular evening, we would be careful to have someone else come along, purely and simply on the advice of my brother who had told me to be careful and to—not to see too much of Leopold, and if I did to be sure there was somebody else around."

"Wasn't that an intolerable condition to exist, two fellows that were very friendly and wanted to be together and could not be together without the world suspecting they were cocksuckers?" Crow asked.

"No."

Crowe wouldn't ease up, sensing he had hit a nerve with this subject.

"Wouldn't it be better if you had broke off, saying 'Now listen, there is a lot of suspicion as to our relationship here, you better go your way and I will go mine and stop all this talk?'"

"We never did that," Dickie explained. "But for quite a while there we saw very little of each other. It is just due to the fact that this here—that we were going to the U. of C. and that we were together a great deal and that there was much more conversation."

In another room on the sixteenth floor, Savage and Sbarbaro began to probe into Babe's personal life. They wanted to know about the Harvard School and an instructor named Mitchell. Babe said the last time he saw Mitchell was on the afternoon of May 22. It was Mitchell, Babe said, who told him of Bobby Franks's death.

"My judgment [about Mitchell] is formed from opinions by what I have heard since," Babe told the detectives, "but my impression is that he looked rather worried, that his color was not good as usual, and his face looked longer than usual."

Savage and Sbarbaro wanted to know if Babe had ever heard any rumors about Mitchell being queer.

"I have heard some wild rumors, yes."

"By queer you mean what?" Savage asked.

"I mean a sexual pervert."

"And for how long have these rumors been floating around, to your knowledge?"

"Ever since I can remember, almost," Babe said.

"You have no knowledge as to whether or not the rumors are true?"

"No, sir."

Changing the subject, Savage asked Babe what languages he knew. Babe said he studied fifteen languages and spoke six fluently: English, German, French, Italian, Spanish and Modern Greek. "I can order breakfast in any Greek restaurant," he said.

Deep into the night, it continued this way—with Savage and Sbarbaro moving from subject to subject, trying to keep their suspect off guard.

They wanted to know about the ransom letter, if Babe had read it. When he said he had, Savage asked if Babe thought he could compose such a letter. "Without any trouble whatsoever," Babe said.

"Do you own a typewriter?"

"Yes, a Hammond Multiplex." Babe explained it could write Greek or italics or mathematical symbols just by changing the type shuttle. He added that he didn't own a portable.

"What about your pals?" Sbarbaro wanted to know.

Babe mentioned Dickie, Dick Rubel, and his fellow birders George Lewis and Sidney Stein.

"Loeb and Rubel, did you ever commit any acts of perversion with these boys?"

"No, sir." Babe's nerves remained secure, although he smoked heavily. Occasionally, he walked across the room to an open window and looked down at the Loop's theater district. Sixteen floors below, lights danced across the marquees, and car headlamps dotted the night.

"Or they on you?"

"No, sir."

"Are you positive?"

"I am positive of that."

Just as Babe became tense, the detectives shifted gears again.

"What is the color of your car?" Savage asked.

"Red."

"And it has a top?"

"Yes."

"It is a summer car?"

"Yes."

"You have the curtains up in this weather?"

"In the back, not in the front."

"Who is Sappho?" Savage asked.

"A great Greek writer of old, a homosexualist," Babe said.

"By homosexualist, you mean pervert?"

"Yes, sir."

"What have you read about her?"

"Merely that she was a famous poetess, homosexualist," Babe said.

"And was Oscar Wilde a pervert?"

"Yes, sir."

"And he wrote some number of works?"

"Yes, sir."

"You read them?"

"Read some of them."

"And they are supposed to deal with perverts?"

"No, sir."

"What is *Dorian Gray*?"

"*Dorian Gray*," Babe said, "is a novel by Oscar Wilde dealing with the painting of a picture by an artist of a man for whom he had very deep regard. In light of what later came out about Oscar Wilde, it has often been said that he had homosexualist tendencies."

"Did you read *Dr. Jekyll and Mr. Hyde*?"

"No."

"What about Stevenson's works?"

"Yes, *Treasure Island*."

"What about *Kidnapped*?"

"Yes."

Babe felt comfortable, in a rhythm, and almost cocky. He answered the string of questions quickly and confidently, especially when the subject turned to religion.

"What is your idea about the existence of God?" Savage asked.

"I do not believe there is a God," Babe said.

"If you die, what becomes of you?"

"Your ashes return to ashes and dust to dust."

"Is there any difference between my death and the death of a dog?"

"No, sir."

"In other words, when I die I am dead all over?"

"Naturally dead."

"There is no hereafter or any hope of return or any reward or punishment?"

"That is my belief."

"For how long a time have you entertained that belief?"

"Some seven or eight years."

It was midnight when detectives Johnson and Crot made another trip to Kenwood. The state's attorney and chief of detectives wanted to compare the typeface of Babe's Hammond Multiplex to that of the ransom note. Mike Leopold made the trip, too.

Johnson and Crot searched the house thoroughly. They found a leather Almer Coe eyeglass case and several bottles of arsenic, ether, and strychnine in Babe's bedroom. They also gathered several typewritten notes. Johnson searched Babe's red Willys-Knight and discovered Illinois Central and Michigan Central timetables, a copy of *Kidnapped*, and a heavy object wrapped with a newspaper and tied with string.

At the LaSalle Hotel, Dickie continued to tell his interrogators that he couldn't remember his movements of May 21st. "After all," he said, "that's more than a week ago." Babe continued answering the myriad of questions from Savage and Sbarbaro. Finally, at 4 A.M., Crowe put an end to the interrogations. Dickie spent the rest of the night at the police station at Forty-Eighth and Wabash, while police drove Babe to Central Headquarters. Mike watched detectives escort his kid brother from the hotel.

## INTELLECTUALLY EMANCIPATED

By Friday morning, May 30, Decoration Day, reporters jumped on the story from all angles. Two sons of millionaires held in connection with the murder of their young neighbor—the makings of a great tabloid event.

After just a few hours of sleep, Babe talked with a handful of reporters. Eating a ham-and-egg sandwich and using a pencil to stir cream in his coffee, Babe nonchalantly talked about the one bit of circumstantial evidence.

"There's no question in my mind the glasses are mine," he said. "They fit me when I tried them on. They must have been in the suit I wore the last time I went there and dropped from my pocket. It's queer, but I have been following the Franks case closely all along, and from the first I had a feeling that those glasses were mine."[136]

Alvin Goldstein and James Mulroy followed up on a tip that Babe belonged to a small law-student study group. They visited Arnold Maremont's home and learned that Maremont and three or four fellow students had worked on "dope sheeting" at Babe's home during the winter. Maremont, a friend of Babe's for four years, told Goldstein and Mulroy that Babe always typed out the group's discussion notes and gave carbon copies to everyone. *Dope sheeting*, Maremont explained, helped group members prepare for upcoming law exams.[137] Maremont said Babe usually used a large Hammond Multiplex, but last February, he switched to a small portable.

A portable. The two reporters hoped they might be on to something. Maremont said they could borrow some carbon copies of the notes. Goldstein and Mulroy rushed the dope sheets to the *Daily News* newsroom, where editors had arranged to have a typewriter expert compare the notes to the ransom letter.

H. P. Sutton of the Royal Typewriter Company examined the dope sheets. He noticed several distinctive characteristics: a twisted *i*, crooked *t* and *m*,. and the *t* printed top-heavy. Very similar to the typeface on the ransom letter, Sutton concluded.[138]

An official at the *Daily News* immediately relayed this information to the state's attorney, who began to round up the other members of the study group.

The city editor at the *Evening-American* sent Howard Mayer out to interview Dickie and Babe. Mayer quickly learned from police sources that the young men were giving two different stories, and it didn't look good for either of them.

Mayer found Babe at the state's attorney's office in the Criminal Courts Building. Babe repeated the alibi to Mayer. But Mayer told him that Dickie was telling police that he couldn't remember a thing. Babe asked Mayer to deliver a message to Dickie: "Tell him to remember what happened on Wednesday."[139]

Mayer, who considered himself a good friend of Dickie's, rushed to the lockup at Forty-Eighth and Wabash. Police allowed him to talk to Dickie in his cell. Mayer told him what Babe had said, but Dickie refused to discuss the matter with Mayer. After Mayer left, Dickie, alone in his cell, weighed his options. Should he tell his interrogators that he now remembered his activities on May 21, or should he continue to say nothing? *But the young prisoner felt no fear, only self-pity. He reveled in the attention. After all, he was a famous criminal, and this was the pleasure all masterminds must endure.*

Dickie summoned a police officer and asked that someone from the state's attorney's office come to his cell. When John Sbarbaro and Bret Cronson arrived, Dickie constructed an alibi to match Babe's. After nearly twenty-four hours in custody, the Master Criminal and his confederate were finally on the same page.

Reporters thought it was odd that two influential millionaires like Nathan Leopold Sr. and Albert Loeb would allow their sons to be held in custody for so many hours without being charged. Why wouldn't their attorneys file a writ of habeas corpus?

Howard Mayer called Allan Loeb and told him he'd better get a lawyer for his brother. Things will work out, Allan told him. Nathan Leopold Sr. and his brother Oscar, a friend of Crowe, visited Babe late Friday afternoon at the state's attorney's office. Crowe offered them privacy, but Babe's father refused.

"Mr. Crowe," Leopold said, "all I want to tell the boy is that if there is anything at all he knows that could be helpful to you, he must tell you. I have nothing private to say to him, nothing you can't hear.

"Babe, if there is any way you can help, anything you know, tell it to Mr. Crowe," the father told the son. Leopold gave Babe some bed linens, pajamas, and toiletries and said good-bye to his son.

Reporters swarmed around Leopold on his way out. He didn't answer questions, but he gave them a brief statement.

> While it is a terrible ordeal to my boy and myself to have him under suspicion, our attitude will be one of helping the investigation rather than retarding it. And even though my son is subjected to

hardships, he should be willing to make sacrifices, and I am also willing, for the sake of justice and truth, until the authorities are thoroughly satisfied that this supposed clue is groundless. I probably could get my boy out on a writ of habeas corpus, but there is no need for that sort of technical trickery. The suggestion that he had anything to do with this case is too absurd to merit comment.[140]

While Crowe and Hughes tried to strengthen their circumstantial case against Babe and Dickie, the press—because of the easy access reporters had to the suspects—portrayed them as strange, intellectual giants, especially Babe. The *Daily News* told its readers that Dickie and Babe were too much for the police to handle.

In Nathan Leopold and Richard Loeb, the University of Chicago students on whom the shadow of the Franks murder mystery fell today, the police and the State's Attorney's staff have a type entirely new to them—a baffling type, too agile intellectually to be handled as bootleggers and bandits and confidence men are handled. Inquisitors skilled at talking secrets out of sharp gangsters couldn't dent the bland assurance of Leopold . . . and Loeb, his little less prodigious chum.[141]

Edition after edition painted a bizarre picture of this "intellectually emancipated" pair. Chicagoans devoured the story with their morning coffee and their evening meals. The *Tribune* called Babe "sophomoric, as a Scott Fitzgerald hero who's showing off after his first drink of gin." Babe loved the attention, especially his sparring with the press.

"You newspaper folks," he said. "You've made me out a conceited smarty, haven't you? But don't you know that when a man's on the defensive he has to have a consistent attitude? Don't you know that? Once a man on the defensive has adopted a certain policy, he's got to stick. If you move any, you've got to take all your soldiers out of one trench and send them to another. Don't you see?"

One writer described Dickie and Babe's conduct as "independent of conventions and taboos. They scorn the judgment of other students, glorying in their superior wealth, their sharper wit, their greater capacity for morbid pleasures."

The *Daily News* suggested, "The fact that Franks was killed as a 'laboratory experiment' in perversion or even cruelty, a perversion itself, was added to the many other possibilities that are under consideration."[142]

With each edition, anger festered rapidly within Chicagoans.

## SVEN

The usually dapper State's Attorney Robert Crowe appeared rumpled. He knew he neared the end of the line; even his signature white handkerchief drooped from his jacket pocket.

For more than thirty-two hours, he had held Babe in custody—almost as long for Dickie—without charging either one with a crime. Crowe had no solid evidence—except the eyeglasses, circumstantial at best. It was time for one last try.

While most of their college chums enjoyed a Jazz Age Friday night, Arnold Maremont, Howard Obendorf, Lester Abelson, and Maurice Shanberg joined Babe at a long conference table in the Criminal Courts Building. They presented their dope-sheet carbons to Crowe and his staff. Each student said Babe had typed the notes on his portable. Babe angrily denied the portable was his. He tried to accuse one of the members of bringing the typewriter to his home. "It certainly does not belong to me," he said.[143]

Crowe had Babe in a corner. No implausible explanation would do here. Babe needed something solid. They all waited for his answer. Finally, he admitted that he had used a portable, but he didn't own it. "It belonged to Leon Mandel," Babe said. Babe would pin it on a U. of C. friend with whom he had studied Italian. Unfortunately, Babe added, Mandel was in Europe.

Savage attacked his story.

"Well, if Leon Mandel owned the machine, he either took it prior to leaving for Europe, or it is still at your home, Mr. Leopold."

"Yes, that is right," Babe said.

"Your servant said the machine was at your home two weeks ago. If that is correct, then Leon Mandel did not take it with him, did he?"

"No, sir, then the machine must be at my house, and I will go out and look for it for you."

Yet another trip to Kenwood.

Savage and Hughes led a team of detectives to Babe's home. Babe was unsure just how much damaging information Crowe and Hughes had on him. He used the ride south to try to gain an insight.

"I'm beginning to get a bit nervous," Babe said. "This chain of circumstantial evidence looks bad. But on the square, I'm just as anxious as anybody to clear up this despicable murder."

No one in the car responded.

At the house, Babe went through the motions. With the police watching his every move, he opened closets and looked into cabinets and linen chests. No portable typewriter. Hughes searched the library himself, and then he woke up the maid. Yes, she told him, there had been a portable in the house a few weeks ago.

The detectives found no portable typewriter, but they discovered two loaded Remington automatics in Babe's bureau drawer.[144]

Detectives returned Babe to the Criminal Courts Building after midnight, well past Crowe's deadline for ending the interrogation. He still had no evidence, and he knew the boys' influential fathers would soon demand he free their sons. Dickie and Babe continued to answer questions, but it was clear to everyone that Crowe's investigation was at a standstill.

Cronson was on his way to the washroom when he noticed an old man in a chauffeur's uniform sitting outside Crowe's office. He wanted to help Mr. Babe, Sven Englund told Cronson. Impatient reporters who crowded the benches in the hallway watched Englund walk into the state's attorney's office but thought nothing of it.

Englund, who had served the Leopold family for eighteen years, was there to help the boys, he said. The loyal servant told Cronson that Mr. Babe could not have been involved in the Franks murder because his red Willys had been in the garage that day.

"I worked on the car all day," Englund said.[145]

Cronson asked if he were sure that he worked on Babe's car on May 21. Sure, Englund said, because that was the day his wife visited her doctor, who wrote her a prescription. Cronson called Mrs. Englund. That's right, she told him, the druggist even stamped the date on her pill box—May 21, 1924. Cronson immediately sent someone to the Englund apartment to retrieve the pill box.

This was it—what the prosecutors had been hoping for. The alibi Dickie and Babe had used—that they drove around in Babe's red Willys-Knight on the day of the crime—was now shattered. Armed with this information, Crowe tightened the interrogation. Sbarbaro and Shoemacher drilled Dickie in one room while Savage and Hughes questioned Babe in another.

The Master Criminal wouldn't budge. No detective could solve his crimes, and the country was in awe of Dickie Loeb, who hid from no one.

But Sbarbaro wouldn't let up. "You and your friend are guilty," he yelled at Dickie. "There was no driving around in Leopold's car. No birding in Lincoln Park. No girls."

"Says who?"

"Sven Englund, Leopold's chauffeur."

The facial tremors that distorted Dickie's face whenever he became upset returned. His gentle face twisted, his boyish charm vanished.

"Leopold's car was in the garage," Sbarbaro barked. "Englund was fixing the brakes. What do you say about that?"

"I'd say he was a liar."

Dickie tried to free himself, but it was impossible. His perfect crime. His elaborate planning. Nothing could help him now. Unlike Jimmie Dale, Dickie Loeb was not smarter than his crime. A servant—Babe's chauffeur, for God's sake—ruined everything.

"You came back that night about 10:30 and took Leopold's car out of the garage."

Dickie's face wouldn't stop trembling. The Master Criminal crumbled.

"My God, get me a glass of water. I'll tell you the entire story."

A few hours later, at four in the morning, the state's attorney sat down with Babe, who had become more arrogant as the night wore on.

"Let me ask you a hypothetical question," he asked Crowe.

Babe probably never noticed, but Crowe had a refreshed air about him. His hair was neatly combed, his eyeglasses were cleaned, and a new handkerchief blossomed from his jacket.

"Very well, what is it?"

"Supposing John Doe has committed this murder, and John Doe's family is as wealthy and influential as mine and could hire able criminal lawyers and get a friendly judge and bribe the jury, don't you think he could beat this case?"

"Well," said Crowe, "I will let you try it out."

"What do you mean?"

"I'm going to charge you with this murder."[146]

"Why, you haven't anything on me except some flimsy circumstances. You will never do that."

Like a pirate, Crowe came at the young law student. He stood up and walked briskly toward Babe.

"You don't know, Nathan Leopold, your pal Dick Loeb is telling the details of this murder, do you?"

"No, my God, he is not doing it. He would stand until hell freezes over."

"What about the Morrison Hotel?" Crowe screamed. "The Rent-A-Car. Looking for Johnny Levinson. The drive to Indiana."

The state's attorney circled Babe and rattled off more facts of the crime—facts Dickie had supplied in a room down the hall.

Babe sat stunned. He knew only Dickie knew this information.

"If Loeb did not tell us that, who did? And besides, he said you were the one who killed Bobby Franks."

Disaster had finally come his way. Babe said nothing at first, but he was visibly shaken. Crowe gave him a few minutes to compose himself.

Angered by Dickie's accusation that he killed the young boy, Babe told Crowe, "Well, if Loeb is talking, I will tell you the real truth."

## OFFICIAL CONFESSIONS

Reporters have always been an impatient lot. In the predawn hours of May 31, restless scribes filled the press room in the Criminal Courts Building. A rumor that Dickie and Babe were confessing gathered momentum, but there was no official word from Crowe. Most of the reporters stayed by their telephones, but a few inventive types took matters into their own hands.

And Jack McPhaul played no small role. Crowe's office door was shut, but the transom remained open. Hoisted high on a reporter's shoulders, the diminutive copyboy from the *Herald and Examiner* peered into the state's attorney's dominion. He saw Dickie and Babe seated at a table. Crowe, his staff, and detectives surrounded the two young men. McPhaul saw Babe talking "as if he were explaining a business deal to a board of directors."[147]

McPhaul actually witnessed a portion of the official confessions. Two court reporters, using shorthand, read each boy's confession out loud. The Master Criminal and his confederate—the Slave and His King—stared at each other and argued. Each accused the other of striking the blows that killed Bobby Franks.

"The plan was broached," Dickie confessed, "by Nathan Leopold, who suggested that as a means of having a great deal of excitement, together with getting quite a sum of money."[148]

Dickie explained that they "planned the thing quite carefully, every detail." Especially the car.

"His (Babe's) car is very conspicuous; and for that reason we deemed it inadvisable to use it and therefore decided to get a car—rent a car from the Rent-A-Car people. Also in fact that such a car, if obtained under a false name, would not be incriminating, were it to be discovered with the crime."

Dickie told how his confederate opened a bank account—with Dickie's money—under the name of Morton D. Ballard, a salesman from Peoria. "Following out the same plan, I went down to the Morrison and registered under the name of Morton D. Ballard, carrying with me a suitcase, an old suitcase carrying some books," Dickie said.

Babe began his confession by talking about the most difficult part of the crime—getting the ransom money.

"We had, oh, several dozen different plans, all of which were not so good, for one reason or another," Babe confessed. "Finally, we hit upon the plan of having the money thrown from a moving train, after the train had passed a given landmark. The landmark we finally chose was the factory of the Champion Manufacturing Company at Seventy-Fourth Street and the I. C. tracks."

Babe outlined in great detail the elaborate plan to obtain the ransom money: "a number of relays. The man was to receive a special delivery letter telling him that his son had been kidnapped . . . to secure $10,000 . . . unmarked bills, placed in a cigar box, wrapped in white paper, the ends sealed with sealing wax. He would then receive a phone call in the afternoon instructing him to proceed to a 'Keep the City Clean' box . He would find a note telling him to proceed to a specific drugstore with a public phone booth. He'd be called at that booth, which was near the I. C. station. He'd be told to buy a ticket for the next train [to Michigan City], then proceed to the rear car, look in the box for telegraph blanks for another letter. This letter instructed him to go to the rear platform of the car, face the east, and look for the first large red-brick factory adjacent to the tracks, which had a black water tower bearing a white inscription, 'Champion,' count to two or three and after that, throw the box as far to the east as he could."

Babe didn't give Crowe's staff a chance to ask any questions during the early part of his confession. He went directly from the planning to the actual killing.

"The next problem was getting the victim to kill. That was left undecided until the day we decided to take the most likely looking subject that came our way. The particular occasion happened to be Robert Franks. Richard was acquainted with Robert and asked him to come over to the car for a moment. This occurred near Forty-Ninth and Ellis Avenue. Robert came over to the car, was introduced to me, and Richard asked him if he did not want a ride home."

"Richard who?" Crowe asked.

"Richard Loeb. He replied 'no,' but Richard said, 'Well, get in a minute, I want to ask you about a certain tennis racket.' After he had gotten in, I stepped on the gas, proceeded south on Ellis Avenue to Fiftieth Street. In the meantime, Richard asked Robert if he minded if we took him around the block, to which Robert said, 'No.'

"As soon as we turned the corner, Richard placed his one hand over Robert's mouth to stifle his outcries, with his right hand beat him on the head several times with a chisel, especially prepared for the purpose. The boy did not succumb as readily as we had believed, so for the fear of being observed, Richard seized him, pulled him into the back seat. Here he forced a cloth into his mouth. Apparently the boy died instantly by suffocation shortly thereafter."

Dickie's story about the killing was different. He talked about how he and Babe watched the kids come out of the Harvard School and followed a group of them, especially a youngster named Johnny Levinson.

"We watched these boys and noticed that Levinson was amongst them."

"What is his first name? John Levinson?" Crowe asked.

"I think so. We went back to the car, got the car, and drove to the west side of Drexel, opposite to where the children were playing. We looked to see if we could recognize them from that distance, but it was very difficult, so we walked down to Fiftieth Street, through an alley where we could watch them more closely. Even from there, however, it was impossible to watch them very closely unless we showed ourselves, so we decided to go back to his car, drive over to his home, and get a pair of bird glasses."

"You mean field glasses?"

"Well, yes, field glasses—and watch the children through the field glasses. This we did. While he was getting the field glasses, I went to a drugstore on the corner of Forty-Seventh and Ellis, where I looked up the name of Mr. Levinson, so that we would be able to tell where John lived. I incidentally bought a couple of packages of Dentyne chewing gum at the drugstore.

"I picked up Leopold immediately after that with the field glasses, and we went over to the same place on Drexel Boulevard. We watched the children some more through the field glasses and noted that Levinson, with a group of some other children, went down an alley out of sight. But when after a while, he didn't show up, we came to the conclusion that he might have gone home."

Dickie explained that they drove to another lot where they thought the Levinson boy might be playing, but he wasn't there. They then drove north on Ellis, where Dickie, who as a youngster wrote in his *Richard's Magazine* about random killing, saw Robert Franks.

"All this time I was driving. We proceeded north on Ellis Avenue until we caught a glimpse of Robert Franks, coming south on the west side of Ellis Avenue. As we passed him, he was just coming across Forty-Eighth Street. We turned the car down Forty-Eighth Street and turned the car around, Leopold getting in the back seat. I drove the car, then, south on

Ellis Avenue, parallel to where young Franks was, stopped the car, and while remaining in my seat, opened the front door and called to Franks that I would give him a ride home. He said no, he would just as soon walk, but I told him that I would like to talk to him about a tennis racket; so he got into the car.

"We proceeded south on Ellis Avenue, turned east on Fiftieth Street, and just after we turned off Ellis Avenue, Leopold reached his arm around young Franks, grabbed his mouth, and hit him over the head with the chisel. I believe he hit him several times. I do not know the exact number. He began to bleed and was not entirely unconscious. He was moaning. I proceeded further east on Fiftieth and turned, I believe, at Dorchester.

"At this time, Leopold grabbed Franks and carried him over the back seat and threw him on a rug in the car. He then took one of the rags and gagged him by sticking it down his throat, I believe. We proceeded down Dorchester, and then at Leopold's directions, drove into the country."

With Bobby Franks bleeding onto the floor of the car, Dickie and Babe drove southeast along Lake Michigan to Calumet Avenue in Indiana. "We even stopped to buy a couple of sandwiches for supper," Babe confessed. The crime scene, as Babe explained, was a familiar spot.

"We drove up and down this road and then proceeded over the path which leads out toward Hegewisch from 108th and Avenue F to the prearranged spot for the disposal of the body," Babe said. "We had previously removed the shoes, socks, and trousers of the boy, leaving the shoes and belt by the side of the road, concealed in the grass.

"Having arrived at the destination, we placed the body in the robe, carried it to the culvert where it was found. Here we completed the disrobing. Then, in an attempt to render identification more difficult, we poured hydrochloric acid over the face and body. Then we placed the body into the drain pipe, pushed it in as far as we could. We gathered up the clothes, placed them in the robe.

"Apparently at this point the glasses fell from my pocket."

Neither Crowe nor Hughes could tell who was telling the truth about who actually delivered the death blows. Each young man signed his confession, and Crowe ordered a staff member to lock the statements in a bank vault.

## HANGING CASE

Shortly after sunrise, the state's attorney called the restless reporters to his office. Robert Crowe looked exhausted, but his voice shook with new life.

"The Franks murder mystery has been solved," Fighting Bob boasted. "The murderers are in custody. Nathan Leopold and Richard Loeb have completely and voluntarily confessed."[149]

Newsmen scrambled to their phones in the Criminal Courts Building. The *Herald and Examiner*, young Jack McPhaul's newspaper, sold a hundred thousand special editions.[150] The press would now refocus its attention from the dead boy to the two killers, who were not much older than the victim. As the *Tribune* reported, "Never in Chicago, probably never in the records of crime in any city in the world, has there been a similar case.[151] The killing of Robert Franks, fourteen-year-old son of Jacob Franks, multimillionaire, by the sons of Albert Loeb, vice president of Sears, Roebuck and Co., and Nathan Leopold, paper-box manufacturer and head of lake shipping interests, is the only known crime where all principal figures, victim and murderers, were the sons of millionaires."

Crowe wasted no time in attempting to strengthen his case.

At 8 A.M., seven police cars formed a line in front of the Criminal Courts Building. Crowe and Hughes would direct a reenactment of the crime. Dickie and Babe each rode in separate cars. The caravan carried members of Crowe's staff, detectives, and reporters. Crowe called the trip "a search for evidence, not thrills."[152]

At the first stop—the Rent-A-Car Agency—Walter Jacobs pointed out Babe as "Morton D. Ballard." Jacobs, president of the company, told Crowe that when Babe first rented a car, he gave a personal reference— Louis Mason—and a phone number, Calumet 4658.[153]

The phone number belonged to Gertrude Barish, proprietor of a nearby cigar store and delicatessen, the tour's second stop. When Mrs. Barish recognized Dickie, he trembled and fainted. Dickie, posing as Louis Mason, had bought some phone slugs from Mrs. Barish and answered the pay phone when Jacobs called checking on "Ballard's" references. Police rushed Dickie to the Windemere Hotel in Hyde Park, where he went to sleep for the rest of the day.

The cars then stopped at a hardware store at Forty-Second and Cottage Grove. Loeb had bought the cold chisel and rope at the store. Next stop, a nearby drugstore on Cottage, where Babe had purchased the hydrochloric acid. Hughes then escorted Babe into a Hyde Park police station. Hughes showed Babe the blood-stained cold chisel that Bernard Hunt found on the night of the murder. Before heading to Babe's home, the police cars stopped at the empty lot on Drexel, where Dickie and Babe had watched the kids play before they picked up Bobby Franks.

At the Leopold home, Babe dug through a closet to find the hip boots he wore while dragging the dead body through the swampland. The caravan then drove to the bridge near the golden Lady Liberty in Jackson Park. Babe explained how Dickie tossed the twisted typewriter keys into the lagoon. About a thousand feet south, the caravan stopped again. Babe said they threw the portable Underwood —in its case—over the southeast side of the stone intake bridge. Babe got out of the car and pointed to the exact spot in the water where the typewriter fell.

"I'd like to jump off this bridge," he told Hughes.[154]

"If you ever went over this bridge, you never would come back."

"That would suit me," Babe said as Hughes led him back to the police car.

The long line of cars, their police bells clanging to clear traffic, followed the edge of the lake to Seventy-Third Street. There, Babe led everyone to a small mound of ashes near the water.

"It's the blue-black plush robe I took out of the garage, the one we wrapped the body in after we put the gag in his mouth," Babe said. Detectives carefully collected the ashes and small bits of cloth.

The party continued southeast, following Babe's directions. They took several country roads before stopping on a deserted road in Heseville, Indiana, near the town of Hammond. Babe told the driver to stop. He pointed to a clump of bushes in a field. He said Bobby's shoes and belt were somewhere in the brush.

"I'm not sure where they are," he said. "We just threw them from the car."

Babe then directed the search.

"Now, half of you go up this side of the road, and the rest of you look along the other side," he ordered the team of Chicago's finest detectives.

They searched for half an hour, but Babe decided that Dickie would remember better. Crowe and Hughes put an official end to the search, but he told two cars of detectives to stay back and search the area again. Four cars returned to the Criminal Courts Building; Shoemacher drove Babe to the Windemere Hotel.

Just before dark, detectives found Bobby Franks's shoes in the brush. The detectives drove to the Franks house in Kenwood and asked Jack Franks if he could identify the shoes. "I remember them perfectly," Bobby's brother said. "He bought them six weeks ago at Marshall Field's. I was with him when he bought them."

Across the street, no lights glowed in the sprawling Loeb mansion.

A mile to the north, Isadora Wilbert looked out the window in her daughter's bedroom high above Woodlawn Avenue. She watched a large automobile pull up in front of her home. A noble-looking man with a shiny mane of silver hair, his long, black cape flying in the breeze, had come to visit. Isadora Wilbert hurried downstairs. Frank Lloyd Wright was no stranger. They greeted each other in the secluded entrance court and then walked through the house together, as they did each time Wright came to call. On this particular Saturday afternoon, he told her he would love to live in the house, but he hadn't much money. And then he left. Frederick Robie's home, built in part to protect his children from "accidents of serious nature," continued to be "the most ideal place in the world."

At the Windemere Hotel, Babe's valet arrived with pajamas and a fresh set of clothes for the two boys. Room service brought turkey dinners to each boy's room. After eating, Dickie and Babe, with police guards stationed outside their doors, fell asleep again.

Crowe, back in his office following the reenactment, summoned reporters.

"I have a hanging case," he said. "And I would be willing to submit it to a jury tomorrow. I shall present the facts to the grand jury early next week."

He added that the only piece of evidence still needed was the portable typewriter and that he ordered a search of the water under the intake bridge in Jackson Park.

"We have the most conclusive evidence I have ever experienced in a criminal case either as a judge or prosecutor. We have the shoes and portions of clothing young Franks wore when he was murdered. We found these things at every instance at the places where Loeb and Leopold led us, places where they told us they would be found.

"The case against these two young men absolutely is conclusive. I can see no way they can get away from it. Our whole afternoon was spent checking and organizing the evidence. I have no hesitation in saying I would be ready to go to trial tomorrow."

Late Saturday night, as police moved Dickie and Babe from the Windemere to a police lockup, the doorbell rang at Clarence Darrow's grand apartment at the tip of the Midway Plaisance.

At age sixty-seven, the celebrated defense attorney was a weary man. Known for his advocacy of the downtrodden, Darrow was tired from fighting public opinion, what he called "the greatest enemy that ever confronted man." Many legal minds considered the former country lawyer from Ashtabula, Ohio, to be a man for all seasons. "I had little respect for the opinion of the crowd," Darrow said. "My instinct was to doubt the majority view. I have always felt that doubt was the beginning of wisdom, and the fear of God was the end of wisdom."[155]

Darrow also defended the privileged and wealthy, and no client of his had ever met a hanging rope.

That was why Jacob Loeb, Dickie's uncle, stood at his door.

Darrow's wife told Loeb that her husband was in bed, but Loeb rushed past her and confronted Darrow in his bedroom.

"Get them a life sentence instead of death," Loeb pleaded.

Darrow sat up in his bed. Unruly gray hair hung over his eyes. Deep furrows gave his weathered face a timeless quality.

"We'll pay anything, only for God's sake, don't let them hang," Dickie Loeb's uncle pleaded.

The young waitress at the Hyde Park coffee shop enjoyed her lively banter with Babe.[156] She served him a hefty breakfast of scrambled eggs, doughnuts, rolls, and coffee the morning of Sunday, June 1. Babe, who had very little sleep during the past few nights, seemed to be running on nervous energy. He joked with the pretty girl throughout the meal, stopping only to take a bite of food or to light another cigarette. Chief Detective Michael Hughes, who sat next to him, noticed that Babe's fingertips were stained brown from nicotine.

Dickie, seated next to Captain John Pendergast, secretary to the chief of police, said nothing. He refused to speak to Babe. Dickie's fresh, glowing baby face had turned pale and drawn. Reporters who joined the killers on the second day of their reenactment wrote in their notebooks as Babe entertained the waitress. When the group left the restaurant, one of the writers told the girl she had been talking to Leopold and Loeb. "My God," she gasped. "And I served them."

Babe rode with Hughes and Wallace Sullivan, a reporter with the *Herald and Examiner.* Pendergast, Dickie, and the *Tribune's* Ty Krum followed in a second police car. Sunday's tour became melodramatic. Crowds formed in various spots along the route, especially in Jackson Park. Three thousand people gathered on and around the intake bridge to watch divers—equipped with an electromagnet—search for the typewriter in the murky water.

Krum and Sullivan each had a private audience with the Master Criminal and his confederate. Dickie talked readily, although his emotions swayed—from cocky to fearful to hopeful. Krum observed, "Richard Loeb is slowly slipping from his lofty pinnacle. He is no longer the sure-footed, well-poised steeplejack, scaling the spires of vagrant imagination . . . and the descent is terrifying."[157]

Dickie's fall was bitter. "If Nathan says I killed Robert, he's a liar—and he knows it," Dickie told Krum. His spirits lifted when he saw all the people trying to get a glimpse of him as the cars went through Jackson Park. But, as they sped through the curious, Dickie became sullen and depressed, only to revive his emotions with childhood imagination and hope.

"This thing will be the making of me," Dickie said from the back seat as the car sped to the Indiana state line. "I'll spend a few years in jail, and I'll be released. I'll come out to a new life. I'll go to work, and I'll work hard, and I'll amount to something—have a career."

"But you've taken a life, you've killed a boy," the policeman who drove the car said. "The best you could possibly expect would be a life sentence to an insane asylum. How can you say this will be the making of you?"

Dickie didn't say a word. In the front seat, Krum filled his notebook. The young killer's hands shook as he tried to light a cigarette.

In the other car, Babe's arrogant persona remained intact. He cast his destiny with the press as an overeducated, snobbish product of the Jazz Age. With a shadowy smile—some people called it a Semitic smirk—he leaned across the seat and touched Wallace Sullivan on the knee. "Now you've been contaminated," Babe said. "You've been touched by a murderer."

Babe proudly told his fellow travelers that he was an intellectual anarchist and an atheist. "A thirst for knowledge," he said, "is highly commendable, no matter what extreme pain or injury it may inflict upon others. A six-year-old boy is justified in pulling the wings from a fly, if by so doing he learns that without wings the fly is helpless."

In Heseville, Dickie left the car and searched the heavy brush for Bobby's belt. After several minutes, he found the gold buckle, the webbed belt, and the loops. Dickie explained that he separated the belt into three sections to make it more difficult to find. On the way back to the Criminal Courts Building, Dickie talked softly to Krum about the victim.

"The only thing that came to my mind was the sight of that happy little boy, swinging down the sunlit sidewalk, swaying from side to side in his happiness, his innocence," Dickie said. "I have thought of that several times. He was such a fine kid. His little tennis racket, no, I guess he didn't have the tennis racket as we dragged him into the car, but oh, his face, the sunlight, the happiness in his eyes."

Krum wanted to know if Dickie was a tool in Babe's control.

"Well, I wouldn't say that exactly. Of course, he is smart. He is one of the smartest and best-educated men I know. Perhaps he did dominate me. He had nothing on me . . . but maybe I just followed him."

"It was all Loeb's idea," Babe said as his car raced along the shores of Lake Michigan. "I realize that I am equally guilty and that we both face the same penalty. It gets me nothing, then, to accuse him. Nevertheless, he planned the kidnapping, and I helped carry it out by writing the extortion letter. Yes, I wrote it—every word of it. It was Loeb, though, who enticed the boy into the car, and it was Loeb who struck him on the head the next instant.

"Why, weapons which might injure a person are so repugnant to me that I loathe the sight of them. I could not—it would not have been physically possible for me to have struck the blow that killed Robert Franks. Loeb knows this, too."

Babe then asked Sullivan to give Dickie a message. "Tell him I am very much surprised that he fears death. Tell him I'm surprised that he was so weak as to confess in the first place and that I was surprised when he was so weak as to faint under the strain. Just a weakling, after all."

When the car neared Hyde Park, Hughes ordered the driver to go past the Franks home. "The one place where I don't want to go," Babe said. The young murderer buried his face in his hands as the car approached the big, yellow house.

It was well into the afternoon when the two police cars arrived at the Criminal Courts Building. Hughes and Pendergast turned over the young men to Crowe. A reporter asked the chief of detectives if he believed a conviction would result from a trial.

"I don't know," an exhausted Hughes said. "Millions of dollars can do many things but—if I were a jury, I'd hang the two of them—quick."

## PHOTO OP

The Pirate took no chances. Robert Crowe had a few surprises waiting for Dickie and Babe when they returned from their Sunday reenactment. Expecting an insanity defense, Crowe hired three prominent forensic psychiatrists to examine Leopold and Loeb.

The trio of alienists, without any attorneys, court reporters, or other, questioned Dickie and Babe in Crowe's office. It was the first of many psychological studies they would go through. This was a time when the disturbing sexual theories of Sigmund Freud fueled parlor analysts across the nation. Unconscious forces—and the mind turning in upon itself—fascinated the tabloid press, as Dickie and Babe would soon discover.[158]

Drs. Hugh Patrick, Archibald Church, and William Krohn all agreed—the boys showed "no signs of any mental disorder or disease."[159]

When asked if he at any time felt like backing out of the murder, Dickie answered, "I did, but I didn't want to be called a quitter."

The alienists gave Crowe want he wanted—a consensus that the confessed killers were sane. The doctors described Dickie and Babe as "nonchalant" and "not understanding the significance of their act. No regret is discernable in their demeanor. When the time comes that each is alone in a cell and given opportunity to think—they will go to the depths of despair. The higher the crest of the waves they have ridden, the lower their fall."

The small courtyard behind the Criminal Courts Building hosted Crowe's next move—a 1920's photo op. Reporters congregated around a dirty Willys-Knight touring car. Photographers snapped pictures of the car, and Dickie and Babe readily answered questions.

"Is this the automobile in which you killed Franks?" the state's attorney asked.

Babe, playing to all the cameras, slowly walked around the car. He inspected its every detail, like a buyer in an automobile showroom. When he ran his hand across the blood-stained area inside a door, he announced, "This is the automobile." Then, at the request of the newsmen, Babe sat behind the wheel for more pictures. Dickie refused to get into the car with his former confederate.

## BELIEFS

His neighbors had killed his Baby, an act far beyond Jacob Franks's comprehension.

"I am relieved a bit to know who killed my boy and how he was murdered," Franks said as he walked with reporters. "I can't, however, understand it. Why did they do it?"[160]

The newspapermen by his side had no answer.

"What could have possessed them to kill my boy, except that they are murderers at heart? Think of the smallness of it—to take my son's life for $10,000—and they were heirs to millions. If a poor man did a thing of this kind, one might say he was influenced by circumstances but these boys, with nothing to crave for, why should they commit such a heinous crime?"

From time to time, pedestrians stopped Franks to offer condolences. He politely shook their hands and thanked them. As he walked up Hyde Park Boulevard, a few blocks from his home, he suggested that a higher authority had something to do with the arrest of Dickie and Babe.

"Young Leopold has said there is no God. He now will know there must be. He has said he is an atheist. He now will realize that God alone could have caused him to drop those glasses that the murderer of my boy might be discovered."

Franks said that he had not heard from the young men's parents but added, "What could they say? I am really sorry for them."

Franks walked the last few blocks in silence. He took long, deep breaths, filling his lungs with the refreshing evening air. He knew what awaited him at home.

"They ought to hang," he said as he walked past the police guards in front of his house.

Inside, Flora Franks remained in her stupor. She spent most of her days and nights in her upstairs bedroom. She occasionally gathered up Bobby's belongings, saying, to no one in particular, "Robert is all right. He should be coming home soon. He won't be much longer."[161]

At the vine-covered Loeb mansion, two uniformed policemen across the street kept the curious away. Like Flora Franks, Anna Loeb believed her son would return home. No one in the family, especially Albert, who was confined to his bed because of a heart ailment, believed Dickie's confession.

As the *Herald and Examiner* reported, "They were so sure their boy was above such a thing that they were willing to leave him with his questioners indefinitely. No habeas corpus for them! The boy was innocent and truth was safe anywhere."

With tears in his eyes, Nathan Leopold stood on his front porch and faced a cluster of reporters.

"Impossible, ridiculous. Nathan—my boy—I can't believe it—I won't believe it,"[162] the father said.

He tried to smile, to look strong, but his heart feared the truth.

## IMAGES

For ten days, passionate Chicagoans argued who could commit such a murder. Now they demanded to know why.

"I have the deepest sympathy for the parents of all three boys," Mayor Dever said. "It is sad that such a tragedy should be visited upon these people and invites the sympathies of all. The whole story is critical—and it shows how necessary it is for us to clean out all the influences which prey on our youth."[163]

The Franks crime bewildered giddy Jazz Age sophisticates. This was a time for breakneck speed, for flaming youths. It was a time for giants—for Babe Ruths, for Mary Pickfords, for Man of Wars. "America was going on the greatest, gaudiest spree in history," F. Scott Fitzgerald wrote. The public began to see the killing of Bobby Franks in moral terms—a sign of the times. Billy Sunday, baseball player turned evangelist, said Dickie and Babe killed because of "precocious brains, salacious books and infidel minds." Sunday said the boys should be hanged.[164]

No longer was it a senseless crime. Fueled by the tabloid press, many people blamed the crime on an "erotic age."

"We are in an age which we recognize to be erotic, when we see about us many morbid and decadent manifestations and we smile them away," declared author Edwin Balmer for the *Herald and Examiner*. "Especially in the last few years—and these have been the years when Nathan Leopold Jr. and Richard Loeb were undergoing their formative experiences—we have permitted and encouraged and even praised a literature morbidly obsessed with the low and depraved and perverted in human conduct."[165]

The crime shocked Jews. Some Jewish leaders placed quick blame on the boys' parents.

"If the parents of these two boys had given the children a Jewish education," wrote the *Jewish Courier*, "if the boys had borne on their shoulders individual responsibility, if they had interested themselves in Jewish problems, if their hearts had bled for their people, if they had been consciously Jewish with Jewish souls, they would certainly not have deviated their entire time to 'pleasure and good times,' and would not have had the possibility of going wrong."

Within a day after their confessions, Dickie and Babe became public specimens. The *Herald and Examiner* published two large photos of the boys' heads. A nationally-known psychoanalyst, Charles Bonniwell, outlined a character study of the killers' physiognomy.

Babe's heavy eyebrows with their joining shows passionate, jealous nature. His short upper lip—love of approbation. Narrow space between eyes—lack of fighting instinct. General shape and contour of ears—uncanny shrewdness. Length of face—a dominance of feminine characteristics.

Dickie's balanced head is of a boy who is likely to prove highly suggestible. Width of face across eyes only average—combative instincts. Shape of eyes and space between—selfishness. Fair eyes without any dominating trait. Curve of jaw from chin to ear distinctly feminine.[166]

Other newspapers would follow with similar photos of the boys, their heads graphically dissected by numbers and lines. The two young killers peering out at Chicagoans from the broadsheets—Babe with his dark, Semitic looks and Dickie, the baby-face frat boy, clearly a suggestible kid. Images that would last for an entire summer.

Dear Sir:

As you no doubt know by this time your son has been kidnapped. Allow us to assure you that he is at present well and safe. You need fear no physical harm for him provided you live up carefully to the following instructions, and such others as you will receive by future communications. Should you however, disobey any of our instructions even slightly, his death will be the penalty.

1. For obvious reasons make absolutely no attempt to communicate with either the police authorities, or any private agency. Should you already have communicated with the police, allow them to continue their investigations, but do not mention this letter.

2. Secure before noon today ten thousand dollars, ($10,000.00). This money must be composed entirely of OLD BILLS of the following denominations;
$2,000.00 in twenty dollar bills
$8,000.00 in fifty dollar bills
The money must be old. Any attempt to include new or marked bills will render the entire venture futile.

3. The money should be placed in a large cigar box, or if this is impossible in a heavy cardboard box, SECURELY closed and wrapped in white paper. The wrapping paper should be sealed at all openings with sealing wax.

4. Have the money with you prepared as directed above, and remain at home after one o'clock P.M. See that the telephone is not in use.

You will receive a future communication instructing you as to your future course.

As a final word of warning - this is a strictly commercial proposition, and we are prepared to put our threat into execution should we have reasonable grounds to believe that you have committed an infraction of the above instructions. However, should you carefully follow out our instructions to the letter, we can assure you that your son will be safely returned to you within six hours of our receipt of the money.

Yours truly,
GEORGE JOHNSON
GHR

Elaborate ransom letter and envelope.

MR JACOB FRANKS
5052 ELLIS AVE
CITY
SPECIAL

Peo Ex 1
Aug 28/1924

CHICAGO
MAY
31
1 AM
1924
ILL.

Investigators examining the culvert where the body of Bobby Franks was found.

Babe Leopold's horn-rimmed glasses, found near the culvert.

State's Attorney Robert Crowe (*left*) and the diver (*middle*) who salvaged the
battered Underwood portable typewriter used to write the ransom letter.

Babe Leopold, who called his brilliant academic achievements "ten percent work and ninety percent horse shit."
Chicago History Museum, DN0077057

Dickie Loeb, whose "childlike face" was irresistible to Jazz Age coeds.
Chicago History Museum, DN0077052

Crowds outside Chicago's Criminal Courts Building during the summer of 1924.

Charles Darrow arguing his point in a hot Chicago courtroom before Judge John Caverly.

The dapper and theatrical Robert Crowe demanding the death penalty "for these cold-blooded, cruel, vicious murderers."

Chicago History Museum, DN0077491

Clarence Darrow sitting (*at right*) with his two defendants, Babe Leopold (*looking straight at the camera*) and Dickie Loeb (*to Darrow's right*) in a crowded courtroom.

Chicago History Museum, DN0078021

Flora Franks, wrapped in black and staring into the sunlight as she describes the late-night May 21 telephone call from "Mr. Johnson."
Chicago History Museum, DN0077520

A weakened Jacob Franks (*left*), escorted by his brother-in-law Edwin Gresham.
Chicago History Museum, DN0077049

| Height | 65.8 | L. Foot | 25.8 | Col. of Eyes | | Age, | 19 | Beard, | Ck. Dk |
|--------|------|---------|------|--------------|--|------|------|--------|--------|
| Eng. H'ght | 5.5¼ | L. M. Fin. | 11.9 | On Dark | | Apparent Age, | | Hair, | Ck. Dk |
| Hd. Length | 19.9 | L. L. Fin. | 9.4 | St. Blue | | Nativ. | Illinois | Comp. | Med |
| Hd. Width | 13.9 | L. Fore A. | 47.0 | | | Occu. | Student | Weight, | 137 |

Remarks Incident to Measurement

| Build | Med | Chin | Med. Rather sharp pt. |
|-------|-----|------|------------------------|
| Teeth | Good | | |

Remarks

F.P.C.  1   U   OI   8
        1   U   OO   15

Measured at Joliet, Illinois, State Penitentiary.   Sept 12, 1924

H. L. Pelly

New look for the former Jazz Age sophisticates
Nathan F. Leopold Jr. (*left*) and Richard Loeb.

| Height | 74.7 | L. Foot | 27.0 | Col. of Eyes | Age, | 19 | Beard, | *Ch Dk* |
|---|---|---|---|---|---|---|---|---|
| Eng. H'ght | 5.83¼ | L. M. Fin. | 11.6 | *Hzl, Grish,* | Apparent Age, | | Hair, | *Ch Dk* |
| Hd. Length | 19.6+ | L. L. Fin. | 8.9 | *Sl. Blue* | ~~Illinois~~ | | Comp. | *Med* |
| Hd. Width | 15.2 | L. Fore A. | 47.8+ | | ~~Student~~ | | Weight, | 160 |

**Remarks Incident to Measurement** _____

9305

| Build | *Med.* | | Chin *Med, Heavy & Sto Ball fro* |
|---|---|---|---|
| Teeth | *Good* | | |

Remarks _____

FPC 5    R    17
    17    Uv    15

Measured at Joliet, Illinois, State Penitentiary.    *Sept 12, 1924*

By    *H. L. Pilly*

Clarence Darrow, who grew weary fighting what he called "the greatest enemy that ever confronted man—public opinion."
Chicago History Museum, DN0077499

Nathan F. Leopold Jr. meeting the press on his release in 1958 from Stateville Prison.
McCormick Library of Special Collections, Northwestern University Library

The eyesore of the block, the former Franks home at 5052 Ellis as it sits today.
Author's collection

The Franks mausoleum in the old Jewish section of Chicago's Rosehill Cemetery. The family graves of Leopold and Loeb are nearby, just beyond a curve in the road.
Author's collection

# Part Three

## Apologia

Clarence Darrow, the Old Lion (*seated, center*), and his young
defendants, Babe Leopold (*left*) and Dickie Loeb.

## BE POLITE . . . SAY NOTHING

Monday, June 2. The first business day following the Decoration Day weekend dawned bright and cool. Nathan Leopold Sr. stepped from his touring car in the shadow of the Criminal Courts Building, a Romanesque behemoth that swallowed an entire city block. Inside the entry lobby, Leopold paused near the double marble staircase with brass handrails and iron balusters. He was early, but that was his way. He rode the elevator to five and then walked up a flight of stairs to the sixth floor.

In less than an hour, the courtroom of Chief Justice John Caverly would hear a petition for a writ of habeas corpus. Leopold took a seat in the middle of the room. The defense table, where they would bring his son, sat directly in front of him. Leopold studied the courtroom. High, recessed-panel wainscoting wrapped around three walls. The south wall held a series of nine giant windows, stretching twelve feet to the ceiling, flooding the space with sunlight. Behind him were the press rows and the visitors' gallery. To his right, by the large double door, a long hat rack awaited the many fedoras that would soon enter the room. Leopold, a short, timid-looking man of sixty-four with gray hair and mustache and delicate wire spectacles, held his own hat on his lap. And waited.

For the past four days, the state's attorney had moved Dickie and Babe from police lockup to police lockup. In an effort to stop the maneuvering—and to keep Robert Crowe's alienists away from the boys—Clarence Darrow and his co-counsel, Benjamin Bachrach, Dickie's cousin, petitioned the court to free the boys from Crowe's custody and send them to the Cook County Jail, where they would be accessible to their attorneys and families.

Movement arrived slowly at first—a few spectators at the rear of the courtroom. Leopold didn't bother to look. A clerk readied papers on Caverly's desk. Reporters, in small groups, took their seats, two, three at a time. Uncle Jacob Loeb sat next to Leopold. The room suddenly got smaller. Swarms of people filled the seats with a shaky rhythm of sounds. Scraping chairs and pockets of hushed conversations broke the silence. With his hands folded across his lap, Leopold watched the courtroom take in people. Like white caps rushing the beach, they flowed toward Caverly's bench. And there, in the middle of it all—Nathan's son. People stood to get a clear look at the killers. Father and son never made eye contact.

When the arguments finally started, Nathan Leopold Sr. cupped a hand behind his ear. He couldn't see his son amid the mass of bodies. He couldn't understand how Babe could be a murderer. And now he couldn't hear. Caverly looked out at a sea of faces. Clarence Darrow, his arm leaning on the judge's bench, was face-to-face with the chief justice of Cook County's Criminal Court. Jacob Loeb and his nephew Dickie stood between Darrow on his left and Babe and the state's attorney.

Crowe admitted having custody of the boys—the petitioners—without due process of the law. "Robert Franks was kidnapped and murdered on May 21, and his body buried in a drain pipe out near the Indiana border line. A pair of spectacles was found alongside where the body was concealed. We learned last Thursday that glasses of the same prescription and frame were sold to Nathan Leopold. I sent for him, and he came to my office. I kept him in a hotel. I sent for Richard Loeb and kept him in custody.

"Both confessed they kidnapped and brutally murdered the boy. If the grand jury were in session, I'd present the evidence against them. I shall do so tomorrow. There is an inquest at 11 o'clock this morning, and I wish to have the prisoners there for identification purposes. After the inquest, I will bring them back here and allow their counsel and relatives to see and talk with them, and I therefore ask that this hearing be continued until 4 o'clock."[1]

"That's a most extraordinary request," Darrow shouted out before the judge could comment. "These boys can't testify at the inquest. If there is any charge against them, the state can easily file a complaint here and now with Your Honor. It can be drawn up in five minutes."

"If we had a pickpocket here, we'd be allowed to hold him until we could place a charge against him in municipal court," Crowe argued. "This is a cold-blooded, vicious murder confessed to by these boys. I'll have them indicted by tomorrow night and arrested on the mittimus [writ]."

"What an outstanding proposition," Darrow shouted. "I never heard the likes of it in court before. These boys are minors and under the constitution entitled to more than ordinary protection from the court. The court has no right to put them anywhere but in jail."

Caverly granted a portion of Crowe's request. He ordered Dickie and Babe to attend the inquest and then be permitted to see their attorney and relatives at the state's attorney's office. After that, they would be in the sheriff's custody at the Cook County Jail.

Following the hearing, Dickie and Babe met briefly with their lawyers behind Caverly's courtroom.

"Say nothing," Bachrach told them.

"Be polite," Darrow warned, "but don't answer any more questions."

Within minutes of these orders, the boys were put to the test. As they walked through a corridor in the Criminal Courts Building, Charles Ream stepped out from a group and pointed a finger at them. The young cab driver who was abducted and castrated the previous November charged Dickie and Babe with the crime.

"Do you think that I could forget the face of the men who have taken so much out of my life?" Ream said. "Leopold and Loeb—I knew them when I first saw their pictures in the paper. Loeb drove the car on the night I was kidnapped. Leopold is the man who prepared the ether bandage. How well I remember."[2]

Assistant State's Attorney Joseph Savage announced that Dickie and Babe were also under suspicion for the murder of Freeman Louis Tracy, the University of Chicago student police found murdered in a Hyde Park street five days after the Ream castration.

When asked about these crimes, Dickie and Babe followed the advice of their attorneys. "I must respectfully decline to answer" each said.

## COOK COUNTY JAIL

Each in his own way, the newest inmates at the Cook County Jail settled in.

Dickie shared his new home—cell 717 in the juvenile section—with a robber named Edward Donker. Babe, one floor below, in cell 604, also bunked with a bandit, Thomas Doherty. Dickie had little trouble adjusting to his new environment.[3] He easily picked up the jailhouse lingo: "I think so-and-so will get the rope . . . I think so-and-so will get the street."[4] And he quickly befriended inmates, even teaching one young highwayman the puzzles of the alphabet.

Babe kept his distance from the prisoners. He stayed on the sidelines during exercise time in the bullpen. As one inmate said, "He thinks he is too good for us guys." Another one said, "He better lay off that ritzie stuff and get down to earth, or he will find himself in a hell of a place."

Outside, crowds of young women gathered day and night on North Dearborn Street. They assembled in small groups and pointed to the upper floors of the jail. Police allowed them to gaze for a while before moving them along.

Clarence Darrow waited for his two young clients in the jail's "lawyers' cage"—a tiny room with bars on one end. It would be a short meeting—a get-to-know-you-better session. But an important one. Darrow would again order the boys to keep their mouths shut—say nothing and cooperate fully with doctors and alienists during the next few weeks while Darrow and Bachrach planned their defense.

Darrow's appearance was bleak. Time had battered his face. He wore a wrinkled seersucker jacket on this warm June day, a soiled shirt, and galluses.[5] An unruly tie, fashioned by an uncaring hand, complemented a mousy shock of hair that fell over his forehead. Babe's initial impression of his lead attorney was "an innocent hay-seed, a bumpkin who might have difficulty finding his way around the city."[6] At nineteen, Babe lacked the wisdom to study the Darrow's dark eyes where, he would soon learn, the truth lived.

But this aging "bumpkin" had saved more than a hundred clients from the gallows.[7] Darrow knew his only defense in this passionate case was the mental conditions of the boys.[8] To that end, Darrow sent the junior member of his defense team—Walter Bachrach (Benjamin's brother)—to Atlantic City, New Jersey. Bachrach's mission: seek out the best and the brightest from the American Psychiatric Association convention being held that week. Crowe had already enlisted the top psychoanalysts in Chicago, so Darrow needed to go out of town to find alienists to examine his clients. The press would call the case "The Battle of the Alienists."

While Darrow planned strategy, the Loeb and Leopold families made sure their sons continued to eat in millionaire fashion. At meal times, guards at the Cook County Jail slipped soggy cardboard plates of jailhouse grub under cell doors. Except for cells 717 and 604. Under these bars came fine cuisine from nearby restaurants, including cigarettes and smuggled booze from Uncle Jacob Loeb's Kenwood cellar.

## INDICTED

For the three days of June 4, 5, and 6, they told their stories to the men and women sitting in the grand jury box.

Tony Minke, who found Bobby's cold body and frantically waved down railroad workers; Paul Korff, the crew chief, who found the eyeglasses and pulled the young victim from the culvert; Korff's three crew members, who carried Bobby up the embankment to the handcars; Dr. Emil Deutsch, who prescribed Babe's horn-rimmed spectacles; chauffeur Sven Englund, who unwittingly sealed the fates of Dickie and Babe; William

Harndon, who rented "Morton D. Ballard" the Willys-Knight touring car; Bernard Hunt, the Kenwood watchman, who saw the cold chisel fly from the car late at night; Albert Hubbinger, the hardware clerk, who sold the cold chisel and rope to Dickie; Irving Hartman, Bobby's schoolmate, who walked along Ellis Avenue moments before Bobby disappeared; the conductor on the Michigan City train, who found the letter instructing Jacob Franks how to throw the ransom money; an assortment of testimony from police officers, including Michael Hughes, William Shoemacher, William Crot, Frank Johnson, James Gortland, Edward Anderson and Hugh Byrne.[9]

On June 6, the grand jury, who heard seventy-two witnesses, handed down two indictments—one for murder, the other for kidnapping for ransom, both capital offenses. The murder indictment included eleven counts; the kidnapping, sixteen. Crowe sought two indictments because if a jury failed to convict the boys of murder, he still had a chance to send them to the gallows on the kidnapping for ransom indictment.

Jurors heard court reporters read Babe's confession. Crowe felt that Babe's narrative of the crime was more coherent and explicit than Dickie's. Upon hearing the confession and also learning that the killers confiscated fifteen cents found in Bobby's trouser pocket, the grand jury voted the indictments. Crowe beamed with confidence. "Undoubtedly a hanging case," the state's attorney said.

Jacob Franks agreed with the state's attorney.

"I would feel it to be my duty," Franks told reporters when asked if he could be the hangman. "Yes, I could pull the trap. I know my son never would have grown up to be like these boys. They were not brought up rightly. They were given too much freedom. For two years it was common gossip in the neighborhood that they drank and ran about at all hours of the day and night. Of course, I realize the death of these two cannot bring my son back to life, but my duty now is to the other parents with sons. Even if they are judged insane, they should be hanged just the same."[10]

Crowe built his murder case on a string of material evidence covering eighteen points:

1. Babe's spectacles. The state had proven the glasses found near the dead body belonged to Babe.

2. Crime scene. Because of his birding activities, Babe was intimately familiar with the area where the body was found.

3. Sven Englund. The Leopold chauffeur's attempt to help the boys proved to be their undoing. Englund shattered their alibi—automobiling

in Babe's car—when he told prosecutors that he had worked on Babe's Willys all day.

4. The killing car. Babe and Dickie admitted the blood-stained Willys-Knight that Crowe displayed in the courthouse courtyard was the rental auto used in the crime.

5. Blood washing. Sven Englund told police he saw the boys washing blood off the rental car.

6. Blood-stained clothing. Dr. William McNally testified that he found blood stains on the clothing worn by Dickie and Babe on the night of the murder. He also discovered blood stains on Babe's boots.

7. Handwriting. Crowe's handwriting experts told him that some writing samples of Babe's matched the hand-written ransom envelope.

8. Ransom directions. Railway authorities found the letter giving directions to Jacob Franks about how to deliver the ransom money. It was in the telegraph box in the Pullman car 507—just where the boys said it would be.

9. Stationery. The person who sold the paper on which the ransom note was written identified Babe during the reenactment.

10. Underwood portable typewriter. Four of Babe's fellow law students—and the Leopold maid—said Babe had used an Underwood portable at his home. A typewriter expert determined that such a machine was used to write the ransom letter. After one week of searching, a salvage diver rose from the murky lagoon water in Jackson Park. He carried a muddy Underwood portable—Crowe's final link of material evidence. Police quickly traced the Underwood to its owner: Pierce Bitker, a University of Michigan student, of Ann Arbor, Michigan. "Everything is in except the verdict," Crowe said following the discovery.

11 through 14. Reenactment. Dickie and Babe led police and prosecutors to four key locations: the cigar store where Dickie and Babe executed their plans to get a rental car; the spot on the Lake Michigan beach where they burned the auto robe; the isolated Indiana roadside where they hid Bobby's belt and buckle; and the brush area where they threw the victim's shoes.

15. Bobby's friend. Crowe proved that Dickie through his friendship with Bobby Franks was able to lure the child into the car.

16. Chisel. The specially prepared cold chisel was in police custody, thanks to Bernard Hunt.

17. Lucie Smith. An eyewitness testified that she saw Dickie and Babe at 113th Street and Michigan Boulevard, not far from the crime scene, in a Willys-Knight at 9:30 on the night of the killing.

18. Gag. Also in custody—the gag that the killers forced down Bobby's throat.

## THEIR FATHERS' WORDS

As Robert Crowe tightened his case against Dickie and Babe, the young men's millionaire fathers told Chicagoans that money would not influence the trial. The June 7 statement made front-page news.

> In view of the many statements that large sums of money will be used in the defense of Nathan F. Leopold, Jr. and Richard A. Loeb, the families of the accused boys desire to say that they have lived in Chicago for more than fifty years, and the public can judge whether they have conducted themselves in their relations with the community in such a way as to earn a standing of truthful, decent, upright, law-abiding citizens, conscious of their duties and responsibilities to the community in which they live.
>
> Assuming that the facts of this case are substantially as published, then the only proceeding they favor is a simple, solemn investigation under the law, touching the mental responsibility of their accused sons.
>
> They emphatically state, that no counsel for the accused boys will be retained, other than those lawyers now representing them, with the possible, but not probable, retention of one additional local lawyer. There will be no large sums of money spent, either for legal or medical talent. The fees to be paid to medical experts will be only such fees as ordinary and usual for similar testimony.
>
> The lawyers representing the accused boys have agreed that the amount of their fees shall be determined by a committee composed of the officers of the Chicago Bar Association.
>
> If the accused boys are found by a jury to be not mentally responsible, their families, in accordance with their conscious duty towards the community, agree that the public must be fully protected from any further menace by these boys.
>
> In no event will the families of the accused boys use money in any attempt to defeat justice.
>
> Nathan F. Leopold, Sr.<br>Albert Loeb[11]

Crowe anticipated an insanity defense. He quickly responded to Leopold and Loeb's public statement. He held two indictments, and he was prepared to go to trial on both.

"The indictments returned are separate and distinct cases, one charging the murder of Robert Franks, the other kidnapping him for ransom," said a state's attorney attaché. "It's an old saying among lawyers, 'you never can tell what a jury will do.' Suppose there was an acquittal or a verdict of insanity. Then, if the State's Attorney so wills, Leopold and Loeb may be tried on the kidnapping charge which also carries the extreme penalty on conviction."[12]

In four days, at the Wednesday, June 11 arraignment, Clarence Darrow, the old "bumpkin," would lead his two young clients before Judge John Caverly, and the city would hear their plea. The Pirate would be ready.

## MORAL RESPONSIBILITY

The tabloid press never allowed the passions of Chicagoans to cool. Doctors, educators, and psychoanalysts continued to find voice in the newspapers. A philosophy professor from the University of Michigan said the boys should be classified as "antinomians"—people who suffer from delusions of genius. "They think they are above the codes they despise," said Robert Wenly, "that those codes are all right for common people, but not for them."[13]

Another U. of M. professor—W. B. Pillsbury—offered a similar diagnosis: "This exaggerated ego eventually led them to commit a murder merely to delight their pride and intellect by getting away with it. They wanted to baffle society and the police so they might enjoy what to them was the delicious feeling of being superior to common mortals."

To some trained eyes, it was all about the curve of a skull or the line of an ear. The latest character study of the boys—presented by Dr. James Fitzgerald—concluded that Babe possessed the "dominant will. Leopold is the male; Loeb is the female, when it comes to a comparison of the temperaments of these two."

Babe's skull, according to Dr. Fitzgerald, showed "he is lacking in the reflective and reasoning faculties, in the moral and religious faculties, in benevolence, respect, and faith." The doctor declared that Babe's cerebellum protruded, meaning his "sex feelings predominate in his social ideals."

Dickie, said the doctor, "is the female type. His desire is to be popular. That is why he has fitted into the life of the jail, whereas Leopold has not. Loeb will suffer while Leopold will not. Leopold is a moral simpleton, while Loeb is a weakling. The prominent chin (in Loeb) denotes a love of excitement, which would cause him to lose his head if aroused."

Dr. Fitzgerald concluded, "It has been Leopold all along. His is the ego that allowed no law but his own desire. Loeb was clay in the hands of potter Leopold."

In Marquette, Michigan, a gathering of six hundred Masons discussed Babe's queer system of ethics. An Episcopalian minister said he had talked with Babe at a Boy Scout camp a year ago. "He is an atheist who believes he is a law unto himself and that he has a right to commit a crime if he wants to take a gamble," Rev. Mr. Laurence told the Masons.[14]

The pastor quoted Babe as saying, "It's only a question of whether I want to take the gamble. If I have a better mind than others and choose to do something else than they do, that is my privilege. There is no future life or punishment. If I could commit a crime without being caught, I could do so without compunction of conscience. It is only a question whether I care to gamble on the possibility of punishment by lesser minds."

The day before the arraignment, the *Tribune* editorial echoed the views of most Chicagoans. The newspaper placed the murder on a national scale: "There have been few crimes in the history of the United States that have more important implications than the killing of Robert Franks." The editors focused on the issue of moral responsibility:

> The relevant question, apart from the proof of fact, is the question of responsibility. . . . In the Franks case, the accused have confessed to a course of action, involving complicated planning, forethought, and deliberate purpose. Both are of exceptional mental attainments, developed by considerable knowledge and elaborate mental training. If the crime was committed according to the confessions, it was one of the most acute, complex, and thoroughly reasoned crimes in the history of crime, revealing not only exceptional mentality but an even more exceptional lack of moral perception or inhibition.
>
> Thus it would seem that the question of penalty involves our fundamental conception of moral responsibility for criminal acts. To the lay public, the facts being established, the application to the criminal law in such a case can hardly seem doubtful, and the failure to apply it, a reversal of our accepted doctrine of responsibility and our policy for punishment of crime.[15]

## SUPERIOR COURT, BRANCH NO. 1

On the morning of his nineteenth birthday, June 11, 1924, Dickie Loeb prepared for a big day. After a shower in the juvenile section of the county jail, it was time for a haircut. He sang as a jail barber shaved his soft face.[16] Inside his cell, he put on a new suit and tie; he slicked back his long, brown hair. He'd have to pose for the flashlight photographers; his hair must be perfect.[17]

A floor below, in cell 604, Babe Leopold also paid close attention to his appearance. A pressed suit, starched shirt, and four-in-hand knot were the order of the day. Like Dickie, Babe combed back his hair in Valentino fashion. This was supposed to have been the day Babe sailed for Europe.

In a few minutes, the boys would meet at the sixth-floor walkway— "the bridge of sighs"—that connected to jail to the courthouse.

While Dickie and Babe dressed for their formal arraignment, huge crowds—some said the largest ever to converge on the Criminal Courts Building—filled Judge Caverly's courtroom. They arrived three hours before the 10:00 A.M. start, jamming the lobby and corridors on the sixth floor. When a clerk finally opened the courtroom doors, the mob rushed for seats and tore the large doors from their hinges. More than three hundred people attacked every inch of the room. Men and women stood in the aisles and on benches behind the visitors' gallery. Some crawled up window sills, their backs pressed against the large windows. Many stood on chairs to get a good view of the defendants. Reporters spilled out of the press rows, and news photographers, their bulky Speed Graphics ready, lined the wall behind Caverly's desk.

Darrow, wearing a rumpled powder-blue shirt, walked to the defense table with Benjamin Bachrach. They nodded to Robert Crowe. The state's attorney sat with several assistants. The grand jurors filled the jury box to Caverly's left. In the middle of the packed room, Uncle Jacob Franks sat with his legs crossed, holding his black derby on his lap. Neither Albert Loeb nor Nathan Leopold Sr. attended the arraignment.

As Judge Caverly approached his bench, a clerk opened the door leading to the bridge of sighs. Like fireworks, loud pops of camera flashlights exploded behind Caverly. The photographers jostled for position in an attempt to get the perfect shot of the two young killers. Sheriff deputies escorted Dickie and Babe to the defense table. Superior Court, Branch No. 1, had begun.

With the smoke from the flashlights still swirling toward the ceiling, the clerk began, "Nathan Leopold and Richard Loeb. On June 6, the grand jury indicted you, Nathan Leopold Jr., and you, Richard A. Loeb for murder. Do you plead guilty or not guilty?"

"Not guilty, sir." Dickie and Babe stood together before Judge Caverly and answered quickly.[18]

Crowe stood and asked the clerk to arraign the boys separately. The clerk then repeated the murder indictment and the kidnapping-for-ransom indictment to each in turn. Their answers were the same: "Not guilty."

"Your Honor," Crowe said, "we would like to have this case assigned."

Caverly said it had been assigned to Branch No. 1 and asked: "Have you gentlemen agreed to a trial date?"

"I suggest that the case be set for trial on July 15 at the latest," Crowe answered.

"That is a very short time, Your Honor," Bachrach said. "The state knows very well that the defense cannot get ready for trial in so short a time. The court must be aware of the state of the public mind. And the newspapers have been publishing statements daily that the state's attorney intends to have the defendants hanged if possible."

"I am not responsible for what appears in the newspapers," Crowe countered.

Darrow then entered the argument. "I don't think there is a man in this city who hasn't read of this case. The defense will require a lot of preparation. We are anxious, however, to get through with the case as soon as possible."

Judge Caverly quickly ordered a trial date for Monday, August 4; Monday, July 21 would be the day to hear all motions.

Soon after the arraignment, Darrow asked Cook County Sheriff Peter Hoffman for permission to allow alienists into the jail to examine his clients in private.

Crowe, meanwhile, continued to prepare to face an insanity defense. He and one of his lead assistants, Milton Smith, interviewed the dean of the University of Chicago law school, James Arthur Hall. Hall said he believed Babe was sane and rational. Crowe also asked that Babe's law exams—taken just a few days after the murder—be returned from Harvard University, where Babe had planned to transfer. Crowe believed these exams would convince a jury that they were written by a sane mind.

## ECHOES

The heat of summer in Chicago is abrupt. Suddenly it's upon you.

As Robert Crowe finessed his hanging case, Clarence Darrow's doctors probed his clients, and Flora Franks waited for Bobby's return, summer swallowed the city. Daily temperatures soared to the mid-nineties and stayed there until well past nightfall.

And with the heat, passions turned to hate.

A few nights after the arraignment, a giant, burning cross lit up the sky in Kenwood. Someone—"Kluxers," neighbors said—set fire to a four-teen-foot-high cross in an empty lot at Forty-Ninth Street and Drexel Boulevard, a few blocks from the Loeb and Leopold homes.[19] Hundreds of people gathered on the hot night to watch the blaze. The cross had been wrapped in gasoline-saturated cotton. Police said the fire was a consequence of the Franks case.

In the early twenties, the Klu Klux Klan had more than twenty neigh-borhood Klan units in Chicago. Kenwood Klan No. 33 was an early Illinois charter. In the summer of 1922, the Klan boasted nearly thirty thousand members, mostly lower-income, white-collar workers, small-business owners, and laborers.[20] Its twenty-four-page newspaper, *Dawn*, originally printed in Hyde Park, kept Kluxers aware of Klan activities across the city. Local businesses supported its ad page. One Woodlawn jewelry store advertised miniature fiery crosses for $3.[21] Although the Invisible Empire had lost much of its strength by the summer of 1924, many of its followers continued to echo the Klan's hate practices. The Franks case offered three conspicuous targets—a well-known, liberal defense attorney and two arrogant Jewish defendants.

A few blocks from the burning cross, two policemen stood guard at young Irving Hartman's home on Ellis Avenue, just down the street from the Franks house. Irving's father, a millionaire furniture merchant, had received two handwritten letters demanding $10,000 ransom: "Is your son's life or anybody else's in the family worth anything to you. Then read this. We are going to kidnap your son and maybe serious injuries may come to any member of your family, but before we go ahead we are giving you a warning."[22]

Hartman called police immediately and then sent his son to Balti-more to stay with relatives. Mrs. Hartman blamed the copycat threat on Dickie and Babe. "If these two boys are not hanged," she said, "I'll go to California, where I can raise my boy in safety."

Goose Island, a dark and dangerous swatch of land on the north branch of the Chicago River, was called Little Hell. Home to tanneries, brew-eries, and soap factories, it was a foul-smelling, noxious place. On the night of Monday, June 23, Jacob Franks emerged from the shadows and placed a small package—a decoy—at a designated site near a coalyard fence. The ransom letter he received the day before demanded $8,000 . . . or Josephine would be the next to die. When Chief of Detectives

Michael Hughes asked Franks if he would be willing to take the decoy to Goose Island—as the letter instructed—Franks answered, "Nothing could frighten me after all I've gone through."

Detectives watched Franks from the dark corners of a gasworks plant. A few minutes after Franks dropped off the decoy, three men ran through the night and picked up the package. Police quickly ambushed them and took them into custody. The men turned out to be teenagers—three eighteen-year-olds.[23]

## DEATH CELL

"That's all bunk," Benjamin Bachrach told reporters.[24]

Bachrach was fed up with rumors that the defense—the "million-dollar defense" as some people called it—would hire fifty alienists. Speculation as to Darrow's defense strategy ran wild in the newspapers. Some reporters—and the state's attorney—felt certain that Darrow would seek a sanity hearing on July 21 instead of going to trial on murder charges.

Darrow hired only three lead alienists—all secured by Walter Bachrach at the American Psychiatric Association convention in Atlantic City: Dr. William Alanson White, president of the American Psychiatric Association and superintendent of St. Elizabeth's Hospital in Washington, D.C., Dr. William Healy, a Boston specialist in criminal psychiatry in juvenile delinquents, and Dr. Bernard Glueck, medical advisor to New York's penal institutions. Unlike Crowe's alienists who first examined Dickie and Babe, these doctors were liberal in their approach, believing the unconscious mind provides answers to behavior. Chicago's newsmen called them "the Three Wise Men from the East."

Darrow also hired two physicians to conduct extensive neuropsychiatric examinations of the teenagers: Dr. Karl Bowman of Boston, a specialist in the observation of mental disorders resulting from the maladjustment of glands in the body; and Dr. H. S. Hulbert of Oak Park, Illinois. The results of their two-week study, which probed the physical and psychological condition of Dickie and Babe each, would be the foundation for Darrow's defense tactics.

It was called the "Death Cell"—an inmate's final stop before the gallows. In the final two weeks of June, Drs. Bowman and Hulbert transformed the Death Cell into their private laboratory. The second-floor room, completely isolated from noise and contact with inmates, held a large table, chairs, a bed, and a sink with hot and cold running water. Its window overlooked the jail's courtyard, where condemned prisoners met their fate.

Warden Westbrook cooperated fully with the doctors, securing their lab from outside influence, the only breach an enterprising reporter stationed in a building across the street, who used a spyglass to peer through the Death Cell's window.

"The planning of it gave me pleasure," Dickie told the doctors.

Comfortable in jail, Dickie spun a vivid, personal narrative for Drs. Bowman and Hulbert, touching all aspects of his life, including his reaction to the crime.

"I knew it would make a stir in the newspapers," he said. "I got an intense thrill out of the plan. The cleverness of the crime appealed to me. It kept me busy. If I had been busy, I might not have done it."

The doctors asked Dickie whether he would go through with the crime again if he felt certain he would not be discovered. "I believe I would if I could get the money," he answered.

At times, Dickie acted unconcerned. The report stated that Dickie felt "very, very sorry for his parents, especially his father" when the doctors asked him about his family. The doctors, though, didn't buy into his compassion. "His manner was not at all convincing," they wrote in the three-hundred-page report. They described Dickie as "selfish and wrapped up in his own thoughts and feelings."

Dickie had no trouble talking about the crime. He had no hatred toward Bobby Franks, and the ransom money, he claimed, was an afterthought. But an important afterthought. "Five thousand is five thousand," he told the doctors about his share of the hoped-for cash.

"The patient lists as his reasons for committing the crime," the doctors wrote, "first, the pleasure of planning it; second, the notoriety which the papers would give to the crime and the fact that he could talk it over with other people and derive a thrill from his feeling of superiority, in that he knew the facts about the crime; and third, the money to be gained."

Moral judgment never played a big role in Dickie's life. Nor did religion. Albert Loeb, a German-Jew, and his wife, Anna, a German-Catholic, provided no religious foundation for Dickie. He attended Jewish temple twice in his life, and he stepped inside a Catholic church twice, both times for his cousins' confirmations.

But he told the doctors he often discussed religion and morals with his confederate. Babe advised him that the only wrong he could do was to make a mistake. According to Babe, anything that gave you pleasure was right to do. "I took this statement with a big dose of salt," Dickie said with a wide smile. "No grain of salt, and its only effect on me was to make me more stuck-up."

Dickie believed he was superior to others, and moral conventions, therefore, should not bind him. "This feeling of superiority," the doctors concluded, "made him indifferent to the feelings of others."

In the privacy of the Death Cell, Dickie spoke frankly about his complicated relationship with Babe. "In a way, I have always been sort of afraid of him. I had always considered him a bad influence on me." But, he added, he needed a comrade to carry out his crime.

The idea of killing Babe crossed his mind. He thought about shooting Babe with a revolver but decided he couldn't do it alone. "If I could have snapped my fingers and made him pass away in a heart attack, I would have done it," he said. He also revealed that he frequently contemplated suicide, especially while in jail. However, it would be much better for his family, he said, if he went to the gallows.

Drs. Bowman and Hulbert reported that Dickie battled depression: "These spells of depression apparently started following punishment, a sense of exclusion during childhood. They have continued up to the present time. These spells of depression come on whenever he is alone but disappear whenever he is occupied with companions. As a result, he cannot bear to be alone and demands constant companionship."

At one point during his discussions, Dickie sat on the edge of his chair and said that he sometimes wondered if he was "all there."

A "wishful world of fantasy" was how the doctors explained Dickie's childhood. In his fantasies of crime, Dickie enjoyed a dominant role; it satisfied his emotional life. And Miss Struthers, Dickie said, controlled his young life.

"I always obeyed her," he said. "As a boy, I didn't do the things other boys did. When she left, I kind of broke lose."

After his arrest, Miss Struthers visited Dickie in jail. She told him she would help him any way she could. Drs. Bowman and Hulbert interviewed Dickie's former governess: "She denied any imperfection in herself while she was governess, and she denied any imperfection with the boy during her stay with the family. She said he was quite all right at fifteen years of age, at which time she left his home. Others . . . thought him to drink and go out with girls."

The doctors agreed, Miss Struthers's influence on Dickie was negative: "She was too anxious to have him become an ideal boy and would not allow him to mix with other boys. She would not overlook some of his faults and was too quick in her punishment and therefore he built up the habit of lying without compunction and with increasing skills. She was quite aware that he had become a petty thief and a play detective, but she was with him so constantly the parents did not scrutinize him particularly."

When asked, Dickie recalled some of his dreams while in jail. "I was in a swimming pool and in some way was summoned into a room where about four or five men were present. They told me, or in some way I found out, that my father had failed in business, and that the failure had been dishonorable. I pleaded with the men for clemency and then they explained that they were going ahead with the thing and that they were going to raise money at 3½ percent interest.

"I was in a locker room in a gymnasium. I went to what I thought was a football field but then somebody told me I was not in the football field and that the football field was covered with snow. I then went upstairs into the locker room and was given a pair of heavy boots, coming up to my knee, instead of the oxford sport shoes I was wearing. I asked who would pay for them and I was told that they would go on the expense account.

"There were a number of fellows in some sort of a contest riding horseback, and they were all naked. I tried to ride, too, but was troubled by severe pains in one of my legs."

In their psychiatric observation, the doctors concluded, "The patient's intellectual functions are intact, and he is, obviously, of high intelligence." Dickie's extensive neurological physical examination did not show any pathology except a low basal metabolism, maybe related to his relatively low sexually potency.

After hearing Dickie's life story in the Death Cell, Drs. Bowman and Hulbert believed that Dickie "never derived any satisfaction from seeing other people suffer."

It was all about getting attention.

"The only thing that he desired of other people was that they look up to him, consequently he had no close friends bud did have a close confederate in crime who deferred to the patient's superiority in intelligence and criminalism," the doctors concluded.

"Horseshit," Babe told the doctors. Babe's attitude and reaction to his examination was sardonic and arrogant. "I suppose the function of this is to prolong my life as something worthwhile. I can't correlate that with my philosophy, but it is usually considered a worthwhile life. My folks have decided on all this. Of course, I am desperately trying to cooperate with them. As for me, I think this medical psychiatric stuff is all horseshit."

At first, Babe cooperated with the doctors. He enjoyed being the center of attention. But as time dragged on and as the doctors took several medical tests, Babe became irritable and less friendly. When the doctors wanted to do a lumbar puncture, Babe begged for an anesthetic or for hypnosis. If he did not receive either, he warned them they would have "a nervous tantrum" on their hands.

An obsessive, abnormal governess—Sweetie—shaped Babe's childhood. She "produced a profound, unwholesome effect" on Babe, the doctors reported.

"She had a very great influence over my mother and myself," Babe said. "She displaced my mother. She was a scheming woman, who used children as a barrier to shield herself. I was thoroughly devoted to her."

Sweetie, Babe explained, took indecent liberties with Babe and his brother Sam. She bathed with Sam and wrestled on the bed with him. She allowed the boys to examine her while she undressed. And she taught the Leopold boys nicknames for her breasts and nipples.

"She produced definite antagonizes between the patient and his parents and brothers, which later was developed by the patient as a revolt against authority," Drs. Bowman and Hulbert wrote in the summation of their report. "She gave the patient a very abnormal and unhealthy introduction to sex topics, and he has never been able to secure a normal viewpoint on this subject."

Babe continued to show no remorse about the crime. He did nothing morally wrong, he told the doctors, because he didn't believe in morals. "He maintains that anything which gives him pleasure is right, and the only way in which he can do any wrong is to do something which will be unpleasant to himself," the doctors wrote.

At times, Babe had a difficult time relaxing in the Death Cell. He paced frequently and was easily distracted. He wandered away from the discussion at hand and could not stay focused. When the doctors discussed his eyesight, Babe mentioned that a physician had prescribed eyeglasses for a stigmatism and said with a grin: "I am sorry I ever got them."

Babe's school notebooks provided a graphic look at his wandering mind. Babe had filled the margins in his college and law-school notebooks with countless crude sketches that reflected his abnormal imagination:

- a large crucifix, a woman kneeling, birds, sheep, a man with a beard, and a man with hair dressed like a Pharaoh, several violins, a man with a head shaped like an egg and his nose bends downward like a pendant penis

- a dog's head, a muskrat coming out of his hole, a butterfly, two eyes, an airplane, a dissected penis, a clown's head, a man with a flag for a head, a caricature of a bird with two ears pointed upward, a pig's snout to which is attached a flag marked with the Greek letters—Phi Beta Kappa

- a man underneath the wording "Woody?" and beneath it, "I'll say he could."

- two boys play football, a woodpecker on a tree, an owl, a girl's hand, a man without a penis, a five-pointed star, men with one or two legs or just a head and shoulders, a typewriter, Siamese twins, birds of various kinds, three hooded men each marked with a *K*

- a sketch of himself marked "Leopold," in which the eyes and the mouth are most prominent, a boy with his back turned with his pants down

Babe was quite aware of his distorted imagination. In a college paper, "Impressions While Sick," he writes, "I know of no more unpleasant condition than to awake at night and feel positively that one is sick, although entirely ignorant of the nature of the malady. At such a time one's imagination is on the 'qui vive' and one is very susceptible to hallucinations." Babe says that on this particular night he fears he is having an appendicitis attack: "I had a pain, and upon considering it closely, I decided that it was on the right side, where I had been taught by hearsay that the appendix has its domicile."

He writes that a doctor was summoned. An examination determines that nothing is wrong—"a slight organic attack"—and that Babe should be well in a few days. "This tends to show that most things (about) which we worry never materialize."

The doctors concluded that Babe had always had "strong and vivid" fantasies since childhood. And these fantasies have "a definite bearing on his behavior, particularly with respect to the commission of crimes."

Over the past few years, Babe wove Dickie into his fantasies, especially his King-Slave fantasy, in which, as the doctors wrote, "one individual was under the complete domination of the other.

"He brings over certain ideas from his world of fantasy into the world of reality, and from his world of reality into his world of fantasy. This resulted in his becoming pathologically suggestible to ideas in the world of reality which could fit in with his world of fantasy and made him uncritical of abnormal ideas," the doctors concluded.

And sex was a big part of his worlds.

"Sex dominated his thinking," Drs. Bowman and Hulbert wrote. "Psychologically, sex has always played an enormous role in his life. Since he has had a marked sex drive, and has not been able to satisfy it in the normal heterosexual relations, this has undoubtedly been a profound, upsetting condition in his emotional life."

The doctors also agreed that the death of his mother to Bright's disease, contracted while she was pregnant with Babe, was another upsetting condition in his emotional life. It was the only time he expressed guilt: "My presence is the cause of her absence."

Babe's physical examination showed evidence of endocrine disorders involving the pineal and the pituitary glands. The doctors believed this was linked to Babe's marked intelligence and sexual drive. But his mental condition, Drs. Bowman and Hulbert wrote, "is an acquired one."

## SPECULATION

In July of 1924, radio was an infant communicator. Although there were six hundred radio stations across the country, most people perceived the medium as a technological marvel, a luxury item.[25]

News came into homes on broadsheets, not through radio receivers. But the *Chicago Daily Tribune* had an idea. On July 17, the *Tribune* asked its readers if its new radio station—WGN (world's greatest newspaper)—should broadcast the upcoming court proceedings. A page-one ballot asked Chicagoans, "Want the Tribune to radio the Franks trial? Vote 'yes' or 'no.'" The paper directed those interested in voting to clip the ballot coupon and mail it back to *Tribune* editors. The *Tribune* would broadcast the trial "only if the public wants it." Its front-page story, though, made a passionate plea.

> Millions of Americans, from New York to San Francisco, have read of the murder of the son of Millionaire Jacob Franks with more than a morbid fascination—with a curiosity that grows out of the fact that this murder touches closely more than one intimate phase of human experience.
>
> Telegraph editors, heads of syndicates receiving daily cable queries from Australia, Havana, Buenos Aires and Saskatchewan for news of the Franks case know how vital is this thirst for details.
>
> When Nathan Leopold and Richard Loeb go to trial some 300 persons will pack the courtroom. Judge, jury, bailiffs . . . newspaper men and women are there because through their calling, they have been endowed with the mantle of representing in a sense the people who read what they write.
>
> Visiting jurists and lawyers are there, drawn by the unparallel importance of the case.

And when all these are crowded in it will be found there is no room for the public itself, who in the primary sense make all laws and have the right and should feel the responsibility of watching over this enforcement.[26]

More than eight hundred people voted on the first day: 420 said no and 385 said yes.[27]

NO: "I'd like to see the two boys, Loeb and Leopold, in the courtroom. I'd rather not hear it over the radio, for I don't like the radio anyway."
—Elizabeth Glesfsky, housewife

NO: "The details of the case are not good for the people's minds. This is a good time to inaugurate a drive for clean minds. . . . Give us, not this case, but WGN with its good music, and its announcer's voice."
—Miss Mickey Mulseen, stenographer

NO: "It sounds like a modern new method, but I believe it establishes a bad precedent—yellow journalism. The radio and newspapers should serve entirely different purposes. I'll take music and other things on the radio, but I believe the newspapers can give us a good enough account of the trial."
—Mr. O. A. Danielson, builder

YES: "Because it's an interesting case. We have never heard anything like that before. . . . I like music on the radio, but this case is so interesting we could put music aside for a while."
—Helen Soboroff, student

NO: "I think it is bad enough as it is, without getting murders and scandals every time you turn a dial on a radio. Let's keep the radio as a source of enjoyment and not for scandals and murders."
—Beatrice Vahle, stenographer

YES: "The trial of the Franks slayers would give the public the benefit of what only a select few otherwise might be permitted to hear."
—A. J. Dolan, salesman

NO: "Some of the testimony may be objectionable. It is not the proper thing to do in the trial of a criminal case."
—John Owen, attorney[28]

Robert Crowe thought it would be a good idea to broadcast the trial. "Whether radio is the proper means of bringing about such popular interest we cannot know as yet, of course, but I am inclined to think that it is highly worth trying."

More than ten thousand readers of the *Tribune* cast ballots over five days. Sixty-five percent voted no. The trial would belong exclusively to the newspapers.

For nearly seven weeks, state and defense alienists had examined the minds of Clarence Darrow's two teenage clients. But Darrow had remained silent.

"What will Darrow do? The defense will contend that the boys must be insane to do what they did," the *Tribune* speculated.[29]

In truth, Darrow had no defense except the mental condition of Dickie and Babe. State's Attorney Crowe prepared a prosecution aimed at quashing any attempt to prove the killers insane. He bristled at stories that suggested a jury would find them insane.

"The report that Leopold and Loeb are insane is nothing more than propaganda sent out by the defense to throw dust into the eyes of men who may be called to serve on the jury," Crowe said. "No reputable alienist would testify the two murderers are insane."

One report indicated the defense would claim the boys were victims of folie à deux, or "madness for two." This rare mental disease results from the coincidental and intimate association of two personalities in a disastrous manner, such as delusive beliefs or ideas.

While Crowe reacted to newspaper stories, Darrow refused to show his hand. A few days before he was to argue motions before Judge Caverly, though, Darrow did offer a glimpse as to his defense.

"Leopold lives in a different world from that in which you and I exist," Darrow said. "In his mind, he had built a wall which shuts him from the conventionalities of the present day and makes him superman. The alienists who have examined him during the weeks have read him. He does not believe in the laws which rule us, and the police are but obstructions which might stand in the way of living the life he has built."

Darrow admitted he would not attempt to free the teenagers of all blame. But, he would make sure that justice—and all Chicagoans—understood the peculiar twists that darkened two bright minds.

## MOTIONS

Dickie and Babe sat at the defense table toward the front of the packed courtroom. They stared at the backs of five men who stood in front of them. State's Attorney Robert Crowe and four of his assistants blocked the teenagers' view of their attorney. Dickie and Babe barely heard Clarence Darrow's soft voice as he addressed Judge John Caverly. And they couldn't see the sweat dripping down the neck of their weary advocate.

But they knew what was coming.

"Your Honor," Darrow said, "we have determined to withdraw our pleas of not guilty and enter a plea of guilty."[30]

Quietly, serenely, the "Old Lion"—as the press would call him—buried the courtroom with a one-word avalanche. Guilty. The word gathered momentum and spun out of control. It bounced from row to row, "What did he say, guilty?" The word echoed all the way to the back of the room, where Jacob Loeb, his head bowed, wept. National correspondents, who sat in the jury box, jumped to their feet to file the news. Local reporters ran for the doors. The bailiff called for order.

The Old Lion rocked back and forth on tired legs and continued:

"Your Honor, we dislike to throw this burden upon this court or any court. We know its seriousness and its gravity, but a court can no more shirk responsibilities than attorneys. And, while we wish it could be otherwise, we feel it must be as we have chosen."

Darrow knew who he was talking to. Caverly, a former judge on the Municipal Court, had been instrumental in forming Cook County's Juvenile Court. Darrow believed Caverly to be kind and discerning in his views of life, a fair and caring man.[31] And the Old Lion was willing to bet two lives on it. By changing the plea to guilty, Caverly—not a jury—would rule on the punishment. If Darrow had sought a sanity hearing, the teenagers' fate would be left to a jury, a risk he was not willing to take.

Darrow would offer evidence on both indictments—murder and kidnapping for ransom—to be disposed of at the same time. On a plea of not guilty, Crowe could prosecute the charges separately. If he failed to win a murder conviction, he could try for a kidnapping verdict, also a capital crime. Darrow had court history on his side. In the last thirty years in Illinois, only five men had been sentenced to hang on a guilty plea to murder. And, more importantly, of the ninety men hanged in Illinois before 1924, no one who pleaded guilty was under the age of twenty-three. Illinois had only sent two youths under the age of twenty-one to the gallows—one eighteen, the other nineteen. And both were a jury's verdict—to a plea of not guilty.

Caverly motioned for Dickie and Babe to approach the bench.

The judge looked at Babe, whose customary smirk had disappeared. Babe looked squarely at the judge. And listened.

Caverly took his time. He slowly and carefully explained the ramifications of Babe's guilty plea. His words drifted through the courtroom, like a faraway plane moving in and out of the clouds. "If your plea is guilty, you may be sentenced to death. You may be sent to a penitentiary for the rest of your natural life. You may be sent away for not less than fourteen years. Do you still desire to plead guilty?"·

"I do," Babe said.

Caverly entered the plea. He then repeated the process for Dickie, who affirmed the guilty plea. The judge then asked them about the kidnapping for ransom charge (minimum sentence five years). Again, the both pleaded guilty.

Judge Caverly then decided that the trial would start in two days—on Wednesday, July 23.

Darrow would attempt to show Judge Caverly—and the world—that Dickie Loeb and Babe Leopold led abnormal childhoods—evidence that influenced their mental condition and, the Old Lion hoped, would mitigate their penalty. Darrow would not try to prove the teenagers insane but rather show an enraged city that these two killers were not normal. And never had been normal. Insanity, a legal term, had very specific parameters, but abnormality was a gray area, open to conjecture. A very elastic defense strategy for the cagy Old Lion.

Crowe was indignant. "The fact that these two murderers have thrown themselves on the mercy of the court does not in any way alleviate the enormity of the crime they committed," he told reporters after the proceedings. "As I informed the court, the State is going to prove not only that these two boys are guilty, but they are absolutely sane and should be hanged. Every exhibit will be laid before Judge Caverly. There is but one punishment that will satisfy the prosecution—that they be hanged."[32]

## PIRATE VERSUS OLD LION

Wrapped in black, Flora Franks held Sam Ettleson's arm and walked into the Criminal Courts Building. Her pale face carried no emotion, only heavy shadows of grief. She and Ettleson hurried through the crowded lobby and disappeared into the elevator.

Outside, mounted police managed crowd control. Three thousand people had shown up on this hot July morning. Only three hundred would make it inside Judge Caverly's courtroom, mostly friends of the court and news reporters. Caverly issued pink admission cards to be shown to guards at the front door. The public had its choice of seventy seats—on a first-come, first-served basis.

The center of all this attention—Dickie and Babe—dressed and readied themselves in their cells at the County Jail. Each studied his looks in a mirror, smoked cigarettes, and joshed with reporters. It was as if they prepared for a Broadway opening, rather than a murder trial.

"I heard you fellows had a hard time describing our clothes the other day," Babe said. "Now, I don't want you to make any mistakes this time. Remember, this is an important day. Now look at me. What am I wearing? If I walked away this minute, not one of you could tell—accurately. So, I'm going to help you out. Dick's hat is a soft fedora, as you can see, it's dull gray. Mine is slate gray. Did you get all that straight?"[33]

Within the hour, deputies would slap handcuffs on the two young killers and lead them across the bridge of sighs.

By ten o'clock, Chicago's temperature had reached eighty-four degrees. It would soar past ninety by mid-afternoon, making the courtroom unbearable. Sunlight surged through the giant windows. Most men held their suit jackets, and a long line of straw skimmers filled the hat rack. An electric fan sat on Judge Caverly's desk, but its efforts seemed to go unnoticed.

Caverly walked into a courtroom bursting with people. They filled every seat. There was no jury, but twelve telegraph operators sat in the jury box, along with a handful of national correspondents.[34] Several rows of benches held the many local reporters. Families of the defendants—and the dead boy—sat toward the front of the room, behind the counsel tables. In the back, the visitors' gallery overflowed—mostly with young girls. More women—from the well-heeled to giddy flappers—attended than men. They would hang on every word, every lurid detail. They were the lucky ones. Two bulky guards at the double doors held back a huge crowd who jammed the sixth-floor corridor, snaked down the iron staircase, and clogged the hallways of the fifth floor. These people would never get a chance to see the stars of the show.

Dickie and Babe glowed in sartorial splendor. Dickie's smile complemented a black worsted suit, powder-blue shirt, gray bow tie, and tax oxfords. A white handkerchief with tan trim adorned his jacked pocket. Babe wore a mixed-tweed coat, button-down white shirt and dead-black four-in-hand tie.[35]

As Caverly entered, he took a long look at the crowd and said, "Those who are not seated will have to leave the courtroom." He then asked the defendants if they wanted change their guilty plea. When they declined, he motioned for the prosecution to begin.

"Fighting Bob" Crowe seized the opportunity.

For one hour, he moved across the front of the courtroom and delivered his opening statement in a series of well-choreographed maneuvers:

He'd raise a fist in the air to signify anger, stop to wipe off his eyeglasses to emphasize a point, and pose in all points of the room so everyone had a chance to get a clear look.

"These two defendants entered into a conspiracy, the purpose of which was to gain money," he told his audience, "and in order to gain it they were ready and willing to commit a cold-blooded murder."

Minutes after he began, the heat had turned his starched, white shirt soggy with sweat. The Pirate threw his arms high in the air and left no stone unturned as he meticulously outlined the teenagers' actions:

". . . stealing a typewriter in Ann Arbor . . . planned their crime over the winter . . . even showed ingenuity in testing the plan. . . . The first overt act beyond the acquiring of the stolen typewriter will be a newspaper folded in a compact manner and tied to a string, which these defendants experimented with by throwing it from the rear of a moving Illinois Central train to see where it would land so they might give direction later on to their victim as to how to throw the money that they hoped and intended to get."[36]

Crowe described the Rent-A-Car Agency, Morton D. Ballard of Peoria, the Morrison Hotel, Louis Mason, the ransom letter, even where the stationery was purchased, the letter Dickie placed in Pullman car 507, the acid, the cold chisel, the ether. But he was at his best when he painted a dramatic picture of Dickie looking for his victim.

"Loeb went to look over . . . prospects to see what little boys might be there that they knew whose fathers were wealthy men and who would be able to produce the $10,000 the following day," Crowe said, adding how Dickie and Babe used field glasses to look for Johnny Levinson. Instead, they spotted the Bobby Franks.

The teenagers had found "a boy who knew Loeb very well and intimately, a boy who the day before, on the 20th of May, had played tennis with Loeb in his yard, named Bobby Franks. He also was a student at the Harvard School. He was the last boy to leave the grounds, and he walked down in the direction of the car where sat these two cold-blooded calculating murderers."

Crowe's Poe-like narration put the women on the edge of their seats. And he relished it.

"He was immediately struck four times over the head with a cold chisel, and then the man in the back seat grabbed this little, fragile, dying, innocent boy and pulled him back, shoved a gag down his mouth, and then the evidence will show, threw his hand over his mouth and held it so firmly and tightly that the marks were discernable after the dead boy was found, and so held him until life left this fragile body."

Crowe took his audience on the death journey to the Indiana state line, where Babe "had been many times with classes of ladies and children, teaching the science of birds." Crowe didn't miss a single detail. He wrapped his bounty of evidence in a graphic, tabloid package—from stuffing Bobby's nude body into the culvert, to throwing the cold chisel from the car, to Dickie's and Babe's eventual confessions.

"The state will show that the motive that prompted the defendant Loeb to confess was his caution and craft to protect himself. He knew that the man who beat that little boy to death was his companion, the defendant, Leopold."

And then, looking directly at Dickie, Crowe said: "He thought he would ingratiate himself by helping to fasten the rope around his friend's neck."

Dickie rolled his head and looked up at the ceiling. A wide smile cut across his face.

Crowe then completed a powerful performance:

"The state will show to Your Honor by facts and circumstances, by witnesses, by exhibits, by documents, that these two men are guilty of the most cruel, cowardly, dastardly murder ever committed in the annals of American jurisprudence. . . . In the name of the people of the of the State of Illinois, in the name of womanhood and fatherhood, and in the name of the children of the State of Illinois, we are going to demand the death penalty for both these cold-blooded, cruel, vicious murderers."

Darrow didn't allow Crowe's dramatic close to take hold. He stood before Caverly.

"Your Honor, I want to say a few words at this time. The defendants in this case have entered a plea of guilty. Now, in all cases with any prosecutor, it seems to me, who is interested in purely administering justice, it would not have been possible to go into all the details that have been gone into this morning and make all the covert threats that been made."[37]

Darrow's calm rebuttal diluted Crowe's theatrics.

"Everyone knows that this was a most unfortunate homicide. That it is the cruelest, the worst, the most atrocious ever committed in the United States is pure imagination without a vestige of truth, and everybody knows that. These words are litany of State's Attorneys, and that is all."

Crowe jumped to his feet. Darrow was not making an opening statement, he said, but rather an argument.

"Well, was it the proper time for you to make it?" the Old Lion shot back.

"If I stepped outside the bounds, it was your business to object. I insist this be conducted like a lawsuit and not like an experiment."

"Oh, Your Honor, he has learned that somewhere in the book," Darrow said. "This will be tried like a lawsuit."

"I object, if Your Honor please, to an argument of this sort," Crowe fired back. "I insist that he should confine himself to a statement as to what he expects to prove."

"Your Honor, it comes with poor grace for counsel after for more than an hour he sought to stir up feelings in this community, where he had repeatedly sought to stir it up that justice may be blind in this case."

"Your Honor, I insist on a ruling," Crowe pleaded.

Caverly paused for a moment. "Well, counsel for the state went further than he should have gone, and if counsel for the defendants had objected, of course, I would have to sustain it. It is true that this isn't the time for argument. The argument of counsel for either side or both sides will be after the evidence is introduced."

The judge allowed Darrow to continue.

The Old Lion took his time. He had won the opening skirmish. He paced slowly in front of the bench, the way a man does when something is troubling him, and then said he was "outraged" at the state's attorney's opening statement. He hooked his thumbs in his galluses and continued.

"No one on the part of the defense claims that there was not a conspiracy, that there was not a murder, that it was not done by these two boys, that it was not done in a way that they have already given to the press. . . . It would be without precedent if these two boys of this age should be hanged by the neck until dead, and it would in no way bring back Robert Franks or add to the peace and security of this community. I insist that it would be without precedent, as we learned, if on a plea of guilty this should be done."

Darrow then attacked Crowe's plan for rehashing every detail of the crime.

"We think the court should not permit for the pure purpose of rehearsing again to this community, to stir up anger and hatred in this community that may result in many other crimes. . . . We got and listened to this statement, utterly incompetent and meant only to appeal to the passion of men. When this case is presented, I know the court will take it, take it calmly and honestly, in consideration of the community and in consideration of the lives of these two boys, and that any echo that may come back from the extravagant and unlawful statement and from the lurid painting in this courtroom, which was made for nothing excepting that a hoarse cry of angry people may somehow reach these chambers—we know Your Honor would disagree that and do in this case what is just, fair and merciful, and the court must always interpret justice and mercy together."

Edwin Gresham, Bobby's uncle, took the stand first for the state. Gresham told the court what he saw that afternoon at the Hegewisch morgue.

"The body had absolutely no clothing on it. It was laying on its back. It had on glasses. I removed the glasses to make sure that the body was the boy's. I noticed further—I looked to see that there were marks on the boy's teeth. When the boy was a child, he had rickets, and that had left marks on or pearls in the teeth, and I looked at the teeth to make sure that the pearls were there. They were there. It was beyond the question of a doubt in my mind that the boy was Robert."[38]

Dr. Joseph Springer, the county's coroner's physician who had performed the postmortem, then described Bobby's wounds. Assistant State's Attorney John Sbarbaro asked Springer to explain the examination he made of the body. The doctor graphically recounted the condition of the body. He concluded, "He came to death from an injury to the head, associated with suffocation."[39]

At noon, after the testimony of Jacob Franks, Crowe called Bobby's mother to the stand. Tension filled the courtroom. People turned their heads toward the huge double doors at the side of the room. Flora Franks, at the arm of Sam Ettleson, walked by the jury box, past her son's two killers, and slumped into the witness chair. Shrouded in a long, black mourning garment and a cloche hat, she appeared lifeless. Numb. White gloves covered her limp hands, which peaked out from the blackness and rested on her lap, as if they were useless. Her head leaned toward the sun-drenched windows. Her large, brown eyes looked nowhere.

Crowe began his questioning. In a compassionate voice, he asked her about the phone call from the killers.

In a slow, monotone voice, Flora Franks strung her words together.

"Well, the phone rang and I went to the phone and they asked for Mr. Franks and I said Mr. Franks was not home, but I was Mrs. Franks, and I asked them what they wanted, and they said, 'Your son has been kidnapped, he is all right, further news in the morning,' and I said, 'Who is it?' And they said, 'Johnson.' I wanted to ask something else but they rang off."[40]

"Are you familiar with your son's clothing?" Crowe asked.

Piece by piece—the crumpled shoes, stocking, belt, buckle, class pin—Crowe placed bits of his bounty of evidence on her lap. She handled each item tenderly. Yes, she told him, they all belonged to Bobby.

With that, her husband and Ettleson led her out a rear door.

After Flora Franks's emotional appearance, Crowe picked up the pace. A string of witnesses paraded before the court: J. B. Cravens, room clerk at the Morrison Hotel; Thomas Taylor, the Morrison house detective; Charles Ward, Arthur Doherty, and Clara Vinnedge of the Hyde Park State Bank; David Barish and Max Tuckerman of the Kenwood cigar store where "Louis Mason" talked on the phone with the Rent-A-Car Agency and vouched for "Morton D. Ballard" of Peoria; Walter Jacobs, William Herndon, and Margaret Fitzpatrick of Rent-A-Car.

Much of their testimony overlapped, irritating the defense attorneys. At one point, Benjamin Bachrach objected.

But Crowe jumped in before Caverly had a chance to rule on the objection.

"If Your Honor, please. I wish to present my case. I intend to show by a mountain of evidence that when these two defendants pleaded guilty, there was nothing else for them to do. I want to go into every detail of the case."

Caverly allowed Crowe to continue his course but cautioned him against duplicating testimony.

Darrow and the Bachrach brothers sat passively through much of the day's testimony. They cross-examined only once. They would follow this strategy for the rest of the trial, believing cross-examining witnesses would only drag out the proceedings and cast more light on the brutal specifics of the crime.

At day's end, Babe sat in his cell and talked through the bars with *Tribune* reporter Ty Krum. The young killer looked out a small window into the setting summer sun.

"You have undoubtedly seen a lot of men hanged during your experience, have you not?"

"Well, I have seen a dozen, if I remember correctly."

"And tell me, how did they die? I have often wondered how a man would act when he walks to the gallows. From your experience, what is the ratio of men who died with a smile against those who died like babies?"

"Well, I can say there is no set ratio. I remember Carl Wanderer sang a love song just before the gallows dropped; Nick Viani sang a bit; a couple of colored gents stood there and spoke pieces as though they were in school, and another young boy at Pontiac sang out to his brother, who stood before him, 'So long, Ben, take good care of mother,' as the trap dropped."

"Tell me something about some who did not die game, as they say around the jail."

"Sam Cardinella, who used to be just about the toughest gunman on the West Side, was carried to the scaffold by a couple of deputy sheriffs. They say he was tough but he died like a baby who couldn't face the music."

"How would you suppose you would act if you were sent to the gallows?"

"I can't say now because I am free and have no reason to wonder. But how do you think you will act if you are sent to the gallows?"

"I have sought for an answer to the question. Lots of times I ask myself what there is for me. I can't find an answer anywhere. I think sometimes I would welcome it, and other times I feel life is everything. Sometime I hope to find the answer. But now I am in a quandary."

## NO FAKING

One by one, they took the stand on day two of the hearing, thirty-three in all, bit players in Robert Crowe's "passion play": Andrew Russo, electrician for the Pullman Company, who found Dickie's note instructing Jacob Franks how to toss the ransom money; Elizabeth Sattler, the Leopold maid, who said Babe had two typewriters, "a big Hammond" and "a small Underwood;" and Arnold Maremont, who belonged to Babe's law-school study group.

"Do you know what 'dope sheeting' is?" Crowe asked Maremont.

"Yes, sir."

"Please explain."

"Well, in studying law, in preparing for examination, in preparing for comprehensive study, one must go over the lecture, after all the subject of law is taught primarily by studying cases and collaborating—"[41]

"One moment," the state's attorney said. Crowe spun around, threw one arm high in the air, and faced the defense table. "I would suggest Mr. Darrow listen to this."

Without hesitation, the Old Lion defused the Pirate's remark with sarcasm of his own, "I thought it was about the races, Bob."

The day's most interesting testimony came from a Kenwood chauffeur, Carl Ulvigh, who told the court he actually saw Dickie driving on Ellis Avenue at 4:30 on the afternoon of the murder.

"What kind of car was he in?" Crowe asked.

"I don't know, it was a dark-color car . . . a touring car."[42]

"And what about the curtains?"

"There were curtains all around it."

"Was there anybody with Richard Loeb?"

"Yes, sir."

"Who was with him?"

"I don't know," the chauffeur replied.

"Where was Richard Loeb sitting in the car?"

"He was sitting behind the wheel."

"Driving?" Crowe asked.

"Yes."

"And where was the other man?"

"He was on the side of him."

Ulvigh then said that he and Dickie waved to each other.

Babe sat up in his chair and whispered in Darrow's ear, "That man is not telling the truth, or he is badly mistaken."

Darrow turned to talk to his client while Ulvigh's testimony continued.

"What do you mean?" Darrow asked.

"We were not there at the time, and the car did not have the curtains up," Babe said. "We did not pass anybody and wave to them. Let me cross-examine him, Mr. Darrow, and I will show the court he is mistaken."

Babe then said the same thing to Benjamin Bachrach. When Crowe completed his direct, Bachrach cross-examined the chauffeur, with Babe handing his attorney questions on note cards. Babe seemed delighted in the exercise, although Bachrach's questioning didn't alter Ulvigh's testimony—that it was Dickie, not Babe, who drove the killing car on the afternoon of May 21.

Crowe's parade of witnesses continued on Friday. "So unnecessary," Darrow told the press. The *Tribune* seemed to agree: "From various arcs of the circle of experience they came. But with the unanimity of a Greek chorus, they chanted an antiphonal echo to Prosecutor Crowe's demand: 'Hang the boys.'"

Three detectives who played major roles in the case had their day in court. And Babe was on their minds.

"Well, we got talking the case over," said Sergeant William Crot. "He (Leopold) stated that he had originally planned that the State's Attorney wouldn't have him. He said, 'I had a plan where I would have twelve headache powders in a box of some harmless nature, and one of them would be strychnine which would be the same color. If I expected to be picked up, and afterwards if it looked bad for me, I was going to take one of these powders. I thought I might be able to talk myself away again, and if I were searched and these things were found on me, it probably would be looked on with suspicion.' Then we go talking about the night we were at his house looking for the glasses. He said, 'If I knew that Loeb was going to peach, I could have killed myself that night, and while I was doing it, I could have took a couple of coppers.' I said, 'Why a couple of coppers.' He said, 'What is the difference?'"[43]

"Why did he say that?" Crowe asked.

"He was referring to a weapon that was in his room, in the upper left hand drawer, a magazine gun."

Sergeant Frank Johnson then took the stand. He talked about part of the reenactment when Babe talked about the extensive newspaper coverage.

"Nathan said to me, 'I can't understand why the papers say this is such an atrocious murder.' I said, 'Why was it necessary you had to kill him?' He said, 'Well, he knew Dick Loeb, and we couldn't afford to take a chance of having him come back and say it was Dick.' I said, 'He didn't know you?' He said, 'Well, I live in the neighborhood; it is just a question of time before he would see me.'"

Sergeant James Gortland testified that he also asked Babe about the motive.

"He says, 'Well, adventure and money, but you don't think I am entirely a fool. Don't you think I am entitled to reserve something for my defense?' I said, 'What do you think your defense will be?' He said, 'That will depend on the wishes of my father and my lawyers. Of course, if they [father and lawyers] wish me to hang, I will plead not guilty, and the jury will hang me, or I will plead guilty before a friendly judge and get life imprisonment. I have lots of things I want to work at which would be of benefit to the world; also there is the insanity plea.' Then I asked him whether he was sorry for Robert Franks, and he said, 'Not at all.' I asked him if he was sorry for the Franks people, and he said, 'I don't give a damn if they croak this minute.'"[44]

Gortland went on to tell an angry courtroom that Babe also told him, "'Up to the age of eight, conscience was drilled into me, but after the age of eight I drilled that conscience out. Murder in my code is not a crime; my crime was in getting caught.'"

Judge Caverly, his chin resting on the palm of his hand, listened intently and took notes.

Later that evening, Ty Krum visited Dickie and Babe, as he did most every night during their stay at the Cook County Jail.

Babe didn't seem upset about today's events in court, including Gortland's testimony. "As far as being remorseful," he told Krum, "I can't see it. Life is what we make it, and I appear to have made mine what it is today. That's my lookout and nobody else's."

Krum then made his way to Dickie's cell, where the young killer was reading the afternoon papers.

"Dickie, the people on the outside are thinking you are about the coldest-blooded mortal in the world because of the way you are acting in court," the reporter said. "You laugh and josh and appear to be having a good time."[45]

Dickie put down his newspaper and smiled. "Well, what do they want me to do?"

"I don't know, I suppose they want you to act natural."

"That's exactly what I am doing. I sit in the courtroom and watch the play as it progresses. When the crowd laughs, I laugh. When it is time to be serious, I am that way. I am a spectator, you know, and like to feel myself as one."

Dick stood up and walked to the bars and looked Krum straight in the eyes. "You can tell the people on the outside that there is no faking or pretending. I have watched you in the courtroom across the table, and you laugh, smile, yawn, look bored, and all the other things. Why should I do different?"

Krum had no answer.

## ON ACCOUNT OF YOUTH

For three days, Jacob Franks had sat a few feet from his son's killers. He watched eighty state witnesses, including his wife, take the stand. He heard eighty stories tying Dickie and Babe to Bobby's murder. He saw strangers handle his boy's clothing, part of the state's attorney's mountain of evidence. He said nothing as a court reporter read the lengthy confessions.

As Robert Crowe neared the end of his case, Franks gave a statement to a reporter.

"I have been watching these two boys for the last three days, and they have got me utterly baffled," he told a newsman during a brief recess. "I thought I was a pretty good judge of human nature during my long experience, but I find I have encountered an insolvable problem. It is impossible for me to believe as I sit here and watch these boys, that they're the ones who killed my child. They are so gentle mannered and refined looking."[46]

A few feet away, Nathan Leopold Sr. talked with his oldest son, Foreman. They smiled at Babe each time he made eye contact with them. Uncle Jacob Loeb and Dickie's oldest brother, Allan, represented the Loeb family. At the end of each day, Allan would call his mother in Charlevoix, Michigan, where she tended to her ailing husband.

On Wednesday, July 30, Crowe rested his case. But the state's attorney's meticulous prosecution was not the talk of Chicagoans. They were still devouring the portions of the findings of Drs. Bowman and Hulbert, that had splashed with precise timing across Monday's front pages of the morning editions of the *Tribune* and *Herald and Examiner*. Someone stole—or leaked—the document from Clarence Darrow's office. Darrow then gave it to other newspapers. He also sent a copy to the state's attorney. Crowe was livid. He believed Drs. Bowman and Hulbert *implied* that the boys were insane but never specifically and directly stated so in writing. Crowe knew Darrow would take the same tact in the courtroom—hint that the boys were insane but never use the word.

People changed their perception of the killers after the report hit the papers. No longer did they see the arrogant Babe as the leader. Now it was Dickie. They learned all the details: his boyhood obsession with detective stories, his fantasies as the Master Criminal, his nightly picturizations, his shadowing, and his compact with Babe—"For Robert's Sake." They saw Babe under Dickie's control, as the Slave in Babe's King-Slave fantasy. They read about the boys' families, their strange governesses, and their many criminal activities, including Dickie's elaborate plan to kidnap a child.

It was more than Crowe wanted the public to know. But for Darrow, it was a public-relations victory. The teenagers were not normal, people agreed after reading their life stories. And never had been normal. It was the Old Lion's opening assault—albeit a clever one—on the Pirate's mountain of evidence.

"I am the superintendent of St. Elizabeth's hospital in Washington, a government hospital for the care of the insane from the army—"[47]

"Just a minute," the state's attorney roared. "I object to that, if Your Honor please?"

"Why?" Judge Caverly asked.

"It is incompetent, irrelevant, and immaterial."

"Why?" Judge Caverly asked again.

Robert Crowe wasn't about to allow Dr. William Alanson White—Clarence Darrow's first witness—to set the stage for a defense that would lean toward insanity. Crowe had read the Bowman-Hulbert report. He knew that Darrow's alienists would try to show that the defendants' abnormal childhoods led them to a life of crime. He wasn't about to let Darrow take the focus away from the brutality of the murder.

"The purpose of it would be to lay a foundation for him to testify as an expert on the question of sanity or insanity of the defendants,"

Crowe said. "On a plea of guilty Your Honor has no right to go into that question. As soon as it appears in the trial, it is Your Honor's duty to call a jury."[48]

Caverly overruled Crowe, but Crowe would not sit down. His voice shot up a few octaves and his Irish face blushed with anger.

"In other words, if Your Honor at the conclusion of this trial, after having gone into the sanity proposition, should sentence these boys to hang, your judgment would not be worth the paper it was written on. The Supreme Court would set it aside. If you enter a judgment that was satisfactory to the defendants, they wouldn't have to appeal, and the State has no right to appeal. In other words, the State cannot appeal from any order Your Honor enters. The defendants have a right to appeal from all orders. I would have to confess error in the Supreme Court if Your Honor hung these men after hearing evidence of insanity."

Crowe took a deep breath, regained his composure, and walked toward Darrow.

"What is the defense trying to do here? Are they trying to avoid a trial upon a plea of not guilty with defendants before twelve men that would hang them, and trying to produce a situation where they can get a trial before one man that they think won't hang them?"

"The defense," Caverly answered, "hasn't said they are going to put on alienists to show that these men are insane, and I don't think they are going to attempt to show that they are insane."

"Well, then what is the evidence for, what are they going to show?"

"You will have to listen to it. They have said they are going to put evidence on in mitigation of the crime," Caverly said. He then made it clear that there are "degrees of punishment in a murder case and the punishment that a court metes out must be guided by the evidence introduced."

But Crowe wasn't finished.

"But here is a cold-blooded murder, without a defense in fact, and they attempt, on a plea of guilty, to introduce an insanity defense before Your Honor, and the statute says that is a matter for a jury."

"Has anybody said that they are going to introduce an insanity defense?" Caverly asked.

"Well, what is the purpose of putting on expert on the stand?"

Caverly was losing his patience with Crowe.

"The state of mind of one who is in possession of his ordinary faculties, without any mental disease, I have a right to know that, and that doesn't excuse him from the offense he has committed. . . . Now if he is affected by mental disease, then he is insane. If that is true, then this court might, and probably would, insist that the defendants withdraw their plea of guilty and enter a plea of not guilty, so that a jury could pass on the question of his sanity or not."

Walter Bachrach then stood up.

"We are not interested in this inquiry, in the legal question of insanity. That is a question which relates solely to the knowledge of the accused as to right and wrong and the ability to choose between the two. But what we propose to show here is a medical condition, which has absolutely no relation to the legal question presented in an insanity issue, and I have the authorities here."

Caverly then asked Bachrach and Crowe to sit down. He said both sides could present legal arguments. For the rest of Wednesday afternoon, all day Thursday and into Friday, they read from law books. Thomas Marshall argued for the state, while Walter Bachrach presented cases to support the defense. But it was impossible to find on-point legal precedent for testimony from alienists as a mitigating defense in a murder case. This historic hearing would set the precedent for the entire nation.

Late Thursday, Darrow had his chance. The Old Lion knew weary courtroom spectators were bored from listening to complicated legal arguments. But he was only interested in one man—Judge Caverly. If Darrow was to save the lives of his clients, he needed to deliver a strong argument of his own.

"Is youth a mitigating circumstance?" he asked. "Well, we have all been young, and we know that fantasies and vagaries haunt the daily live of a child. We know the dream world we live in. We know that nothing is real. We know the lack of appreciation. We know the condition of the mind of a child. And has the court a right to consider age a mitigating circumstance, and if so, why?

"Here are two boys who are minors. The law would forbid them making contracts, forbid them marrying without the consent of their parents, wouldn't permit them to vote, why? Because they haven't that judgment that only comes with years. Because they are not fully responsible."

Darrow walked slowly toward the boys. They looked up at him, so refined, so innocent-looking. No longer did their faces carry sarcastic smiles. Darrow continued:

"The reason that youth would be a mitigating circumstance is on account of the mind, nothing else, the lack of judgment, the lack of discrimination, nothing else. I don't know. I cannot understand the glib, light-hearted carelessness of lawyers who talk of hanging these two young boys as if they were talking of a holiday or visiting the races.

"I have never seen a more deliberate effort to turn the human beings of a community into ravening wolves as has been made in this case and to take advantage of anything that they might get every mind that has to do with it into a state of hatred against these boys."

Darrow then spun a personal tale, one that presented a theme of compassion, something missing in a sweltering city anxious to hang two teenage boys. He faced the visitors' gallery and wiped the sweat from his brow. He spoke gently, carefully, the way one would talk when remembering a sad story.

"About seven or eight years ago, a poor boy named Pettit, whom I was asked by some charitable organization to defend, was charged with murder in this court. He was running a delivery wagon. He delivered some goods to a house where there was a baby and a mother, and he found a bread knife on the table and he carved up the baby and the mother. He killed them both, and I was asked to defend him, and I did. And I did what I did here. I entered a plea of guilty, trusting myself to the mercy of the court which could see and determine and understand. And the judge on that case was Judge Barrett, who was once a partner of Mr. Crowe.

"I called in that case his [the boy's] teacher to show how his mental condition on a plea of guilty, and I brought in his marks at school to show that he was backward, and I called alienists who, for the sake of mercy, gave me their time as I did mine, to prove the condition of that poor boy's mind.

"Judge Barrett said he wouldn't hang him. He said he was sorry to send him to the penitentiary, but there was no other place to send him, that he was eight or nine years old. We had a full hearing in court where the boy's mind was looked into.

"And yet Mr. Marshall would have this court to believe that that was no business of the court, and not even a mitigating circumstance that he was a half-wit, that he had lived in darkness, surrounded by visions and dreams and knew nothing of life, the court couldn't consider it. But we would have a holiday for the benefit of the state's attorney and hang him. He should have made his argument in Central Africa somewhere, and not in Chicago."

In closing, Darrow appealed directly to Caverly, saying the judge "will carefully, patiently, and humanely listen to the evidence in this case, and trusting on account of our case, on account of the youth, on account of the mental condition, that we may save their lives, and we have never asked for more."

On Friday morning, Crowe made one final try.

"I don't care by what name Mr. Darrow and his alienists call it, the legal effect, and the effect it has upon the minds of the layman, is that it is a defense of insanity. Under the law, you have no right to hear that defense, any more than you would have a right to hear an alibi. A judgment entered after evidence of insanity is presented to your court is a nullity. . . . I insist, under the authorities, under the rules of logic and reason, that this evidence be excluded."

To the relief of everyone in the hot courtroom, Caverly then stated that he was ready to announce his decision of whether Darrow's alienists should be allowed to testify on the condition of the boys' minds. He would allow "evidence in mitigation, as well as evidence in aggravation."

"The court will hear it and give it such weight as it's entitled to," he ruled.

Caverly then looked over his eyeglasses at Crowe. "The motion of the state—was that your motion?" he asked.

"It was an objection," Crowe snapped.

"The objection to the witness is overruled, and the witness may proceed."

Dr. White, who had remained in the witness chair during the two days of arguments, smiled.

## THREE WISE MEN

At last, Dr. White was free to speak. A practicing alienist for thirty-one years, William White's jet-black hair gave him an authoritative look, one befitting the president of the American Psychiatric Association.

"The inner mental life," he told Walter Bachrach, "signifies the real fundamental needs and aspirations and hopes and wishes of the individual. They give us the real story of what that individual seeks in life."

Inner mental life. This is the road Darrow would take in defending the boy killers. And in a subtle attempt to humanize them, the defense attorneys had instructed Dr. White to refer to the defendants by the nicknames their families called them—Dickie and Babe.

"Dickie lied about all sorts of things," Dr. White said. "He lied to Babe Leopold, his comrade, about his attendance in college. While his marks were on the whole pretty good, he made them a great deal better, so he was continually building up all sorts of artificial situations until he himself says that he found it difficult to distinguish between what was true and what was not true."[49]

Crowe jumped to his feet. "Now, just a minute . . . if what the doctor says is true, he [Dickie] could not distinguish between true and untrue, that means he could not distinguish between right and wrong. Truth is right, the other is wrong. I submit we are getting now clearly into an insanity hearing, and I suggest that a jury be impaneled."

"Motion denied," Caverly said. "You may precede, Doctor."

The subject shifted to Dickie's nightly picturizations.

"He himself was often being abused and beaten," Dr. White said. "He would see people appearing at him through the bars and commenting upon the fact that he was a great criminal, looking upon him with curiosity. These people were often times young girls."

Dr. White told the court that Dickie still had fantasies in his jail cell, just like when he was a child and talking to his teddy bear, "You know, Teddy," and then the fantasies would unfold.

Regarding the killing, Dr. White said that from Dickie's perspective, the motive was to commit a perfect crime. "He is the master criminal mind and wanted to do a great job, wanted to commit a crime that would be perfect, that would be thoroughly and completely planned in all details, that would baffle the police, that would be an object of great concern in the immediate community, that would leave no clues, that would be an intellectual feat to accomplish."

As the witness spoke, the girls in the visitors' gallery moved about, trying to get a good look at Dickie, who sat with his legs crossed and with no expression on his face.

"The boy remains childlike, an infantile level of development," Dr. White said. Emotionally, Dickie and Babe were mere boys—"between five and seven years of age." About Dickie, Dr. White said, "He cannot distinguish between the real world as it is and the fantasy world which has accomplished such enormous proportions within him. He has lost the ability to differentiate and to draw clear lines, to tell where his is."

Dr. White's testimony then focused on Babe.

"He developed in early life a feeling that he himself was more or less set apart from others and that he differed from others in the direction of his superiority. Very early in life he developed a feeling of antagonism toward tender emotions . . . because they made him suffer." Latter in life, Dr. White explained, this attitude turned into "a hedonistic philosophy, a philosophy wholly of pleasure and pain, a philosophy of complete and absolute selfishness, a philosophy of mechanism in which there is no bad, where everything is explained wholly and solely and satisfactory upon the mechanistic property."

Dr. White said he asked Babe what he would do if the case went against him, if he was sentenced to be executed.

"He would," the doctor said, "write down about ten of the world riddles, put them in a safe deposit vault, and appoint a commission of scientists who, after his death, would attempt to get in contact with him for the purpose of seeing whether he could solve the world riddles. He also would write what he called his apologia, which would demonstrate that he went to his end consistently and not as perhaps as some people expect."

To understand the crime, Dr. White said, one needed to understand the relationship between the two killers. Dickie needed an audience. In his fantasies, his criminal gang was his audience. In reality, Babe played the role. "I cannot see how Babe would have entered into it at all alone because he did not have criminalistic tendencies in any sense as Dickie did, and I don't think Dickie would have ever functioned to this extent all by himself. So these two boys, with their peculiarly interdigited personalities, came into this emotional compact with the Franks homicide as a result."

In cross-examining Dr. White, the state's attorney refocused the subject—away from the mental condition of the boys to the actual crime.

"Now, Doctor," Robert Crowe asked, "When you were talking to Nathan Leopold Jr., did you ask him who actually struck the blows that killed Robert Franks?"

"No, I don't think I did."

"Have you an opinion as to who killed Robert Franks?"

"Yes. I believe Dickie did it."

Flappers in the back of the courtroom watched in disbelief, while Jacob Loeb and Allan Loeb glared at the witness. It was the first time someone other than Babe had pointed the finger at Dickie. The fresh-face boy who could "charm the birds out of the trees" leaned forward in his chair but said nothing.

A "most strange and pathological relationship." The words of Dr. William Healy, the second of Darrow's "Three Wise Men from the East," led to the most sensational testimony of the trial. The Boston alienist, who specialized in mental disturbances in adolescents, centered his testimony on Dickie and Babe's friendship. Dr. Healy called it "an incredibly absurd childish compact that bound them, which bears out in Leopold's case, particularly the thread and idea of his fantasy life." For Dickie, Dr. Healy said the association with Babe gave him "someone who could carry out his criminalistic imaging and conscious ideas."

On cross-examination, Crowe asked for details. He wanted Healy to explain this "absurd childish compact."

"I am perfectly willing to tell it in chambers, but it is not a matter to be told here," the doctor said.[50]

Judge Caverly motioned for the attorneys to step up to the bench. A few reporters followed and stood behind Darrow and the Bachrach brothers, but Caverly ordered them to go back to their seats. "This will not go to the papers," he said.

Dickie and Babe could only watch from their chairs. Many people stood in an attempt to hear the hushed conversation. The judge leaned forward toward the cluster of lawyers, and the court reporter began to transcribe Dr. Healy's whispers:

"Leopold would have the privilege of inserting his penis between Loeb's legs at special dates. At one time it was to be three times in two months—if they continued the criminalistic activities together."

Crowe asked when they began this compact.

"Their criminalistic ideas began on the same day when they began cheating at bridge. It was the first time in a [train] berth, and it was when Leopold had this first experience with his penis between Loeb's legs. Then he found it gave him more pleasure than anything else he had ever done. To go on further with this, even in jail here, a look at Loeb's body or his touch upon his shoulder thrills him, so he says, immeasurably."

Like kids trying to listen in on an adult conversation, a couple of reporters quietly made their way to the bench. They crouched down behind the defense attorneys and scribbled in their notebooks. When Caverly noticed them, he slammed down his gavel. "Gentlemen, will you go sit down, you newspapermen. Take your seats. This should not be published."

After Dr. Healy concluded his testimony "in chambers," the attorneys returned to their seats, and the trial resumed in open court. Dr. Healy, turning the pages of a large notebook he held on his lap, read some of Babe's quotes from their private discussions:

"I have reveled in the fact that I have no qualms of conscience."

"I have tried to kill affection for years."

"Making up my mind to commit murder was practically like making up my mind whether or not I'd eat pie for supper. The question was, 'Will it give me pleasure?'"

Dr. Healy then interpreted Babe's comments, "There seems to be profound disorder of judgment as shown in the contradiction of ideas and impulses. With all the self-love there was no normal self-regard. A real superiority of normal judgment would not have taken such an extraordinary chance of ending his career."

The witness ended his analysis of Babe by outlining his abnormal behavior: mixing fantasy and reality; believing he is superior; and entering into a "thoroughly childish and absurd compact" that brought him danger. "On account of all this," Dr. Healy said, "in my opinion, he is thoroughly unbalanced in his mental life, or, to use another term, mentally diseased."

"But is he insane?" Crowe asked during his cross-examination.

"I don't think anything about it," Dr. Healy answered.

"He is not insane. He is sane?"

"I did not use the word sane or insane. I have not thought about it."

Dr. Healy would not be tied down to a legal term like "insanity." He kept his composure and continued, "The crime is possible only because Leopold had these abnormal mental trends with the typical feelings and ideas of a paranoid personality. He needed these feelings and ideas supplemented by what Loeb could give him. There is no reason why he should not commit the crime, with his diseased notions. Anything he wanted to do was right, even kidnapping and murder. . . . In other words, he had established personality before he met Loeb, but probably his activities would have taken other directions except for this chance association."

Regarding Babe's accomplice, Dr. Healy described a cold, calculating criminal. "He seems incapable of viewing his criminal acts with anything like a natural feeling." Dr. Healy called Dickie "charming, very friendly, and well-mannered, but because of his dual personality he is an extensive liar, unscrupulous, unfair, ungrateful, and disloyal in many social relationships."

Dr. Bernard Glueck, medical advisor to the state penitentiary in New York, took the witness stand the next morning, Wednesday, August 6, the start of another hot and steamy day. A small, electric fan on Judge Caverly's desk blew warm air in Dr. Glueck's face as he answered questions from Benjamin Bachrach.

"Did Loeb say who it was that struck the blow on the head of Robert Franks with a chisel?"

"He told me all the details of the crime, including the fact that he struck the blow."[51]

Unlike Drs. White and Healy, Dr. Glueck actually said Dickie had told him he delivered the death blows. He called Dickie "a hardened criminal" but different than other murderers he has known. Most of them, the doctor said, exhibited a crude persona.

"But Dickie is affable and polite," Dr. White said. "As I see them coming in and going from the courtroom, and I see them sitting there in their seats, it impresses me as though they were attending a college play of some sort. I discussed with Loeb the possibility of terminating his life by hanging, and he said in a matter-of-fact way, 'Well, it's too bad a fellow won't be able to read about it in the newspapers.'"

Dr. Glueck's attention then turned to Babe. "He told me of his attitude toward Dickie and how completely he had put himself in the role of slave in connection with him. He said, 'I can illustrate it to you by saying that I felt myself less than dust beneath his feet,' quoting from one of the poems of Lawrence Hope. He told me of his object devotion to Loeb, saying that he was jealous of the food and drink that Loeb took, because he could not come as close to him as the food and drink."

## INJUDICIAL AGENCIES

Throughout the trial, Darrow allowed newspapermen free access to his clients in their jail cells. He hoped the reporters, many of whom were young, would paint a humane picture of the teenage killers if they got to know them on a personal level.

For the press outside Chicago, though, it was a different story.

As Darrow's alienists presented evidence in mitigation, the *Tribune* carried an editorial from the *Montreal Herald* that angered the defense team:

### Babe and Dickie

"I will not hear evidence as to the sanity of the accused but certainly I shall hear evidence as to their mental state."

The foregoing is an extract from newspaper reports of the remarks of the presiding justice in the fiasco being staged in Chicago at the so-called trial of two of the most depraved, conceited, ill-mannered, filthy, hell-begotten monstrosities modern society has produced. The performance is, we believe, being enacted in a place where criminals are supposed to face justice. But why not in a theater, or better on the stage of a cabaret restaurant, where those seeking amusement may have food, drink and dope as the desire comes to them.

The accused educated brutes are referred to in the court as "Babe" and "Dickie." These darlings merely murdered a little boy 14 years of age in the most loathsome manner, and proceeded to make fun of the distracted family of their victim. "Babe" and "Dickie," indeed, and why not?

It means also that the people of the United States are on trial; it means that democracy and republicanism are faced with the greatest danger of their existence. The elected of the people are no better and no worse than the people themselves.

We do not agree with the Ku Klux Klan, but we ask again what recourse have the minority? Is this democracy and if it is, and if "Dickie," "Babe," "Darrow" et al. are its fruits, then we join the illustrious company who ask is democracy safe for the world?[52]

"It's damn unfair," Darrow bellowed. "If the boys hang, the United States might well vote murder indictments against the unjudicial agencies, many of them far removed from Chief Justice John Caverly's courtroom, who are trying to 'fix' public opinion. It's not a question of sanity or insanity of the two defendants that is at issue. It's a question of the insanity of the methods by which certain forces are seeking to direct public opinion to blood, without permitting the world to consider impartially, the findings of certain alienists."

The *Daily Mail* of London, another injudicious agency, disagreed with Darrow:

> The monstrous depravity of Leopold and Loeb is causing their trial to be followed with horror-struck and unparalleled interest. The *Mail* criticizes the "mobilization of a procession pf psycho-analysts" endeavoring to save the accused from the proper penalty on the convenient plea of insanity. The danger to the public in this dubious science here is clearly shown.[53]

### SHEIKS AND SHEBAS

Heavy, gray clouds hung over the Criminal Courts Building on Thursday, August 7. But a youthful splash of style brightened the long lines of the morbidly curious. Young men—with center-parted, patent-leather hair and bow ties and white "Oxford bags"—escorted flappers in colorful rain slickers, short skirts, turned-down stockings, and peek-a-boo hats.

It was Sheiks and Shebas Day at the hearing. The Jazz Age sophisticates took their turns in the witness chair, part of Darrow's plan to show the abnormal behavior of their chums, Dickie and Babe.

Arnold Maremont, Babe's law-school colleague, said Babe had no qualms about murder. "In fact, he made the statement one afternoon that if it gave him pleasure to go out and murder someone, it would be perfectly all right in his philosophy to go out and murder a person, provided, of course, he were not apprehended for the murder and forced to suffer punishment."[54]

John Abt, also a U. of C. law student, said Babe's philosophy dictated that "pleasure was the sole emblem of conduct." Abt also talked about Babe's loyalty to his friends. "He would have no remorse in throwing a friend over, no gratitude or friendship with the one exception of a boy he regarded in the light of a superman, a boy who could do anything until he got caught. As soon as he made a mistake and was caught he would cease to be a superman and would return to the level of ordinary mortals, on the same status as other friends."[55]

Lorraine Nathan, one of Dickie's girlfriends, discussed Dickie's immature behavior during the past several months, including reckless driving and stealing. "We had quarrels," she said. "I told him I found such a change in him that our relationship could not be anything else but brother and sister, and he resented that."[56]

Theodore Shimberg, a U. of C. student, said it was hard to know the real Dickie. "It seemed his actions most of the time were so childish, and we were in the habit of seeing him drunk a great deal, that there were so many times we could not tell whether the boy was drunk or sober."

## DR. HULBERT

He took the witness stand on Friday, August 8, with a large, indexed notebook and a fat portfolio filled with X-ray pictures and photographs. Dr. H. S. Hulbert was ready to talk physiology, neurology, and psychology.

Dr. Hulbert first presented an X-ray image of Dickie's skull. He pointed out a saddle-shaped region and said, "You will notice there is no shadow of the pineal gland in this boy."

Walter Bachrach asked him to explain.

"It indicates the pineal gland in Richard Loeb is not calcified."[57]

"Is that a normal condition in a boy or young man of eighteen or nineteen?" Bachrach asked.

"It should not be calcified at this age, and it is not calcified in this case."

Robert Crowe interrupted, "So, it is normal, Doctor?"

"It should calcify at about [age] 30," Dr. Hulbert said.

"So, this is normal?" Crowe asked.

"Yes."

Dr. Hulbert said he would only give the abnormal results of Dickie's physical and neurological exams.

"No," Crowe said sarcastically, "give them all to us, because I would like to know whether he is 95 percent normal or not."

For the next hour, the courtroom became a science classroom. Dr. Hulbert went into great detail about blood pressure, sugar tolerance, and blood chemistry. "There were fifty-six volumes percent of carbon dioxide in the blood, the normal value being sixty-five percent."

"That throws considerable light on this murder, does it not?" Crowe said.

Dr. Hulbert said Dickie's basal metabolism was "minus seventeen per cent which is abnormally low."

"What does such an abnormally low basal metabolism result signify in an individual?" Bachrach asked.

"A disorder of the endocrine glands and the sympathetic nervous system," the witness answered. "It is one phase of medical evidence to indicate that there is such a disease of the endocrines and sympathetic nervous system.

[The affect of the endocrine glands on a person's mental condition was a new medical theory in 1924. An abnormality in these glands, some doctors believed, affected the brain and caused an abnormal mental condition.]

"My opinion is that the man is not normal physically or mentally, and there is a close relation between his physical abnormalities, largely of the endocrine system, and his mental condition. Intellectually, he far excels the average boy of his age. But his emotional reactions are those—I estimate because I cannot measure—of a boy about nine or ten, certainly less than a boy of puberty. And in the matter of judgment, he is childish. The discrepancy between his judgment and his emotions on the one hand and his intellectual attainment on the other is a greater discrepancy than we find in normal persons. And therefore, I am forced to conclude that he is mentally diseased."

Dr. Hulbert related his findings on Babe, beginning with his King-Slave fantasy. "This fantasy had set the pattern of his ambition in conscious life to be the perfect slave of the most perfect person he could find. He found such a person, he felt, in Richard Loeb. He wanted to be Loeb's perfect slave in any way Loeb should request, even to the point of kidnapping and murder or anything else."

Regarding the Franks crime, Dr. Hulbert said Babe's motive was to please Dickie. "It was a desire on the part of Richard Loeb to commit a perfect crime, and a desire on his [Babe's] to do whatever Richard Loeb wanted him to do."

Dr. Hulbert physiologically dissected Babe: "hair somewhat prominent, curvature of the spine, abdomen protrudes, round shouldered, flatfooted, a disorder of the nervous control of the blood vessels."

Like Dickie, Babe's basal-metabolism test scored very low. And the X-ray pictures of his skull revealed what Dr. Hulbert called "the most pathology." His pineal gland was calcified, Dr. Hulbert said, and the endocrine-gland disorder was responsible for the following mental findings: "His precocious mental development, his rapid advance through school, and his ease of learning. The fact that the cruel instincts show but little inhibition is of endocrine origin. That he fatigues if he overexerts himself and is nonaggressive, the prey of hidden fears, neurotic and unmoral, at the same time keen and witty, is of endocrine origin. The early development and strength of his sex urge is obviously of endocrine origin."

Darrow rested his case on the afternoon of Tuesday, August 12. His "Three Wise Men from the East" had done their jobs well. They gave

Judge Caverly an opportunity to consider Dickie and Babe in a more compassionate light, a humane one. The presentation of physiological and psychological evidence showed the defendants as vulnerable boys who suffered from mentally abnormal childhoods. And the newspapers, in edition after edition, brought this new psychology into people's homes. Dickie Loeb and Babe Leopold, two pampered sons of millionaires who lived upholstered lives, didn't kill just for a thrill, the papers reported. It was abnormal childhoods that led them to the crime. The public now saw the boys as object lessons for raising children. No longer was the focus on the victim, Bobby Franks.

But Robert Crowe would have none of it. He was furious at Darrow's attempt to make the killers appear as pregnable kids. The brutality of the crime—and its young victim—became lost in all the psychoanalysis. Fighting Bob would try to refocus the hearing with his own alienists.

## CROWE'S REBUTTAL

They called themselves "practical psychologists." It was up to them to punch holes in the theories of "mentally diseased" offered by Darrow's alienists.

Dr. Hugh Patrick, a specialist on nervous and mental disorders, smiled broadly. A neatly trimmed mustache and high starched white collar have him a professorial appearance. Dr. Patrick, one of the doctors summoned by Robert Crowe, examined Dickie and Babe on June 1, after they reenacted the crime for the state's attorney and police. The doctors told Crowe they found "no evidence of mental disease."

John Sbarbaro asked Dr. Patrick why they had come to that conclusion.

"The reason for that opinion are these," the doctor said, "that unless we assume that every man who commits a deliberate cold-blooded, planned murder must be mentally diseased, there was no evidence of any mental disease in any of the communication or in any of the statements the boys made regarding it, or their earlier experiences. There was nothing in the examination to show it. There were no mental obliquities or peculiarities of the enormity of the deed which they committed."[58]

In a sarcastic attempt at trivializing the findings of the defense alienists, John Sbarbaro posed a detailed, hypothetical scenario to Dr. Patrick, "Now, Doctor, assume a hypothetical person who on examination disclosed the facts and circumstances that you have gained from your examination of Richard Loeb. And add these other facts that have been testified here.

"That he is immature in his sexual development; that he still has his baby teeth; that the growth of hair on the body is scanty, and he only requires to shave twice a week or three times a week; that he has had several fainting spells during his life; that he has tremors of the hands and tongue and enlarged inguinal glands; that his basal metabolism, when examined on one day, averaged minus seventeen percent. Have you an opinion whether such an individual was suffering from any mental disease on May 21, 1924?"

"I would answer the same—that I see no evidence of any mental disorder."

Next, Dr. Patrick minimized the importance of the Bowman-Hulbert Report. He said Babe's X-ray image that Dr. Hulbert said showed a calcified pineal gland probably was "brain sand that in a picture might look like the shadow of a calcified gland." And when Sbarbaro asked him to comment on other points outlined in the Bowman-Hulbert report, Dr. Patrick gave the same answer: "Trivial or well within the range of psychological health."

After Dr. Archibald Church testified that he found no mental disease in either defendant, Darrow stood to begin his cross-examination. He held a copy of the alienist's book, "Nervous and Mental Disorders," and quoting from it, said one of the fundamental rules for making a psychiatric examination is to "go to the patient as a physician."

Darrow walked slowly to the witness stand and asked loudly, "Did you go as a physician to these boys?"

"I did," Dr. Church said.

"To these boys?"

"Not as *their* physicians, but as *a* physician."

"As Mr. Crowe's physician," Darrow bellowed.

"No."

"You went to examine them for the sake of giving your testimony," Darrow shouted, "and if you could, to hang them. That's why you went there, was it not?"[59]

Crowe boomed out an objection. He rushed to the witness stand as his assistants barked out protests.

"Not at all," Dr. Church said to Darrow. But Caverly couldn't hear the answer amid all the yelling from Crowe's table.[60]

"Not at all," Dr. Church said again.

"I will strike out the '*could*,'" Darrow said.

But he had made his point, and it infuriated Crowe.

"I don't think Mr. Darrow should be permitted to ask a question, and then when he knows the answer is going to hurt him, ask to have it stricken out," he said as he walked up to Darrow.

Darrow threw out an arm as to brush aside Crowe and yelled, "Oh, what's the use of quibbling with me."

Fighting Bob refused to move. The two attorneys stood belly-to-belly, their arms waving about. A rush of blood painted Crowe's face bright red; Darrow's unruly hair covered one side of his face. The rush of words that followed were more about each other than the case at hand.

"I'm not quibbling with you," Crowe yelled, "but I insist—"

"Oh, don't worry," Darrow screamed. "I don't play tricks."

"Yes, and it's a lot of tricks you play."

The spectators leaned forward to get a good look at the attorneys, although few seemed to understand the reason for such a heated exchange. Finally, Judge Caverly leaned over the bench and restored order.

"We will suspend for five minutes, gentlemen, and when you come back, try and be a little calmer."

Before resting his case on August 19, Crowe called two more prominent Chicago alienists—Drs. Harold Singer and William Krohn—to attest to the mental fitness of the defendants. Both men called Dickie's and Babe's mental states "normal."

In cross-examining Dr. Singer, Darrow claimed that the state violated his clients' constitutional rights when they questioned the teenagers without giving them an opportunity to seek counsel. This prompted another war of words between Darrow and Crowe.

"I will confess," Crowe said, "that I violated a number of constitutional rights, and I intend to continue that as long as I am state's attorney. When a man is charged with a crime, I am not going to telephone him and ask him to hire a lawyer before I talk to him."

"Well," Darrow shot back, "I don't think in a well-organized, intelligent community, a man could be elected state's attorney under the statement that when a man is charged with a crime, the state's attorney would violate his constitutional rights. Now, maybe Judge Crowe can get away with it, but it doesn't speak well for this community if he can."

## THESE FIENDS, THESE MURDERERS

Jacob Franks sat in his customary chair, not far from the boys who killed his son. Wearing the strain of the past few months, Franks looked ghost-like in his black suit. He watched Thomas Marshall, on behalf of the state, read from a stack of law books in arguing that Dickie and Babe should be sent to the gallows. If Judge Caverly did not hang the boys, he said, then the executions of the past had been unjust.

Franks's ashen-gray face gave no clue whether he heard Marshall's words. He appeared to be drowning in his thoughts. Two months earlier, on June 22, a letter had arrived at his home demanding $8,000—or his daughter would be killed.[61] Like he had done twice before, he asked Sam Ettleson to go to the police. The extortion plan was the work of two brothers, ages nineteen and eleven. The younger boy eventually was arrested in the middle of the night when he climbed into a garbage dumpster and retrieved a decoy package of torn newspapers. And shortly after that, a gruesome symbol of death appeared at a house across the street from the Franks home. A human head, a pair of withered arms, and a single discolored leg—positioned in the shape of a pirate's skull and crossbones—were discovered on the front steps of a home down the street from the Loeb mansion. An envelope sat between the elbows of the severed arms; written on the envelope was "Chicago. City of Crime." Inside, a message: "If the court don't hang them, we will. K.K.K."[62]

On Wednesday, August 20, Joseph Savage—Crowe's youthful assistant—had been speaking for forty minutes, his booming voice recounting every detail of the crime: the planning, buying the acid, renting the car, driving around looking for a victim, luring Bobby Franks into the car, calling Mrs. Franks, the ransom letter.

"And here, Your Honor," Savage said, his face dripping with perspiration, "here we have a crime, cold-blooded and dastardly, committed without even giving the poor little victim a chance for his life, not even a fighting chance. This boy, fourteen years old, weighing eighty pounds—"[63]

"One hundred pounds," Darrow interrupted. He then winked at a nearby reporter. Dickie and Babe chuckled, while Savage leered at Darrow.

"This fourteen-year-old boy," Savage continued, "was seated in a car as he thought with friends. And then started to pull away . . . "

Savage approached the defendants and pointed at them.

" . . . one of these cold-blooded hands struck that poor boy four times over the head with a chisel. These fiends, these murderers . . . "

It was all too much for Jacob Franks. Tears covered his tired face as he left his seat and walked past his son's murderers. Dick and Babe looked down at the floor. They didn't watch Bobby's father leave the courtroom.

## PLEA

As a young man, Clarence Darrow learned to be an independent thinker, with little respect for the opinion of the crowd. It was his father, a visionary and dreamer, who taught him to question rather than accept. Doubt, Darrow believed, was the beginning of wisdom.[64]

On the afternoon of Friday, August 22, at age sixty-seven, the Old Lion, his weary face showing the strain of the summer, began his plea. His wisdom and his mistrust of the majority would be tested. Silence filled Judge Caverly's overflowing courtroom as Darrow approached the bench.

The opinion of the crowd. It was his first target of assault.

"Our anxiety over this case has not been due to the facts that are connected with this most unfortunate affair, but to the almost unheard of publicity it has received, to the fact that newspapers all over this country have been giving it space such as they have almost never been given to any case. The fact that day after day the people of Chicago have been regaled with stories of all sorts about it, until almost every person has formed an opinion.

"And when the public is interested and demands a punishment, no matter what the offense, great or small, it thinks of only one punishment, and that is death."

Darrow walked over to his defendants and urged the court to consider their young age.

"We are here with the lives of two boys imperiled, with the public aroused. For what? Because, unfortunately, the parents have money. Nothing else. I told Your Honor in the beginning that never had there been a case in Chicago, where on a plea of guilty a boy under twenty-one has been sentenced to death. I will raise that age and say, never has there been a case where a human being under the age of twenty-three has been sentenced to death. And, I think I am safe in saying, although I have not examined all the records and could not—but I think I am safe in saying—that never has there been such a case in the State of Illinois.

"And yet this court is urged, aye, threatened, that he must hang two boys contrary to precedents, contrary to the acts of every judge who ever held court in this state. Why? Tell me what the public necessity there is for this. Why need the state's attorney ask for something that never before has been demanded? Why need a judge be urged by every argument, moderate and immoderate, to hang two boys in the face of every precedent in Illinois and in the face of the progress of the last fifty years?"

He moved cautiously around the front of the courtroom, weaving between the defense table and the rows of chairs. He'd stop occasionally to wipe his forehead or to gaze out the windows, as if answers lay beyond the realm of the court. His long arms waved about as he talked, urging on his tired body. When he wanted to stress a particular point, he'd hook his thumbs in his galluses. This was his pose when he talked motive.

"We have sought to tell this court why he should not hang these boys. We have sought to tell this court, and to make this court believe, that they were diseased of the mind, and that they were of tender age. However, before I discuss that, I ought to say another word in reference to the question of motive in this case. If there was no motive, except the senseless act of immature boys, then of course there is taken from this case all of the feeling of deep guilt upon the part of the defendants.

"There was neither cruelty to the deceased, beyond taking his life—which is much—nor was there any depth of guilty and depravity on the parts of the defendants, for it was truly a motiveless act, without the slightest feeling of hatred or revenge, done by a couple of children for no sane reason. But Your Honor, we have gone further than that, and we have sought to show you, as I think we have, the condition of these boys' minds."

As the afternoon wore on, Darrow discussed his clients' mental states, "their diseased brains."

"How insane they are I care not, whether medically or legally. They did not reason; they could not reason; they committed the most foolish, most unprovoked, most purposeless, most causeless act any two boys ever committed, and they put themselves where the rope is dangling around their heads.

"There are not physicians enough in the world to convince any thoughtful, fair-minded man that these two boys are right. Was their act one of deliberation, of intellect, or were they driven by some force such as Dr. White and Dr. Glueck and Dr. Healy have told this court? There are only two theories: one is that their diseased brains drove them to it; the other is the old theory of possession by devils, and my friend Marshall could have read you books on that, too, but it has pretty well given up in Illinois.

"Why did they kill little Bobby Franks? Not for money, not for spite, not for hate. They killed him as they might kill a spider or a fly, for the experience. They killed him because they were made that way. Because somewhere in the infinite processes that go to the making up of the boy or the man something slipped, and those unfortunate lads sit here hated, despised, outcasts, with the community shouting for their blood."

On Saturday morning, Darrow revisited the afternoon of May 21, when the youngsters of the Harvard School filled the playgrounds and sidewalks of Kenwood.

"Without any excuse, without the slightest motive, not moved by passion or hatred, by nothing except the vague wanderings of children, they rented a machine, and about four o'clock in the afternoon started to find somebody to kill. For nothing. They went over to the Harvard School. Dick's little brother was there, on the playground. Dick went there himself in open daylight, known by all of them . . . and he looked over the little boys.

"Your Honor has been in these courts a long time; you have listened to murder cases before. Has any such case ever appeared here or in any of the books? Has it ever come to the human experience of any judge, or any lawyer, or any person of affairs? Never once. Ordinarily there would be no sort of question of the condition of these boys' minds. The question is raised only because their parents have money.

"They first picked out a little boy named Levinson, and Dick trailed him around. Now, of course, that is a hard story. It is a story that shocks one. A boy bent on killing, not knowing where he would go or who he would get, but seeking some victim. Here is a little boy, but the circumstances are not opportune, as so he fails to get him.

"As I think of that story of Dick tailing this little boy around, there comes to mind a picture of Dr. Krohn; for sixteen years going in and out of the courtrooms in this building and other buildings, trailing victims without regard to the name or sex or age or surroundings. But he had a motive, and his motive was cash, as I will show further. One was the mad act of a child; the other the cold, deliberate act of a man getting his living by dealing in blood.

"Dick abandons that lead. Dick and Nathan are in the car, and they see Bobby Franks on the street, and they call to get him in the car. It is about five o'clock, in the long summer days, on a thickly settled street, built up with homes, the houses of their friends and their companions known to everybody, automobiles appearing and disappearing, and they take him in the car—for nothing.

"If there had been a question of revenge, yes; if there had been a question of hate, where no one cares for his own fate, intent only on accomplishing his end, yes. But without any motive or any reason they picked up this little boy right on a populous street, where everybody could see, where eyes might be at every window as they pass by. They hit him over the head with a chisel and kill him, and go on about their business, driving this car within half a block of Loeb's home, within the same distance of Franks's home, drive it past the neighbors that they knew, in the open highway, in broad daylight. And still men will say that they have a bright intellect, and, as Dr. Krohn puts it, can orient themselves and reason as well as he can, possibly, and it is the sane act of sane men.

"I say again, whatever madness and hate and frenzy may do to the human mind, there is not a single person who reasons who can believe that one of these acts was the act of men, of brains that were not diseased. There is no other explanation for it."

Darrow had the complete attention of everyone in the courtroom as he dramatically described the ride to Indiana: "They stop at the fork in the road and leave little Bobby, soaked with blood, in the machine, and get their dinner, and eat it without an emotion or qualm."

Judge Caverly took notes as Darrow said, "There is not a sane thing in all of this from the beginning to the end. There was not a normal act in any of it, from its inception in a diseased brain, until today, when they sit here awaiting their doom."

As he talked, as he painstakingly moved about, making eye contact with most everyone—reporters, the judge, the state's attorney, the visitors gallery—people listened. And maybe they thought: One death is enough. Would the killing of two more youngsters bring Bobby Franks back to life? Tears covered many faces when Darrow said, "I can picture them, wakened in the gray light of morning, furnished a suit of clothes by the state, led to the scaffold, their feet tied, black caps drawn over their heads, stood on a trap door, the hangman pressing the spring, so that it gives way under them. I can see them fall through space—and—stopped by the rope around their necks."

Darrow positioned himself by the bench. He looked directly at Judge Caverly and asked, "Can you administer law without consideration? Can you administer what approaches justice without it? Can this court or any court administer justice by consciously turning his heart to stone and being half dead to all the finer instincts which move men? Without those instincts I wonder what would happen to the human race.

"If a man could judge a fellow in coldness without taking account of his own life, without taking account of what he knows of human life, without some understanding—how long would we be a race of real human beings? It has taken the world a long time for man to get even where he is today. If the law was administered without any feeling or sympathy or humanity or kindliness, we would begin our long, slow journey back to the jungle that was formerly our home."

"How did it happen?" Darrow asked Monday, August 25, when court resumed. He spent most of the morning answering his own question, beginning by describing the life history of Dickie and his state of mind at the time of the crime.

"Here was a boy at a tender age, placed in the hands of a governess, intellectual, vigorous, devoted, with a strong ambition for the welfare of this boy. He was pushed in his studies, as plants are forced in hothouses. He had no pleasures, such as a boy should have, except as they were gained by lying and cheating. Now, I am not criticizing the nurse. I suggest that some day Your Honor look at her picture. It explains her fully. Forceful, brooking no interference, she loved the boy, and her ambition was that he should reach the highest perfection. No time to pause, no time to stop from one book to another, no time to have those pleasures which a boy ought to have to create a normal life.

"And what happened? Your Honor, what would happen? Nothing strange or unusual. This nurse was with him all the time, except when he stole out at night, from two to fourteen years of age. He, scheming and planning as healthy boys would do, to get out from under her restraint. She, putting before him the best books, which children generally do not want; and he, when she was not looking, reading detective stories, which he devoured, story after story, in his young life. Of all this there can be no question. What is the result? Every story he read was a story of crime. We have a statute in this state, passed only last year, if I recall it, which forbids minors reading stories of crime. Why? There is only one reason. Because the legislature in its wisdom felt that it would produce criminal tendencies in the boys who read them. The legislature of this state has given its opinion and forbidden these boys to read these books. He read them day after day. He never stopped."

Darrow talked about money, how great wealth played a role. "We have grown to think that the misfortune is not having it. The great misfortune in this case is the money. That has destroyed their lives. That has fostered all these illusions. That has promoted this mad act. And, if Your Honor shall doom them to die, it will be because they are the sons of the rich."

During his forty-five years of practicing law, Darrow learned how to make a courtroom his altar. He moved closer to the large windows. And with his weary face and wrinkled suit washed in sunlight, he said, "When I was young, I thought as a child, I spoke as a child, I understood as a child, but now I have put off childish things, said the Psalmist twenty centuries ago. It is when these dreams of boyhood, these fantasies of youth still linger, and the growing boy is still a child—a child in emotion, a child in feeling, a child in hallucinations—that you can say that it is the dreams and the hallucinations of childhood that are responsible for this conduct.

"There is not an act in all this horrible tragedy that was not the act of a child, the act of a child wandering around in the morning of life, moved by the new feelings of a boy, moved by the uncontrolled impulses which his teaching was not strong enough to take care of, moved by the dreams and the hallucinations which haunt the brain of a child. I say, Your Honor, that it would be the height of cruelty, of injustice, of wrong and barbarism to visit the penalty upon this poor boy.

"Now, Your Honor, I want to speak of the other lad, Babe. Babe is somewhat older than Dick and is a boy of remarkable mind—away beyond his years. He is sort of a freak in this direction, as in others; a boy without emotions, a boy possessed pf philosophy, a boy obsessed of learning, busy every minute of his life."

It was the scornful teachings of the philosopher Nietzsche, Darrow said, that guided Babe. "At seventeen, at sixteen, at eighteen, while healthy boys were playing baseball or working on the farm, or doing odd jobs, he was reading Nietzsche, a boy who never should have seen it, at that early age. Babe was obsessed of it, and here are some of the things which Nietzsche taught.

"'Why so soft, oh, my brethren? Why so soft, so unresisting and yielding? Why is there so much disavowal and abnegation in your heart? Why is there so little fate in your looks? For all creators are hard, and it must seem blessedness upon you to press your hand upon millenniums and upon wax. This new table, oh, my brethren, I put over to you: Become hard. To be obsessed by moral consideration presupposed a very low grade of intellect. We should substitute for morality the will to our own end and consequently to the means to accomplish that.'"

Placing a hand on the judge's bench, Darrow looked directly into the eyes of Judge Caverly and asked, "Why should this boy's life be bound up with Frederick Nietzsche, who died thirty years ago, insane, in Germany? I don't know. I only know it is. I know that no man who ever wrote a line that I read failed to influence me to some extent. I know that every life I ever touched influenced me, and I influenced it, and that it is not given to me to unravel the infinite cause and say, 'This is I, and this is you.' I am responsible for so much; and you are responsible for so much. I know—I know that in the infinite universe everything has its place and that the smallest particle is part of all. Tell me that you can visit the wrath of fate and chance and life and eternity upon a nineteen-year-old boy. If you could, justice would be a travesty and mercy a fraud!"

Nearing the end of his plea, Darrow cleaned up some unfinished business—the testimony of James Gortland.

"He came into this court, the only witness who said that young Leopold told him that he might get into the hands of a friendly judge and succeed. Your Honor, that is a blow below the belt. There isn't a word of truth in that statement, as I can easily prove to Your Honor. It was carved out of the air, to awe and influence the court, and place him in a position where if he saved a life someone might be malicious enough to say that he was a friendly judge, and, if he took it, the fear might invade this community that he did not dare to be merciful."

Darrow said, standing next to his clients, "I do not know how much salvage there is in these two boys."

He looked exhausted, besieged by the enormity of his responsibility. After a short pause—either to collect his strength or to create drama—he placed a hand on Dickie's shoulder and continued.

"I hate to say it in their presence, but what is there to look forward to? I do not know, but what, Your Honor, would be merciful if you tied a rope around their necks and let them die—merciful to them but not merciful to civilization and not merciful to those who would be left behind. To spend the balance of their days in prison is mighty little to look forward to, if anything. Is it anything? They may have the hope that as the years roll around they might be released. I do not know. I do not know. I will be honest with this court as I have tried to be from the beginning. I know that these boys are not fit to be at large. I believe they will not be until they pass through the next stage of life, at forty-five or fifty. Whether they will be then, I cannot tell. I am sure of this; that I will not be here to help them. So far as I am concerned, it is over.

"I would not tell this court that I do not hope that some time, when life and age have changed their bodies, as it does, and has changed their emotions, as it does—that they may once more return to life. I would be the last person on earth to close the door of hope to any human being that lives and least of all to my clients. But what have they to look forward to? Nothing. And I think here of the stanza of Housman."

> Now hollow fire burns out to black,
> And lights are fluttering low:
> Square your shoulders, lift your pack
> And leave your friends and go.
> O never fear, lads, naught's to dread,
> Look not left nor right:
> In all the endless road you tread
> There's nothing but the night.

Walking up to the bench, Darrow apologized to Judge Caverly for the time he had taken. He stood before the entire courtroom, his heavy shoulders square, and poured out his emotions in one final, passionate plea.

"This case may not be as important as I think it is, and I am sure I do not need to tell this court or to tell my friends that I would fight just as hard for the poor as the rich. If I should succeed in saving these boys' lives and do nothing for the progress of the law, I should feel sad, indeed. If I can succeed, my greatest reward and my greatest hope will be that I have done something for the tens of thousands of other boys, for the countless unfortunates who must tread the same road in blind childhood that these poor boys have trod—that I have done something to help human understanding, to temper justice with mercy, to overcome hate with love.

"I was reading late night the aspiration of the old Persian poet, Omar Khayyam. It appealed to me as the highest that I can vision. I wish it in my heart, and I wish it was in the hearts of all."

> So I be written in the Book of Love,
> I do not care about that Book above.
> Erase my name or write it as you will,
> So I be written in the Book of Love.

## PIRATE

While Darrow traversed the courtroom strategically, with a passionate eloquence, Crowe stormed it. The Pirate's closing argument took no prisoners.

"As a public official selected by the people, charged with the duty of enforcing the laws of my country, I have no right to forgive those who violate their country's laws," he told Judge Caverly. "It is my duty to prosecute them. Your Honor has no right to forgive those who trespass against the State of Illinois."[65]

Crowe paused to wipe off his eyeglasses. In a mocking tone, he told of the "trip" he had been on during the past several weeks.

"I thought I was going to be kept in Chicago all summer trying this case, and that most of my time would be spent in the Criminal Courts Building. And I find I have been mistaken. I did come to Your Honor's courtroom five weeks ago, and after I was there a little while, Old Doc Yak—is that his name?—the man from Washington—oh, Dr. White. Dr. White took me by the hand and led me into the nursery of two poor, rich young boys, and he introduced me to a teddy bear. Then he told me some bedtime stories, and after I got through listening to them, he took me into the kindergarten, and he presented me to little Dickie and Babe, and he wanted to know if I had any objection to calling them that, and I said no, if he had no purpose.

"And after he had wandered between the nursery and the kindergarten for quite a while, I was taken in hand by the Bachrach brothers and taken to a psychopathic laboratory, and there I received quite a liberal education in mental diseases and particularly what certain doctors did not know about them."

Robert Lee, a *Tribune* reporter called Crowe "panther-like" as he stalked the courtroom.

"Call them babes, call them children? Why, from the evidence in this case they are as much entitled to the sympathy and mercy of this court as a couple of rattlesnakes, flushed with venom, coiled and ready to strike."

As he concluded his first day of closing arguments, Crowe walked toward the two defendants, raised a fist high in the air, and said, "I want to tell, you Your Honor, bearing in mind the testimony that was whispered in your ear, one of the motives in this case was a desire to satisfy natural lust. You have before you the coroner's report, and the coroner's physician says that when little Bobby Franks was examined, his rectum was distended that much—"

The defense table erupted. "Objection!" the Bachrachs screamed.

Crowe walked up to the bench. He waved his thumb and forefinger in the air. "The coroner's report said that he had a distended rectum, and from that fact and the fact that the pants were taken off and the fact that they are perverts, I have a right to argue that they committed an act of perversion."

Judge Caverly ordered the women out of the courtroom. But most of them stayed in their seats. "Now, I want you to leave. If you do not, I will have the bailiffs escort you into the hallway." When several flappers in the visitors' gallery refused, the judge barked, "Why, why do you persist in staying here and listening to such rot?"

The defense attorneys then presented the coroner's report, which stated that although the rectum was distended, there was no evidence of perversion.

But the Pirate had made his point.

The next day Crowe attacked the Bowman-Hulbert report, dissecting page after page.

"Dr. Hulbert and Dr. Bowman said that [Dickie's] fantasies usually occur a half hour before he goes to sleep. That is the time Your Honor and I and everybody else fantasizes. When we get into bed, we dream dreams of what we are going to accomplish, and we scheme and plan, and that is exactly what Dickie Loeb did. And all this other stuff that we have been regaled with is perjury, pure and simple; perjury of a purpose. From Philip Drunk to Philip Sober, from the lying alienists on the stand to a report made by the alienists that they did not think would come to light."

Pointing to Dickie, Crowe raised his voice to a frenzy and read a passage from the Bowman-Hulbert report: "Page 128: 'He says he is not sorry for his present predicament.' It reminds me of a fellow who killed his wife, over in jail, some years ago, and when his lawyer went in to talk to him, he had no defense on earth. At that time these nameless insanity defenses were not thought of, and it looked as if this fellow was going to hang, and he afterwards did, and he told the lawyer, with tears running down his cheeks, 'You know, there isn't anybody in town who feels as bad about this as I do.' There isn't anybody in town that feels as bad as Loeb does about his present predicament."

Crowe made his final push an assault on Darrow. "I want to tell you the real defense in this case, Your Honor. It is Clarence Darrow's dangerous philosophy of life. He said to Your Honor that he was not pleading alone for these two young men. He said he was looking to the future, that he was thinking about the ten thousand young boys that in the future would fill the chairs his clients filled, and he wants to soften the law. He wants them treated not with the severity that the law of this State prescribes, but it wants them treated with kindness and consideration. I want to tell Your Honor that it would be much better if God had not caused the crime to be disclosed. It would have been much better if it went unsolved and these men went unwhipped of justice. It would not have done near the harm to this community as will be done if Your Honor, as chief justice of this great court, puts your official seal of approval upon the doctrines preached by Clarence Darrow as a defense in this case.

"Society can endure, the law can endure, and criminals escape, but if a court such as this court should say that he believes in the doctrine of Darrow, that you ought not to hang when the law says you should, a greater blow has been struck to out institutions than by a hundred, yea, a thousand murders.

"Mr. Darrow has preached in this case that one of the handicaps the defendants are under is that they are rich, the sons of multimillionaires. I have already stated to Your Honor that if it was not for their wealth, Darrow would not be here, and the Bachrachs would not be here. If it were not for their wealth, we would not have been regaled by all this tommyrot by the three wise men from the east."

As the state's attorney completed his argument, he decided to revisit the testimony of James Gortland.

"Did Gortland lie? He said it was told to him by Leopold. I don't know whether Your Honor believes that officer or not, but I want to tell you, if you have observed these two defendants during the trial, if you have observed the conduct of their attorneys and their families with one honorable exception, and that is the old man who sits in sackcloth and ashes and who is entitled to the sympathy of everybody, old Mr. Leopold. With that one honorable exception, everyone connected with the case have laughed and sneered and jeered. And if the defendant, Leopold, did not say that he would plead guilty before a friendly judge, his actions demonstrated that he thinks he has got one."

Caverly looked shocked at Crowe's remarks. He leaned forward and glared at the state's attorney.

Darrow yelled out a protest. "I want to take exception to this statement."

"You brought it up and argued on it," Crowe said. "I am replying to it."

Judge Caverly stood up and pointed toward the court reporter's table. "Let the reporter write up that statement," he ordered. "Let the statement be written up."

Crowe then quickly and respectfully—while Caverly sat down—closed. "I leave this case with you on behalf of the State of Illinois, and I ask Your Honor in the language of Holy Writ to 'execute justice and righteousness in the land.'"

Crowe then briefly and formally dispatched with the kidnapping indictments. Jacob Franks took the stand and the ransom letter was placed in evidence. Franks told of the telephone call from "Mr. Johnson." Then, Captain William Shoemacher discussed portions of the confessions that dealt with the ransom. The defense did not present arguments.

But Caverly, his face still flushed with anger from Crowe's comments, was not finished. He called Crowe's closing remarks regarding Gortland's testimony "a cowardly and dastardly insult upon the integrity of this court."

"It was not so intended, Your Honor," Crowe said.

"And it could not be used for any other purpose except to incite a mob and to try and intimidate this court. It will be stricken from the record."

With Crowe standing in front of the bench, Caverly bellowed, "This court will not be intimidated by anybody at any time or place as long as he occupies this position."

After thirty-two days, the trial was over. An angry Judge Caverly said he would take ten days to study the two-thousand pages of exhibits before announcing his sentencing.

"I will fix the day as September 10th, at 9:30 o'clock, and I will say to those people who are here now that there will be nobody admitted in this room on that day, except members of the press and members of the family and sheriffs and the state's attorney's staff."

## BATTER UP

The stress of the hearing had exhausted everyone—except Dickie and Babe. Within minutes of adjournment, the two boys joined the other juvenile inmates on the jail's indoor baseball diamond. Babe took his usual position at first base for the Alley Rats; Dickie, the captain of the Seventh Floorers, resumed his pitching duties. "They appeared happy and gay," a *Tribune* scribe wrote.[66]

While Dickie and Babe didn't show any strain—at least to reporters—others involved in the case were on edge.

"If anyone molests me during the next few days while I'm deliberating on this case, they will be arrested and sent to jail," Judge Caverly said as he talked with newspapermen in his office.

He said he ordered Cook County Sheriff Peter Hoffman to have a large staff of deputies on duty on September 10 to protect order.[67] "I have received letters from cranks all during the trial telling me that this and that will happen if I do not hang the two defendants. I have also gotten letters saying that I will be killed if I do send them to the gallows. One letter said that the writer would bomb the building if I did not impose the death penalty. Another said I would be shot and then hanged to a telephone pole if I did order them to be executed. I am not afraid of these insane threats but I do not want to endanger the lives of any of the lawyers, the defendants, or members of the Leopold, Loeb, or Franks families. I will see that ample protection is provided all."

As he gathered his belongings, he said he planned to mix in some recreation during the next few days, perhaps taken in a ball game or go to the races. A bodyguard then escorted the judge out of the building and accompanied him to his apartment at the Edgewater Beach Hotel, on the far North Side. Caverly would have twenty-four-hour protection during the next few weeks.

Throughout the summer, the big yellow-brick house on Ellis Avenue had been a Mecca for the morbidly curious. Cars slowed to a crawl as they passed by; pedestrians lingered by the lilac bushes. Day and night, police stood guard. At the end of August, Jacob Franks, who had purchased the corner lot at Hyde Park and Ellis from Albert Loeb fifteen years earlier, sold his home. He and his family would leave Kenwood; leave the tree-lined street that swallowed his son's life, leave the neighborhood where so much evil had festered.

# Part Four

## Justice

BIRDS-EYE VIEW OF ILLINOIS STATE PENITENTIARY.

Illinois State Penitentiary at Joliet.

# RIDDLES

Babe Leopold said many times he was not afraid to die—his philosophy of life did not allow fear. As Babe told Dr. William Alanson White, he anticipated continuing his search for knowledge in the hereafter. To that goal, Babe prepared ten questions—the riddles of the world, he called them. He wrote the riddles in his jail cell and planned to ask a friend to lock the list in a vault—if Judge Caverly imposed the death sentence. Several scientists—appointed by Babe—would, after his death, attempt to get in contact with him to see if he could solve the riddles.

## Babe's Riddles of the World

1. Are the experiences of human life carried into the hereafter?

2. Is the intellectual or the spiritual the dominate note after death?

3. Is the absence of the physical being an advantage or a deterrent to such intellectual or spiritual happiness?

4. Is the hereafter dimensional as on earth or is there complete omniscience?

5. Does one retain reactions to sensations registered on the mind previous to death?

6. Is life on earth a necessary precedent to life hereafter? If so, how long a life?

7. If the intellectual is dominant in the hereafter, is earthly knowledge adequate or insufficient to its enjoyment?

8. Is life on earth a correct balance of the rewards and penalties or is there a higher judgment?

9. If the life hereafter is spiritual, are the cultural experiences of the earth necessary? What of the savage mind?

10. What is happiness?[1]

Babe added a postscript that if he was to be hanged, he would have a speech ready when he reached the gallows. "I will say something that will make the world listen."

Dickie Loeb prepared no riddles. No speech. He had no philosophy to nurture him while he awaited his fate. Dickie seemed to think it would be better to hang than to spend the rest of his days in prison. "When I think of the long life down there, I sometimes feel that it would be better to get it all over with now," he said from his cell. "I don't care a damn whether I am hanged or not. The folks are to be considered, but for myself it doesn't mean much now."

## WEDNESDAY, SEPTEMBER 10

Suddenly, Chicago's heat spell broke. John Caverly awoke to cool temperatures on Wednesday, September 10. The thermometer outside his kitchen window read forty-seven degrees, but a stiff Lake Michigan breeze made it feel much colder. His courtroom would be able to breathe.

Chief of Detectives Michael Hughes greeted the judge inside the lobby of the Edgewater Beach while three squad cars waited at the hotel entrance. Caverly and Hughes climbed into the back seat of the middle car. Two police sharpshooters accompanied them as the small caravan drove south on Sheridan Road.

In Hyde Park, Clarence Darrow left his apartment at the eastern edge of the Midway Plaisance and headed north. In Kenwood, chauffeurs readied automobiles for Jacob Loeb and Allan Loeb and for Nathan Leopold Sr. and Foreman Leopold. Jacob Franks would stay home.

Throughout the morning, people congregated outside the Criminal Courts Building. By 9 A.M.—thirty minutes before Judge Caverly would announce his sentencing—five thousand people had clogged the streets around the courthouse and the adjoining Cook County Jail. One hundred policemen—on foot, on horseback, on motorcycles—controlled order. Seven detective-bureau squad cars protected the front doors. When Caverly arrived, a squad of sheriff deputies escorted him all the way to his sixth-floor chambers.

Judge Caverly looked exhausted when he entered the courtroom. He held twenty copies of his verdict and placed the bundle on his desk. Two armed guards stood at either side of the judge. At exactly 9:30, sheriff deputies led Dickie and Babe into the silent courtroom. Tense smiles cracked their pale faces as they nodded to their families. Babe sat in a chair in front of his father while Jacob and Allan Loeb occupied seats directly behind Dickie.

"In view of the profound—"

The flashes from a battery of press cameras erupted as Judge Caverly began reading his verdict. "When you are through," the judge said, "I will go on." The photographers took their pictures as Dickie and Babe waited. After a few minutes, Caverly resumed.

"In view of the profound and unusual interest that this case has aroused not only in this community but in the entire country and even beyond its boundaries, the court feels it is his duty to state the reasons which have led to the determination he has reached."[2]

The judge peered over his steel-rimmed eyeglasses, which rested on the lower part of his nose, and explained the peculiarities of the case. While the defendants pleaded guilty, he said, they did so in an unusual way. "Moreover, the plea of guilty did not in this particular case, as it usually does, render the task of the prosecutor easier by substituting the admission of guilt for a possibly difficult and uncertain chain of proof. Here the state was in possession not only of the essential substantiating facts but also of voluntary confessions on part of the defendants. The plea of guilty, therefore, does not make a special case in favor of the defendant."

Caverly then discussed the fact that no evidence of insanity was presented. He said the defendants' life histories "and their present mental, emotional and ethical condition has been of extreme interest and is valuable to criminology. . . . The court is satisfied that his judgment in the present case cannot be affected thereby."

Caverly's words crashed down on the defense table. Jacob Loeb and Nathan Leopold slumped in their chairs.

And what followed would be even worse for the young killers.

"The testimony in this case reveals a crime of singular atrocity." The judge talked slowly, with no emotion. "It is, in a sense, inexplicable but is not thereby rendered less inhuman or repulsive. It was deliberately planned and prepared for during a considerable period of time. It was executed with every feature of callousness and cruelty. And here the court will say, not for the purpose of extenuating guilt but merely with the object of dispelling a misapprehension that appears to have found lodgment in the public mind, that he is convinced by conclusive evidence that there was no abuse offered to the body of the victim.

"But it did not need that element to make the crime abhorrent to every instinct of humanity, and the court is satisfied that neither the act itself, nor in its motives or lack of motives, or in the antecedents of the offenders, can find any mitigating circumstances."

No mitigating circumstances. In one sentence, Judge Caverly had shattered Darrow's strategy. Babe showed absolutely no emotion. He sat with his legs crossed and looked directly at Caverly. Dickie's mouth trembled. To most everyone in the courtroom, it looked like a hanging verdict.

News correspondents stirred, ready to break the news that Dickie and Babe would hang.

But Darrow remained calm. Like a lion hiding in tall grass, he waited quietly for Caverly's defining move.

Then, after outlining Illinois statutes for murder and kidnapping, the judge abruptly changed his presumed direction.

"It would have been the task of least resistance to impose the extreme penalty of the law," he said.

The sentence rushed through Babe like a shot of adrenalin. His head jerked forward in anticipation.

"In choosing imprisonment instead of death, the court is moved chiefly by the consideration of the age of the defendants, boys of eighteen and nineteen years."

Judge Caverly looked out at Dickie and Babe.

"In the history of Illinois, only two minors have been put to death by legal process . . . to which number the court does not feel inclined to make an addition."

Nathan Leopold Sr., his eyes glassy with tears, reached forward and put his hand on his son's shoulder. Dickie turned and smiled at his brother.

"This determination appears to be in accordance with the progress of criminal law all over the world and with the dictates of enlightenment humanity. More than that, it seems to be in accordance with the precedents hitherto observed in this state."

As the judge continued, correspondents raced out of the courtroom to file their stories. In less than an hour, newsboys would be hawking the special editions on the streets of Chicago. Caverly recommend no parole and then read the formal sentencing.

"In number 33,623, indictment for murder, the sentence of the court is that you, Nathan F. Leopold Jr. be confined in the penitentiary in Joliet for the term of your natural life. In number 33,623, indictment for murder, the sentence of the court is that you, Richard Loeb, be confined in the penitentiary in Joliet for the term of your natural life.

"In number 33,624, kidnapping for ransom, it is the sentence of the court that you, Nathan F. Leopold Jr. be confined in the penitentiary at Joliet for the term of ninety-nine years. In Number 33,624, kidnapping for ransom, it is the sentence of the court that you, Richard Loeb, be confined in the penitentiary in Joliet for the term of ninety-nine years."

Judge Caverly then rose and slammed down his gavel. Dickie and Babe sprung to their feet and shook hands with their attorneys. Reporters, their notebooks in hand, rushed the defense table as guards hustled the boys out of the courtroom. It was 9:45. Mercy came quickly. It took only fifteen minutes for Caverly to spare the two young lives.

## INITIAL REACTION

As Dickie and Babe headed back across the bridge of sighs, newspaper-men swarmed Clarence Darrow. The Old Lion could not hold back his smile.

"I have always hated capital punishment," he said. Darrow leaned against the defense table as he talked to a cluster of reporters. "This decision at once caps my career as a criminal lawyer and starts my path in another direction. This verdict so encourages me that I shall begin now to plan a definite campaign against capital punishment in Illinois. Perhaps I may be able to take up the matter with the legislature immediately."[3]

Darrow explained that the ninety-nine-year sentencing—in addition to life—meant that Dickie and Babe would not be eligible for parole until after thirty-seven years. "Perhaps, the sentence is worse than a death penalty for the two boys but not for their families."

On the other side of the courtroom, Robert Crowe, who did shake Darrow's hand after the verdict, also talked with the press.

"While I do not intend and have no desire to criticize the decision of the court," he said, "I still believe that the death penalty is the only penalty feared by murderers. Fathers and mothers in Cook County can rest assured as long as I remain state's attorney, I will always do everything within my power to enforce the law honestly, fearlessly, and vigorously without regard to the status of the criminal."[4]

Jacob Loeb, who spoke for the defendants' families, read a prepared statement.

"On behalf of the Leopold and Loeb families there is but little to say. We have been spared the extreme penalty. What have these families to look forward to?

"Nathan F. Leopold Sr. is sixty-four years old. He has lived in Chicago practically his entire life, coming here from Michigan as a boy. He has been an exemplary citizen. His youngest son was his special pride. He justly believed that his boy was a genius, a most brilliant student and a loving son. He honored him with his own name. He hoped that this boy of nineteen would make his mark on the world, be a comfort and solace in his old age, and accomplish tasks for the benefit of humanity. Now Mr. Leopold is crushed in spirit in his declining years.

"Albert Loeb, my brother, has spent his entire life of fifty-six years in the city of Chicago. He came from the ranks: He worked his way through college; He became a lawyer of repute, then a great businessman. He was always interested in every forward movement for communal welfare. His one hobby has always been his wife and children. He considered Dickie, the third boy, particularly talented. This son entered the University of Michigan at fourteen, and he was the youngest graduate of that college. He was always a most affectionate and loving son, never known in his home life to be disobedient but was thoughtful and considerate of his parents and the members of his family until this terrible tragedy overtook them. It is painful that on account of illness, at a time like this, the father and mother are unable to be at the side of their son.

"Again I say, what have these two families, whose names have stood for everything that was good and reputable in the community, to look forward to? Their unfortunate boys, nineteen years of age, must spend the rest of their lives in the penitentiary. What is there in the future but grief and sorrow, darkness and despair?"[5]

The press reached Jacob Franks at his Kenwood home. When told that Caverly had spared the lives of Dickie and Babe, Franks said, "My wife and I never believed Nathan Jr. and Richard should be hanged."

Newspaper editorials across the country generally echoed the same tonality: the boys should remain in prison for the rest of their lives with no possibility of parole. Robert Small of the *Chicago Daily News* perhaps said it best.

> Life imprisonment in the cases of "Dickie" Loeb and "Babe" Leopold may be justified only if these two youthful murders are placed in confinement so deep that they will never be heard from again. This is preponderant in editorial comment gathered from all sections of the United States today on the action of Judge Caverly in the famous Chicago murder case.
>
> Newspapers as well as many judges who have been interviewed hold the view that too much responsibility was placed upon Judge Caverly. It is agreed that no state should permit a person accused of first-degree murder to plead guilty. If a sentence of death follows such a plea, it smacks of legal suicide. If an atrocious crime is palliated by life imprisonment, it shows that tender-hearted judges do not always follow the intent of the law. Most of the states require a jury trial in first-degree murder.

## LIFERS

As dusk approached on the day after the sentencing, sheriff deputies—
holding shotguns and rifles—patrolled the perimeter of the courthouse
and jail. Mounted police kept hundreds of people away from the jail's west
gate, where several cars of newspapermen and sheriff deputies awaited
the prisoner transport to the Illinois State Penitentiary in Joliet, about
fifty miles away.

Inside, the remains of two catered dinners—steaks, onions, french
fried potatoes, and chocolate éclairs—sat on trays in the Death Cell.
Dickie and Babe smoked and chatted with guards. Shortly before seven
o'clock, Warden Westbrook, accompanied by several guards, interrupted
the casual conversation. "Get your hats," he told the boys, "it's time to
go." One of Westbrook's men—deputy jailer Hans Thompson—slapped
a handcuff attached to a three-foot chain onto Babe's right wrist. He
clasped the other handcuff around Dickie's left wrist. Thompson grabbed
the middle of the chain with both hands, and—three-abreast—they followed Westbrook and his guards into the jail's courtyard.[6]

Four cars, their engines running, awaited them. Dickie, Babe, and
Thompson awkwardly got into the back of a black Packard. Westbrook
and his driver occupied the front seat. They would follow a Cadillac filled
with sheriff deputies to Joliet. Sheriff Hoffman's Stutz racer and a police Cadillac followed. With a large crowd of people watching from the
sidewalk, the iron gates swung open, and the small caravan tripled in
size as police cars and motorcycles and autos filled with newsmen joined
the convoy to Joliet.

With sirens blazing, the cars crossed the Chicago River and sped
through the Loop. As they headed west on Jackson Street, the lead auto
swiped a roadster and sent it crashing into a parked car.

"Hey, where's the fire?" Dickie said. "We've got a long time ahead of
us. What's the hurry?"[7]

"Yes," Babe added. "About the time we get out, fifty-three years from
today, you and I will be talking through our whiskers, Dick."

A short time later, as the cars traveled southwest on Archer Avenue,
a former Indian trail, the brakes on the lead Cadillac started to smoke.
Just beyond the town of Argo, just southwest of Chicago, the caravan
stopped so repairs could be made. By this time the twilight had slid into
darkness. Several guards surrounded the prisoners' Packard, rifles and
shotguns ready, as the deputies adjusted the Cadillac's brakes.

Not long after they resumed their journey along Archer Avenue, the
wheels on the Cadillac locked, and the car skidded to a dead stop in the

middle of the road. The Packard, traveling at fifty miles per hour, nearly crashed into the back of the Cadillac. Its driver swung the big machine off the road and onto the Chicago-and-Joliet electric tracks. The car bounced and careened over the trolley tracks for half a block and nearly toppled over before finally coming to a stop. Sheriff deputies eventually pushed the car back onto the roadway.

Dickie and Babe chuckled at all the delays, although they both complimented their driver on his efforts. Sheriff Hoffman then pulled his Stutz racer in front of the Packard. He would lead the rest of the way to Joliet.

At nine o'clock, the convoy of cars arrived at the Joliet penitentiary, a castle-like stone structure set in the city of Joliet. One thousand people stood outside the prison and watched the cars speed through the main gate. Inside the prison grounds, an army of photographers awaited Dickie and Babe. Camera flashlights cut through the summer night as Thompson and his two prisoners climbed out of the Packard. Dickie's hands shook as he stepped off the running board.

Armed prison guards pushed back an army of people who clogged the main hallway of the administration building. In the crush, a rifle accidentally knocked Dickie's fedora off his head. Sherriff Hoffman grabbed Babe's arm while Warden Westbrook held Dickie's arm. They dragged the boys through the crowd and into the security of a locked-down section of the building. Then a huge iron door slammed shut.

Dickie Loeb and Babe Leopold, prisoners 9305 and 9306, awoke in their solitary cells to a breakfast of meat stew and coffee. They each chatted briefly with a prison official. "We're going to do just what's right here," Babe told him.[8] It would be a day of obligatory tasks of haircuts, official photographs, physical examinations, fingerprinting, and, in the afternoon, one final, five-minute chance to talk with the Chicago press.

Dickie and Babe entered the small interview room together. Their mouths broke into sheepish grins when they saw the crowd of familiar reporters. Dickie Loeb and Babe Leopold, the two sleek University of Chicago grad students who spent the summer tantalizing Chicago's "lost herd of fantastic bravos" had nothing to say. Their Valentino look and Brooks Brothers style had vanished. Once Jazz Age sophisticates, they stood before reporters in penitentiary garb: baggy, gray suits and woolen shirts, heavy coarse brogues, a size-and-a-half too large, and blue caps. They were ordinary convicts.

Silence. It seemed like the reporters—the same newspapermen who camped out nightly at the teenagers' cells in the county jail—were afraid to speak. Finally, someone broke the ice.

"Dick, the warden has just told us this is the last time we will see you."

"That's fine," Dickie sneered. It was the Master Criminal's last go-around with the press. He'd leave them wanting more. "That suits us exactly."

Then the questions came. They tumbled one on top of the other. How do you like it here? What do you think of Joliet now? How was breakfast? Haven't you some message for the outside?

The two cons just shook their shaved heads.

"Dick, we've only got five minutes," a desperate voice yelled from the back. "Can't you say something?"

Nothing. The boys, confederates again, stood there. Their smiles had turned to smirks.

"We're sorry," Babe finally said, "but we've been told not to talk."

Just then, a guard opened the room's door. And the boys turned and walked away.

Amid the dense pines of Charlevoix, Michigan, Clarence Darrow tried to relax. Dickie's parents had invited Darrow to rest at the Loeb farm. Darrow, who had neglected his health during the summer, suffered from chest pains and rheumatism. He'd spend a few weeks resting and then maybe go abroad with his wife. At least those were his plans.

One morning, after writing letters to Dickie and Babe, Darrow took coffee in the playroom of Albert Loeb's country estate. He slumped in a lazy chair and looked out at the wooded landscape.

"Look at this—see these things—appreciate them," he muttered. "Then try to tell me that Dick Loeb is sane. Try to make me believe that any boy would leave this. Why, it's beyond imagination."[9]

# Epilogue

## Passages

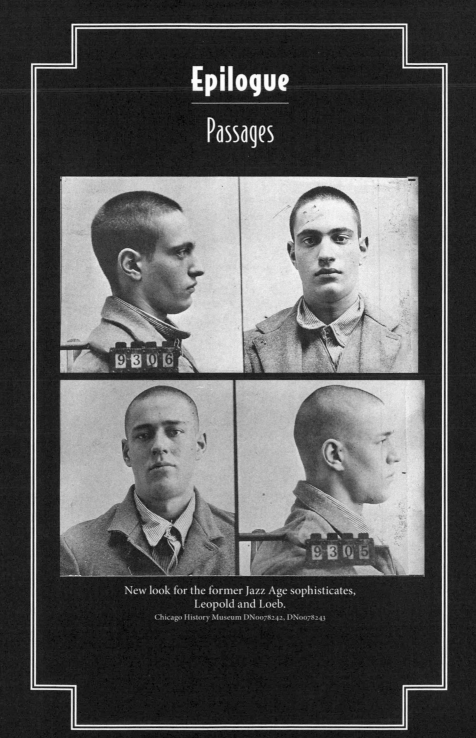

New look for the former Jazz Age sophisticates,
Leopold and Loeb.

## FRANKS FAMILY

It became the eyesore of the block. For the past several years, the large yellow-brick house at the corner of Hyde Park and Ellis has sat vacant and neglected. Plywood slabs cover the first-floor windows. Flora Franks's lilac bushes and terrace lawn are soiled with litter. On most days, Lake Michigan winds blow the debris across the landscaped grounds of Kenwood. The home fares better in winter, when the snows hide its scars.

Many owners, including a few nursery schools, have occupied the house since September of 1924, when Jacob Franks moved his family across the Chicago River to the Drake Hotel. Two years after Bobby's death, Jack Franks wrote a book of poetry dedicated to his little brother. *My Blessed Little Pal* contains several tributes to his family.[1]

> **Elegy to My Little Brother**
> *Who Dwells with Me Perpetually*
> My blessed little pal—he's gone.
> He played with me—and then as the fawn
> Which, frightened, bounds off with a start,
> Thus swift he fled, it rends my heart:
> In body, yes; in spirit, no.

At Rosehill Cemetery, in the Jacob Franks mausoleum, afternoon sunlight slips through a small green and yellow stained-glass window of a river meandering through a valley. Just beyond the curve in the road lie echoes of the past: the graves of Dickie Loeb's grandparents and a white stone obelisk marking the plots of the Leopold family.

## DICKIE LOEB AND BABE LEOPOLD

At the start of Passover, 1925, sixty inmates gathered for a religious ceremony in the chapel of the Illinois State Penitentiary in Joliet.[2] After a meal of matzos, hard-boiled eggs, and coffee, guards allowed the convicts to mingle and chat. For the first time in six months, Dickie and Babe spent time together. A few weeks later, authorities transferred Babe to nearby Stateville, a new facility in the middle of Illinois farmland. It would be 1930 before he and Dickie would see each other again.

They adjusted to prison life in inches. Change came slowly behind bars. From time to time, they'd receive news—mostly bad—from the outside world. In October of 1924, came word that Albert Loeb had died. Then came the sale of the Loeb and Leopold Kenwood homes, the death of Nathan Leopold in 1929, and, perhaps the cruelest news of all, Foreman and Samuel Leopold had changed their name to Lebold.

It took years before Dickie and Babe regained their smiles, their swagger. It was like the warden told them the first day they arrived, "Life in this prison is just what you make. Behave, and you'll get along pretty well. Act badly, and you'll get into trouble. It's up to you."[3]

In 1930, Dickie moved to Stateville. He and Babe battled the monotony by starting a correspondence school. They also reorganized Stateville's library. Although they were not cellmates, this activity allowed them to spend many hours each day together.

Babe earned numerous graduate credits by correspondence from the University of Iowa, Columbia University, University of Michigan, and the University of Chicago. In 1933, while working in the sociologist actuary office, he began his own study on parole prediction. The sociology department at Northwestern University became very interested in his work. Two years later, writing under the name of William F. Lanne, Babe completed his dissertation—"Predicting Criminology." The *Northwestern Journal of Criminal Law and Criminology* published the research in 1936.[4] Babe's name did not appear on the paper because of the massive publicity that resulted from an event at the prison on one cold day in 1936.

At the noon hour, January 28, Dickie Loeb picked up a fresh set of underwear and socks. He followed a small-time crook named James Day into the shower room. What followed proved to be an ironic end to a live consumed by crime and fantasy.

The cover story of *Inside Detective*, under the headline "Justice Catches Up with Richard Loeb" chronicled the gruesome event.

> One moment it was quiet, submerged in the half-silence that marks every prison. The irresistible baton of Time tolled another second, and routine fled in the far corners. Someone mortally wounded had screamed!
>
> The two convicts closest to him stared at the nude figure lurching, staggering, clutching at the chill, white corridor wall—stared in that hypnotic fashion typical of those who fear that even a glance may be offensive to the Wheel of Rules with which Society tries to grind them into better men.

Whence he had come—this slashed and torn human figure with shredded, bloodstained skin and flesh and muscle that suggested a drapery of ragged red lace?[5]

Day, who would claim that Dickie made homosexual advances toward him, had slashed him fifty-six times with a straight razor. He told the warden, "I kept slashing him. I can't remember much more than after some minutes of fighting in the shower . . . used two fingers of his right hand to push in some of the flesh of his abdomen which seemed to be cut open . . . put everything he had into a lunge at me. . . . I slashed it in some more and kept on slashing till he fell, mumbling like."

Like the killing of Bobby Franks, there was no witness.

Years later, when Babe wrote his autobiography, *Life Plus 99 Years,* he called Dickie "the best pal I've ever had."[6]

During World War II, Babe offered himself for malaria-control experiments—and then launched a long campaign to gain his parole. Prison officials denied his first three attempts. Chicagoan Ralph Newman, a prominent Lincoln scholar and close friend of Foreman Leopold, led the efforts to gain parole for Babe. It was Newman who suggested Babe write his life story.

In 1949, Newman asked his friend Carl Sandburg to get involved. After corresponding with Babe, Sandberg penned a letter to the parole board. He pleaded for Babe's release: "I would add that if he were a neighbor of mine, I would want to see him often, if only for benefits from association with a great and rare intellect."[7]

Finally, on March 13, 1958, after serving not quite thirty-two years, Babe walked out of Stateville, a free man. Newman and Chicago attorney Elmer Gertz escorted Babe through the main gate. The jacket pocket of Babe's state-issued suit held an envelope filled with $600 from his prison account. Scores of reporters and photographers were waiting. Babe said very little to the newspapermen and then got into the front seat of Newman's car for the ride to Chicago. Like they did in 1924, several carloads of reporters followed Babe along the highway. The next day, he boarded a plane for Puerto Rico.

Babe settled in a small village—Castaner—near San Juan. As a condition of his parole, he worked as a lab technician at a hospital run by the Church of the Brethren. In 1961, with permission from the parole board, he married Gertrude Feldman Garcia de Quevada. And after completion of his parole, Babe and his wife traveled extensively. They made several trips back to Chicago, visiting old University of Chicago friends. He moved to San Juan and attended the University of Puerto Rico, earning a degree in social work in 1968. Babe died from diabetes-related heart attack in August of 1971. He kept only two mementos of 1924 in his apartment throughout his final years—a framed photo of Dickie Loeb and one of Clarence Darrow.

Dickie Loeb was cremated at Oak Woods Cemetery in Chicago. Babe Leopold willed his body to the University of Puerto Rico for medical research.

## CLARENCE DARROW

Every March, they come to honor him. In 1938, Clarence Darrow, at age eighty-one, died at his Hyde Park apartment, which overlooked Jackson Park lagoon. His family scattered his ashes on Wooded Island. And on every March 13—his death date—a group of people gather on the small bridge that bares his name. Scholars, politicians, historians, priests, and lawyers brave the chilly air to celebrate the Old Lion, who grew weary fighting what he called "the greatest enemy that ever confronted man— public opinion."[8]

According to legend, Darrow, an agnostic, vowed to reappear after his death. From time to time, believers say, the silhouette of an elderly man in a topcoat and fedora wanders the back steps of the Museum of Science and Industry, which faces the Jackson Park lagoon. He gazes across the water and studies the people on the Darrow Bridge. And then he disappears.

## NO LIMITS

More than eighty summers have passed through Kenwood–Hyde Park since Dickie Loeb and Babe Leopold kidnapped and killed Bobby Franks. Many of the blocks still carry an air of entitlement. Million-dollar homes are commonplace, and the University of Chicago remains an elite bastion of higher earning. Students and professors linger on the campus quad on sun-splashed days. Nannies push strollers along quiet streets. Kids play baseball after school.

The national fascination with the crime continues. Our questions mirror those of 1924: How could two privileged, intelligent boys from good homes commit such an incomprehensible, evil act? What would possess them?

"Their minds were not normal and never had been normal," Clarence Darrow wrote in his autobiography, "The Story of My Life." Vivid imaginations are common for children, but it was an intense narcissism—entitlement—that fed Dick and Babe's childhood and adolescent fantasies.

"Most kids are naturally narcissistic," Dr. Paula Cormalleth, a clinical psychologist, said during an interview with the author. "But we then—usually the mother—teach them that other kids have feelings, too. They soon learn they are not the center of the universe. Miss Struthers and Sweetie—the boys' nursemaids—are their mother figures. And they feed the boys' grandiosity. It's where they connect with each other, this belief that they're superior to everyone else. Their narcissism has no limits."[9]

Miss Struthers's passionate desire to make Dickie into the ideal boy inflated his narcissism, while Sweetie was a source of love and also a sexual object for Babe. Sweetie's twisted moral compass was Babe's main connection to humanity. "They must have felt so different than other children," Dr. Cormalleth said. "It's a terrible curse. They look around, see what they have, and see themselves as superior. And this feeling never leaves them."

This intense narcissism, this grandiosity were on display for the world during the summer of 1924 in Judge Caverly's courtroom. The boys dressed for each court appearance as if they were attending the theater. Although they faced the death sentence, they smiled easily for the press photographers and joked with reporters, especially Dickie. And it all began in their fantasies:

*Each night they came into his cell. Stripped of his clothing, the guards had their way with him. They shoved him against the bars and whipped him . . .*

Because Dickie felt inferior to his brothers, this fantasy—with Dickie playing the master criminal—provided him with a sense of superiority. Even the torture he suffered in this fantasy added to his grandiose status. If he could tolerate this type of treatment, he could go through anything. This fantasy morphed into reality at the Cook County Jail, where the Master Criminal held court daily with reporters from his jail cell and enjoyed the hot dinners his family sent him.

*As the master criminal mind of the century, Dickie led other. Of course, they obeyed him. He was the ideal fellow: good-looking, smart, rich. And he knew all about being a criminal.*

"Dickie Loeb needed to be respected, to have an audience," Dr. Cormalleth said. "It is part of narcissistic need, particularly to outsmart the smartest detective. Really good crooks adjust to any environment. A good example of this is his essay *[in Richard's Magazine]* about random victimization during the bombings of World War I. In his mind, the way to escape the randomness—being this grandiose, narcissistic boy—is to be the killer. Take control of the randomness."

*Here's someone I should shadow. Surely she's up to something. Sure, that's it one of those mansions on Drexel. Where are her confederates?*

While other kids in Kenwood played baseball, Dickie stalked the streets to learn his craft. "His world was too small," according to Dr. Cormalleth. "To be powerful, he must actually walk in the footsteps of a master criminal. He's projecting here, following that lady. It's all random, and he makes assumptions—she's picking out a house to rob—a narcissistic fantasy."

*The slave-drivers beat the young boy until he could no longer stand. Bloody and dirty, they left him for dead. The King, tall and strong, came upon the Slave and saved his life. Under the King's command, he grew healthy and fit. The Slave resembled the Hart, Schaffer, and Marx man. In a heroic battle, the Slave saved the King's life. For this brave act, the King offered the Slave his freedom, but the Slave refused. He would always serve the King.*

Babe's fantasy centered on his Nietzschean belief of genuine autonomy. In this fantasy, the Slave actually refused his freedom. "It proves his mastery, "Dr. Cormalleth contends, "because he makes the choice." Babe believed each individual should live without limits, without moral obligation.

*Mother, poor mother, idolized by all who knew you. I know I'll never see you again.*

Babe always believed he caused his mother's death because she contracted a life-threatening disease during her pregnancy with him. This is paramount to his criminal tendencies, according to Dr. Cormalleth. "Babe is omnipotent in his own mind. Since he believes he already killed someone important—his mother—he might as well kill again. It becomes part of his identity. He has a place for it in his mind. Again, no limits."

For more than eighty years, people—psychologists, psychiatrists, physicians, reporters, judges, attorneys, novelists, playwrights, screenwriters, and parents—have presented their own particular interpretations of the crime and the killers. Although Clarence Darrow's brilliant defense that summer graphically portrayed the abnormal lives of Dickie Loeb and Babe Leopold, in the end what moved Judge John Caverly was humanity—their young ages at the time of the crime: "In choosing imprisonment instead of death, the court is moved chiefly by the consideration of the ages of the defendants, boys of eighteen and nineteen years."

It was, as many believe, "a judgment so wise."[10]

NOTES
=====

BIBLIOGRAPHY
=====

INDEX
=====

# NOTES

## Preface

1. Leon Despres, personal interview, April 5, 2005.

## Part One. Fantasies

1. Dr. William Healy, court testimony, court transcripts, August 4–5, 1924.

2. Bowman, Karl, and Harold S. Hulbert, Bowman-Hulbert Report, Richard Loeb. Robert W. Bergstrom Papers, Special Collections, Newberry Library, Chicago, 67.

3. Bowman and Hulbert, Loeb, 12.

4. Bowman and Hulbert, Loeb, 14.

5. Bowman and Hulbert, Loeb, 13.

6. Bowman and Hulbert, Loeb, 74.

7. Frank L. Packard, *The Adventures of Jimmie Dale* (New York: Burt, 1915), 1.

8. Bowman and Hulbert, Loeb, 70.

9. M. R. Werner, *Julius Rosenwald, the Life of a Practical Humanitarian* (New York: Harper, 1939), 67.

10. Chicago Landmark Commission, *Chicago*, July 9, 2003.

11. Warren G. Harding to Albert Loeb, Julius Rosenwald Collection, University of Chicago Library Special Collections, Chicago.

12. *Chicago Daily Tribune*, June 2, 1924.

13. Theodore Roosevelt to Richard Loeb, May 8, 1916, Julius Rosenwald Collection, University of Chicago Library Special Collections, Chicago.

14. Bowman and Hulbert, Loeb, 79.

15. Clarence Darrow plea, court transcripts, August 22, 1924.

16. Marian Rosenwald Ascoli, oral history, July 25, 1988, Chicago Jewish Archives, Spertus Institute for Jewish Studies.

17. Bowman and Hulbert, Loeb, 17.

18. Bowman and Hulbert, Loeb, 18.

19. Bowman and Hulbert, Loeb, 134.

20. Nathan F. Leopold Jr., *Life Plus Ninety-nine Years* (New York: Doubleday, 1958), 26.

21. Erik Larson, *The Devil in the White City* (New York: Random, 2003), 17.

22. Bowman, Karl, and Harold S. Hulbert, Bowman-Hulbert Report, Nathan F. Leopold Jr., Robert W. Bergstrom Papers, Special Collections, Newberry Library, Chicago, 36.

23. *Chicago Daily Tribune,* June 4, 1924.

24. Doug Anderson, personal interview, June 11, 2005.

25. Bowman and Hulbert, Leopold, 8.

26. Bowman and Hulbert, Leopold, 5.

27. Bowman and Hulbert, Leopold, 7.

28. Bowman and Hulbert, Leopold, 18.

29. Bowman and Hulbert, Leopold, 20.

30. Bowman and Hulbert, Leopold, 19.

31. Bowman and Hulbert, Leopold, 56.

32. Bowman and Hulbert, Leopold, 46.

33. Bowman and Hulbert, Leopold, 45.

34. Bowman and Hulbert, Leopold, 47.

35. Nathan F. Leopold Jr. to Walter Darling, July 18, 1964, Nathan F. Leopold Jr. Collection, Chicago History Museum, Chicago.

36. *Harvard Review* yearbook, 1920.

37. Bowman and Hulbert, Leopold, 37.

38. F. Scott Fitzgerald, *This Side of Paradise* (New York: Modern Library, 2001), 21.

39. Fitzgerald, *This Side of Paradise,* 21.

40. Clarence Darrow plea, court transcripts, August 22, 1924.

41. *Chicago Daily Tribune,* June 2, 1924.

42. Paula S. Fass, *The Damned and the Beautiful* (New York: Oxford UP, 1977), 318.

43. Dr. White court testimony, court transcripts, August 3, 1924.

44. Bowman and Hulbert, Leopold, 92.

45. Bowman and Hulbert, Leopold, 80.

46. *Daily Mining Gazette,* May, 2002.

47. Bowman and Hulbert, Loeb, 87.

48. Bowman and Hulbert, Leopold, 95.

49. Dr. Healy court testimony, court transcripts, August 4, 1924.

50. Fass, *The Damned and the Beautiful,* 28.

51. Leopold, *Life Plus,* 269.

52. Leopold, *Life Plus,* 269.

53. Bowman and Hulbert, Leopold, 43.

54. Bowman and Hulbert, Leopold, 68.

55. Bowman and Hulbert, Leopold, 68.

56. Dr. Healy, court testimony, court transcripts, August 5, 1924.

57. Dr. Healy, court testimony, court transcripts, August 5, 1924.

58. Bowman and Hulbert, Loeb, 94.

59. Bowman and Hulbert, Leopold, 94.

60. *Chicago Daily Tribune,* May 31, 1924.

61. Bowman and Hulbert, Loeb, 95.

62. Dr. Healy, court testimony, court transcripts, August 5, 1924.

63. Dr. Healy, court testimony, court transcripts, August 5, 1924.

### Part Two. Realities

1. *Chicago Daily Tribune*, June 6, 1924.

2. William Howland Kenney, *Chicago Jazz* (New York: Oxford UP, 1993), 15.

3. *Chicago Daily Tribune*, November 26, 1923.

4. *Chicago Daily Tribune*, June 3, 1924.

5. *Chicago Daily Tribune*, June 3, 1924.

6. *Chicago Daily Tribune*, November 3, 1923.

7. *Chicago Daily Tribune*, November 26, 1923.

8. *Chicago Daily Tribune*, November 26, 1924.

9. *Chicago Daily Tribune*, June 3, 1923.

10. Richard Lindberg, *To Serve and Collect: Police, Prohibition, and the Crime Syndicate* (Westport, CT: Praeger, 1991), 150.

11. Lindberg, *To Serve and Collect*, 176.

12. John R. Schmidt, *"The Mayor Who Cleaned Up Chicago"* (De Kalb: Northern Illinois UP, 1989), 55.

13. Schmidt, *"The Mayor Who Cleaned Up Chicago,"* 57.

14. Schmidt, *"The Mayor Who Cleaned Up Chicago,"* 442.

15. *Chicago Herald and Examiner*, April 17, 1923.

16. *University Record* [University of Chicago] 10.3 (July 1924): 193.

17. *University Record* [University of Chicago] 10.3 (July 1924): 192.

18. *Chicago Daily Tribune*, April 18, 1923.

19. Schmidt, *"The Mayor Who Cleaned Up Chicago,"* 80.

20. Lindberg, *To Serve and Collect*, 182.

21. Bowman and Hulbert, Loeb, 116.

22. Christian K. Ross, *Charley Ross, the Kidnapped Child, a Father's Story* (Philadelphia: Potter, 1876), 25.

23. Ross, *Charley Ross, the Kidnapped Child*, 48.

24. Ross, *Charley Ross, the Kidnapped Child*, 70.

25. Patterson Smith, "Ransom Kidnapping in America," *AB Bookman's Weekly* 23 (Apr. 1990), 2.

26. Patterson Smith, "Ransom Kidnapping," 3.

27. Donald Hoffmann, *Frank Lloyd Wright's Robie House* (New York: Dover, 1984), 8.

28. Hoffmann, *Frank Lloyd Wright's Robie House*, 12.

29. Hoffmann, *Frank Lloyd Wright's Robie House*, 8.

30. Hoffmann, *Frank Lloyd Wright's Robie House*, 15.

31. Hoffmann, *Frank Lloyd Wright's Robie House*, 94.

32. Bowman and Hulbert, Leopold and Loeb (June, 1924); Loeb and Leopold, confessions to the Cook County State's Attorney (May 31, 1924).

33. Bowman and Hulbert, Leopold, 98.

34. Leopold, *"Life Plus," Chicago Daily News*, November 7, 1957.

35. Bowman and Hulbert, Leopold, 38.

36. *Chicago Daily Tribune*, May 25, 1924.

37. *Chicago Daily Tribune*, May 25, 1924.

38. Cook County Recorder of Deeds, County Building, Chicago.

39. *Chicago Herald and Examiner*, June 2, 1924.

40. Leopold, confession, May 31, 1924.

41. Willys-Knight, advertisement, *National Geographic* (Mar. 1924).

42. *Chicago Daily Tribune*, May 29, 1924.

43. *Chicago Daily Tribune*, May 25, 1924.

44. Hal Higdon, *The Crime of the Century* (Urbana: U of Illinois P, 1999), 34.

45. Jacob Franks, court testimony, court transcripts, July 23, 1924.

46. Loeb, confession, and Leopold, confession, May 31, 1924.

47. Leon Despres, former Chicago alderman, personal interview, April 5, 2005.

48. Loeb, confession and Leopold, confession, May 31, 1924. Loeb's confession was reprinted in the *Chicago Daily News*, June 7, 1924. Leopold's confession was reprinted in the *Chicago Tribune* on June 6, 1924.

49. *Chicago Daily Tribune*, May 23, 1924.

50. Leopold, *"Life Plus," Chicago Daily News*, November 4, 1957.

51. *Chicago Daily Tribune*, May 23, 1924.

52. Bernard Hunt court testimony, court transcripts, July 24, 1924.

53. Charles Enos court testimony, court transcripts, July 23, 1924.

54. Court evidence, Loeb-Leopold trial, July 27, 1924.

55. *Chicago Daily Tribune*, May 23, 1924.

56. Tony Minke court testimony, court transcripts, July 23, 1924.

57. *Chicago Daily News*, May 23, 1924.

58. Leopold, *"Life Plus," Chicago Daily News*, November 4, 1957.

59. Leopold, *"Life Plus," Chicago Daily News*, November 4, 1957.

60. Loeb, confession, May 31, 1924.

61. *Chicago Daily News*, May 31, 1924.

62. *Chicago Daily Tribune*, May 23, 1924.

63. *Chicago Daily Journal*, May 22, 1924.

64. *Chicago Daily News*, May 23, 1924.

65. *Chicago Daily News*, May 23, 1924.

66. Loeb, confession, May 31, 1924.

67. *Chicago Daily Tribune*, May 23, 1924.

68. Leopold, *"Life Plus," Chicago Daily News*, November 4, 1957.

69. Higdon, *The Crime of the Century*, 48.

70. Alvin Goldstein, court testimony, court transcripts, July 25, 1929.

71. *Chicago Evening-American*, May 23, 1924.

72. *Chicago Evening-American*, May 23, 1924.

73. *Chicago Evening-American*, May 23, 1924.

74. *Chicago Daily Tribune,* May 25, 1924.

75. *Chicago Evening-American,* May 23, 1924.

76. *Chicago Daily Journal,* May 23, 1924.

77. Ernest W. Puttkammer, court testimony, court transcripts, July 25, 1924.

78. *Chicago Evening-American,* May 23, 1924.

79. *Chicago Daily Tribune,* May 23, 1924.

80. *Chicago Evening-American,* May 23, 1924.

81. *Chicago Evening-American,* May 23, 1924.

82. *Chicago Daily Tribune,* May 23, 1924.

83. Bowman and Hulbert, Loeb, 110.

84. Bowman and Hulbert, Loeb.

85. Higdon, *The Crime of the Century,* 52.

86. Howard Mayer, court testimony, court transcripts, July 25, 1924.

87. Howard Mayer, court testimony, court transcripts, July 25, 1924.

88. *Chicago Daily News,* May 31, 1924.

89. Joseph Springer, court testimony, court transcripts, July 23, 1924.

90. *Chicago Evening-American,* May 23, 1924.

91. *Chicago Evening-American,* May 23, 1924.

92. Paula S. Fass, "Making and Remaking an Event: The Leopold and Loeb Case in American Culture." *Journal of American History* (December 1993), 22.

93. *Chicago Evening-American,* May 23, 1924.

94. *Chicago Daily Tribune,* May 24, 1924.

95. *Chicago Daily News,* May 24, 1924.

96. *Chicago Daily News,* May 24, 1924.

97. *Chicago Daily Journal,* May 23, 1924.

98. *Chicago Daily News,* May 27, 1924.

99. *Chicago Herald and Examiner,* May 26, 1924.

100. *Chicago Daily Journal,* May 24, 1924.

101. Smith, "Ransom Kidnapping in America," 467.

102. *Chicago Daily Tribune,* May 25, 1924.

103. *Chicago Daily News,* May 24, 1924.

104. *Chicago Daily Journal,* May 24, 1924.

105. *Chicago Daily Tribune,* May 24, 1924.

106. *Chicago Daily Journal,* May 24, 1924.

107. *Chicago Daily Tribune,* May 27, 1924.

108. *Chicago Daily Tribune*: May 25, 1924.

109. *Chicago Daily News,* May 27, 1924.

110. *Chicago Daily Journal,* May 23, 1924.

111. Leopold, *"Life Plus," Chicago Daily News,* November 5, 1957.

112. Jacob Weinstein, court testimony, court transcripts, July 26, 1924.

113. *Chicago Tribune,* May 24, 1924.

114. *Chicago Tribune,* May 24, 1924.

115. *Chicago Daily Journal,* May 24, 1924.

116. Loeb, confession, May 31, 1924.

117. Leopold, *"Life Plus," Chicago Daily News,* November 8, 1957.

118. *Chicago Tribune,* May 24, 1924.

119. Bowman and Hulbert, Loeb, 111.

120. Leopold, *"Life Plus," Chicago Daily News,* November 6, 1924.

121. Leopold, *"Life Plus," Chicago Daily News,* November 6, 1957.

122. Leopold's statement read into court record, court transcripts, July 25, 1924.

123. *Chicago Daily Tribune,* June 2, 1924.

124. Higdon, *The Crime of the Century,* 72.

125. *Chicago Tribune,* June 2, 1924.

126. Ernest Puttkammer, court testimony, court transcripts, July 25, 1924.

127. Leopold, *"Life Plus," Chicago Daily News,* November 6, 1957.

128. Leopold, *"Life Plus," Chicago Daily News,* November 7, 1957.

129. Leopold, *"Life Plus," Chicago Daily News,* November 7, 1957.

130. Leopold, *"Life Plus," Chicago Daily News,* November 7, 1957.

131. Robert Crowe, opening remarks, court transcripts, July 23, 1924.

132. Transcript of Leopold's interrogation, read at the court hearing, court transcripts, July 28, 1924.

133. Leopold, *"Life Plus," Chicago Daily News,* November 7, 1924.

134. Leopold, *"Life Plus," Chicago Daily News,* November 7, 1957.

135. A transcript of Loeb's interrogation was read at the July 28, 1924, hearing.

136. *Chicago Daily News,* May 30, 1924.

137. Arnold Maremont, court testimony, court transcripts, July 24, 1924.

138. *Chicago Daily News,* May 31, 1924.

139. Howard Mayer, court testimony, court transcripts, July 25, 1924.

140. Higdon, *The Crime of the Century,* 89.

141. *Chicago Daily News,* May 30, 1924.

142. *Chicago Daily News,* May 30, 1924.

143. Crowe, opening remarks, court transcripts, July 23, 1924.

144. Leopold, *"Life Plus," Chicago Daily News,* November 9, 1957.

145. Sven Englund, court testimony, court transcripts, July 24, 1924.

146. Crowe, opening remarks, court transcripts, July 23, 1924.

147. *Chicago Sun-Times,* January 9, 1953.

148. Loeb, confession, and Leopold, confession, May 31, 1924.

149. *Chicago Daily News,* May 31, 1924.

150. *Chicago Herald and Examiner,* June 1, 1924.

151. *Chicago Daily Tribune,* June 1, 1924.

152. *Chicago Daily News,* May 31, 1924.

153. William Shoemacher, court testimony, court transcripts, July 28, 1924.

154. *Chicago Daily Tribune,* June 1, 1924.

155. Irving Stone, *Clarence Darrow for the Defense* (New York: Doubleday, 1941), 242.

156. *Chicago Herald and Examiner,* June 2, 1924.

157. *Chicago Daily Tribune,* June 2, 1924.

158. Frederick J. Hoffman, *The 20's: American Writing in the Postwar Decade* (New York: Free, 1949), 234.

159. *Chicago Daily Tribune*, June 2, 1924.

160. *Chicago Herald and Examiner*, June 1, 1924.

161. *Chicago Herald and Examiner*, June 1, 1924.

162. *Chicago Daily Tribune*, June 1, 1924.

163. *Chicago Daily News*, May 31, 1924.

164. *Chicago Herald and Examiner*, June 5, 1924.

165. *Chicago Herald and Examiner*, June 1, 1924.

166. *Chicago Herald and Examiner*, June 1, 1924.

## Part Three. Apologia

1. *Chicago Daily Tribune*, June 3, 1924.

2. *Chicago Daily Tribune*, June 3, 1924.

3. Bowman and Hulbert, Loeb, 114.

4. Bowman and Hulbert, Loeb, 114.

5. Leopold, *Life Plus, Chicago Daily News*, November 9, 1957.

6. Leopold, *Life Plus, Chicago Daily News*, November 9, 1957.

7. Higdon, *The Crime of the Century*, 101.

8. Clarence Darrow, *The Story of My Life* (New York: Scribner's, 1932), 234.

9. *Chicago Daily Tribune*, June 6, 1924.

10. *Chicago Daily Tribune*, June 4, 1924.

11. *Chicago Daily Tribune*, June 7, 1924.

12. *Chicago Daily Tribune*, June 7, 1924.

13. *Chicago Daily Tribune*, June 6, 1924.

14. *Chicago Daily News*, June 21, 1924.

15. *Chicago Daily Tribune*, June 10, 1924.

16. *Chicago Daily News*, June 11, 1924.

17. Bowman and Hulbert, Loeb, 113.

18. *Chicago Daily Tribune*, June 12, 1924.

19. *Chicago Daily Tribune*, June 19, 1924.

20. Kenneth T. Jackson, *The Ku Klux Klan* (Chicago: Dee, 1992), 103.

21. Jackson, *The Ku Klux Klan*, 113.

22. *Chicago Daily News*, June 19, 1924.

23. *Chicago Daily Tribune*, June 24, 1924.

24. *Chicago Daily News*, June 14, 1924.

25. Jean Folkerts and Dwight L. Teeter Jr., *Voices of America: A History of Mass Media in the United States*, 4th ed. (Boston: Allyn and Bacon, 2002), 357.

26. *Chicago Daily Tribune*, July 17, 1924.

27. *Chicago Daily Tribune*, July 18, 1924.

28. *Chicago Daily Tribune*, July 18, 1924.

29. *Chicago Daily Tribune*, July 20, 1924.

30. *Chicago Daily Tribune*, July 22, 1924.

31. Darrow, *The Story of My Life*, 237.

32. *Chicago Daily Tribune*, July 22, 1924.

33. *Chicago Daily News,* July 23, 1924.

34. Maureen McKernan, *The Amazing Crime and Trial of Leopold and Loeb* (New York: New American, 1957), 77.

35. *Chicago Daily News*, July 23, 1924.

36. Crowe, court transcripts, July 23, 1924.

37. Darrow, court transcripts, July 23, 1924.

38. Edwin Gresham, court testimony, court transcripts, July 23, 1924.

39. Dr. Joseph Springer, court testimony, court transcripts, July 23, 1924.

40. Flora Franks, court testimony, court transcripts, July 23, 1924.

41. Arnold Maremont, court testimony, court transcripts, July 24, 1924.

42. Carl Ulvigh, court testimony, court transcripts, July 24, 1924.

43. William Crot, court testimony, court transcripts, July 25, 1924.

44. James Gortland, court testimony, court transcripts, 1924.

45. *Chicago Daily Tribune*, July 26, 1924.

46. *Chicago Daily Tribune*: July 26, 1924.

47. Dr. William Alanson White, court testimony, court transcripts, August 1, 1924.

48. Crowe, court transcripts, July 30, 1924.

49. Dr. White, court testimony, court transcripts, August 1, 1924.

50. Dr. Healy, court testimony, court transcripts, August 4, 1924.

51. Dr. Bernard Glueck,, court testimony, court transcripts, August 6, 1924.

52. *Montreal Herald,* August 2, 1924.

53. *London Daily Mail,* August 1, 1924.

54. Arnold Maremont, court testimony, court transcripts, August 7, 1924.

55. John Abt, court testimony, court transcripts, August 7, 1924.

56. Lorraine Nathan, court testimony, court transcripts, August 7, 1924.

57. Dr. H. S. Hulbert, court testimony, court transcripts, August 8, 1924.

58. Dr. Hugh Patrick, court testimony, court transcripts, August 13, 1924.

59. Darrow, court transcripts, August 13, 1924.

60. Dr. Archibald Church, court testimony, court transcripts, August 13, 1924.

61. *Chicago Daily Tribune*, August 21, 1924.

62. *Chicago Daily Tribune,* August 21, 1924.

63. Joseph Savage, court testimony, court transcripts, August 20, 1924.

64. Darrow, *My Story of My Life*, 32.

65. *Chicago Daily Tribune*, August 27, 1924.

66. *Chicago Daily Tribune,* August 29, 1924.

67. *Chicago Daily Tribune,* August 29, 1924.

### Part Four. Justice

1. *Chicago Daily Tribune*, September 4, 1924.

2. Judge John Caverly, verdict, court transcripts, September 10, 1924.

3. *Chicago Daily News,* September 10, 1924.

4. *Chicago Daily News,* September 10, 1924.

5. *Chicago Daily News,* September 10, 1924.

6. Leopold, *Life Plus,* 80.

7. *Chicago Daily Tribune,* September 12, 1924.

8. *Chicago Daily News,* September 12, 1924.

9. *Chicago Daily News,* September 12, 1924.

## Epilogue. Passages

1. Jack Franks, *My Blessed Little Pal* (Chicago: Self-published, 1926), 3.

2. *Chicago Daily News,* April 9, 1925.

3. *Chicago Daily News,* September 13, 1924.

4. Leopold to Darling, 18 July 1964, Chicago History Museum, Chicago.

5. Harry Read, "Justice Catches Up with Richard Loeb," *Inside Detective* (May 1936), 7.

6. Leopold, *Life Plus,* 270.

7. Carl Sandburg to Illinois Board of Pardons and Paroles, 4 April 1949, Nathan F. Leopold Jr. Collection, Chicago History Museum, Chicago.

8. Darrow, *The Story of My Life,* 232.

9. Dr. Paula Cormalleth, personal interview, August 28 and 29, 2006.

10. Leon Despres, personal interview, April 15, 2005.

# BIBLIOGRAPHY

## Sources except Newspapers

Anderson, Doug. Telephone interview. June 5, 2005.

Asbury, Herbert. *Gem of the Prairie*. New York: Knopf, 1940.

Ascoli, Marian Rosenwald. Oral history, July 25, 1988. Chicago Jewish Archives. Spertus Institute for Jewish Studies.

Asher Library. Spertus Institute of Jewish Studies, Chicago Jewish Archives.

Bach, Ira J., ed. *Chicago's Famous Buildings*. Chicago: U of Chicago P, 1965.

Badal, Oswalda. "The Hyde Park–Kenwood Urban Renewal Story." *Hyde Park Historical Society Newsletter* 17.2–3 (Summer/Fall 1995): 1–9.

Bergstrom, Robert W. Papers. Special Collections, Newberry Library, Chicago.

Block, Jean F. *Hyde Park House, an Informal History*. Chicago: U of Chicago P, 1978.

Bowman, Karl, and Harold S. Hulbert. Bowman-Hulbert Report, Nathan F. Leopold Jr. Robert W. Bergstrom Papers, Special Collections, Newberry Library, Chicago.

———. Bowman-Hulbert Report, Richard Loeb. Robert W. Bergstrom Papers, Special Collections, Newberry Library, Chicago.

Burgess, Ernest W. Papers, Special Collection, University of Chicago.

*Census Data of Chicago*, Chicago: Burgess and Newcomb, 1920.

Chicago Landmark Commission. *Chicago*. July 9, 2003.

Cormalleth, Dr. Paula. Personal interviews. August 28 and 29, 2006.

Court transcripts. Robert W. Bergstrom Papers, Special Collections, Newberry Library, Chicago.

Cutler, Irving. *The Jews of Chicago, from Shtetl to Suburb*. Urbana: U of Illinois P, 1996.

Darrow, Clarence. *The Story of My Life*. New York: Scribner's, 1932.

David, Andrew. *Famous Criminal Trials*. Minneapolis: Lerner, 1979.

Despres, Leon. Chicago Jewish Archives, Spertus Institute for Jewish Studies.

———. Personal interview. April 5, 2005.

Fass, Paula S. *The Damned and the Beautiful*. New York: Oxford UP, 1977.

———. "Making and Remaking an Event: The Leopold and Loeb Case in American Culture." *Journal of American History* (December 1993): 919–51.

Fitzgerald, F. Scott. *The Great Gatsby*. New York: Scribner's, 1925.

———. *This Side of Paradise*. New York: Modern Library, 2001.

Folkerts, Jean, and Dwight L. Teeter Jr. *Voices of America: A History of Mass Media in the United States.* 4th ed. Boston: Allyn and Bacon, 2002.

Franks, Jack. *My Blessed Little Pal.* Chicago: Self-published, 1926.

Gertz, Elmer. *Handful of Clients.* Chicago: Follett, 1965.

Harding, Warren G. Letter to Albert Loeb. Julius Rosenwald Collection. University of Chicago Library Special Collections, Chicago.

*Harvard Review* yearbook.

Higdon, Hal. *The Crime of the Century: The Leopold and Loeb Case.* Urbana: U of Illinois P, 1999.

Hoffman, Frederick J. *The 20's: American Writing in the Postwar Decade.* New York: Free, 1949.

Hoffmann, Donald. *Frank Lloyd Wright's Robie House.* New York: Dover, 1984.

Hulbert, Harold S. Papers. Northwestern University Archives.

Hyde Park Historical Society.

Jackson, Kenneth T. *The Ku Klux Klan in the City 1915–1930.* Chicago: Dee, 1992.

Kenney, William Howland. *Chicago Jazz, a Cultural History, 1904–1930.* New York: Oxford UP, 1993.

Larson, Erik. *The Devil in the White City.* New York: Random, 2003.

Leopold, Nathan F., Jr. Collection. Chicago History Museum, Chicago.

———. Collection. University of Chicago.

———. Confession of May 31, 1924, to the Cook County States's Attorney, Criminal Court Building, Chicago. *Chicago Tribune,* June 6, 1924.

———. "The Kirtland's Warbler in Its Summer Home." *Auk, a Quarterly Journal of Ornithology* 41 (1924): 44–58.

———. *Life Plus Ninety-nine Years.* New York: Doubleday, 1958.

Leopold, Nathan F., Jr., and Richard Loeb. Collection. McCormick Library of Special Collections, Northwestern University.

Lewis, Lloyd, and Henry Justin Smith. *Chicago, the History of Its Reputation.* New York: Blue Ribbon, 1929.

Lindberg, Richard. *Return to the Scene of the Crime.* Nashville: Cumberland, 1999.

———. *To Serve and Collect: Police, Prohibition, and the Crime Syndicate.* Westport, CT: Praeger, 1991.

Loeb, Richard. Confession of May 31, 1924, to the Cook County States's Attorney, Criminal Court Building, Chicago. *Chicago Daily News,* June 7, 1924.

Lowe, David Garrard. *Lost Chicago.* New York: Watson-Gaptill, 2000.

Mayer, Harold M., and Richard C. Wade. *Chicago: Growth of a Metropolis.* Chicago: U of Chicago P, 1969.

McKernan, Maureen. *The Amazing Crime and Trial of Leopold and Loeb.* New York: New American, 1957.

Merz, Charles. "Bigger and Better Murders." *Harper's,* August 1927, 338–83.

Miller, Donald L. *City of the Century.* New York: Simon, 1996.

Neighborhood History Research Collections, Chicago Public Library.

Packard, Frank L. *The Adventures of Jimmie Dale.* New York: Burt, 1915.

Peterson, Virgil W. *Barbarians in Our Midst.* New York: Little, 1952.

Read, Harry. "Justice Catches Up with Richard Loeb." *Inside Detective*, May 1936, 4–11, 42.

Riniolo, Todd C. "The Attorney and the Shrink." *Skeptic* 9.3 (2002): 80–83.

Roosevelt, Theodore Roosevelt. Letter to Richard Loeb, May 8, 1916. Julius Rosenwald Collection, University of Chicago Library Special Collections, Chicago.

Rosenwald, Julius. Collection. University of Chicago Library Special Collections, Chicago.

Ross, Christian K. *Charley Ross, the Kidnapped Child, a Father's Story.* Philadelphia: Potter, 1876.

Sandburg, Carl. *Smoke and Steel.* New York: Harcourt, 1920.

Schaumberg, Ron. "They Killed for Kicks." *New York Times Upfront*, September 18, 2000, 30–32.

Schmidt, John R. *"The Mayor Who Cleaned Up Chicago," a Biography of William E. Dever.* De Kalb: Northern Illinois UP, 1989.

Smith, Patterson. "Ransom Kidnapping in America." *AB Bookman's Weekly*, April 23, 1990.

Stone, Irving. *Clarence Darrow for the Defense.* New York: Doubleday, 1941.

Stuart, William H. *The Twenty Incredible Years.* Chicago: Donohue, 1935.

Sullivan, Edward Dean. *The Snatch Racket.* New York: Vanguard, 1932.

*University Record* [University of Chicago] 10.3, July 1924.

Urstein, Maurice. *Leopold and Loeb, a Psychiatric and Psychological Study.* New York: Lecouver, 1924.

Werner, M. R. *Julius Rosenwald, the Life of a Practical Humanitarian.* New York: Harper, 1939.

Whiffen, Marcus. *American Architecture since 1780.* Cambridge: MIT UP, 1992.

Willys-Knight. Advertisement. *National Geographic*, March 1924.

Wirth, Louis. *Local Community Fact Book.* Chicago: U of Chicago P, 1938.

## Newspapers

*Chicago Daily Journal*
*Chicago Daily News*
*Chicago Daily Tribune*
*Chicago Evening-American*
*Chicago Herald and Examiner*
*Chicago Sun-Times*
*Daily Mining Gazette*
*Jewish Courier*
*London Daily Mail*
*Montreal Herald*

# INDEX

**John Theodore** has been a reporter, writer, editor, and producer at United Press International, WGN, and WGN-TV. He lives with his family in the Chicago area. Theodore is also the author of *Baseball's Natural: The Story of Eddie Waitkus.*